Open Generative Syntax

Editors: Elena Anagnostopoulou, Mark Baker, Roberta D'Alessandro, David Pesetsky, Susi Wurmbrand.

In this series:

1. Bailey, Laura R. & Michelle Sheehan (eds.). Order and structure in syntax I: Word order and syntactic structure.

2. Sheehan, Michelle & Laura R. Bailey (eds.). Order and structure in syntax II: Subjecthood and argument structure.

3. Bacskai-Atkari, Julia. Deletion phenomena in comparative constructions: English comparatives in a cross-linguistic perspective.

Deletion phenomena in comparative constructions

English comparatives in a cross-linguistic perspective

Julia Bacskai-Atkari

language
science
press

Julia Bacskai-Atkari. 2018. *Deletion phenomena in comparative constructions: English comparatives in a cross-linguistic perspective* (Open Generative Syntax 3). Berlin: Language Science Press.

This title can be downloaded at:
http://langsci-press.org/catalog/book/193
© 2018, Julia Bacskai-Atkari
Published under the Creative Commons Attribution 4.0 Licence (CC BY 4.0):
http://creativecommons.org/licenses/by/4.0/
ISBN: 978-3-96110-083-5 (Digital)
         978-3-96110-084-2 (Hardcover)

DOI:10.5281/zenodo.1211896
Source code available from www.github.com/langsci/193
Collaborative reading: paperhive.org/documents/remote?type=langsci&id=193

Cover and concept of design: Ulrike Harbort
Typesetting: Julia Bacskai-Atkari
Proofreading: Ahmet Bilal Özdemir, Andreas Hölzl, Andreea Calude, Barend Beekhuizen, Catherine Rudin, Daniil Bondarenko, Eran Asoulin, George Walkden, Guohua Zhang, Jean Nitzke, Jeroen van de Weijer, Kleanthes Grohmann, Lea Schäfer, Prisca Jerono, Timm Lichte, Vadim Kimmelman, Vasiliki Foufi
Fonts: Linux Libertine, Libertinus Math, Arimo, DejaVu Sans Mono
Typesetting software: XƎLATEX

Language Science Press
Unter den Linden 6
10099 Berlin, Germany
langsci-press.org

Storage and cataloguing done by FU Berlin

Freie Universität Berlin

Für Ralf

Contents

Contents

Acknowledgements

This book grew from my dissertation, published by Universitätsverlag Potsdam under the title *The syntax of comparative constructions: Operators, ellipsis phenomena and functional left peripheries* in 2014. Chapters 2–4 and 6 have been revised and updated from the original, while Chapter 5 is entirely new. I owe many thanks to the reviewer and the proofreaders for their constructive comments and suggestions, as well as Sebastian Nordhoff for technical assistance.

The research behind this book was funded by the German Research Fund (DFG), as part of my research project "The syntax of functional left peripheries and its relation to information structure" (BA 5201/1-1) and formerly as part of the SFB-632 "Information structure: The linguistic means for structuring utterances, sentences and texts". I would like to thank my fellow German taxpayers for making this enterprise possible.

I definitely owe many thanks to many people for assisting me in various ways during the time I was working on this book. I would especially like to thank Gisbert Fanselow and Malte Zimmermann for encouraging me in this endeavour and for helpful discussions during all these years. Extra thanks go to Gisbert for supervising my dissertation back then and for his continued support of my research in my postdoctoral life.

My work, especially regarding ellipsis, benefited a lot from discussions with my late colleague Luis Vicente. It is therefore particularly tragic that I cannot show him the book any more – I can only hope that the result is something he would have appreciated.

I am indebted to Lisa Baudisch, my research assistant in the project, whose help in evaluating the data from surveys and corpora prevented the valuable empirical basis of the whole enterprise from turning into a nightmare.

Further, I am highly grateful to many others of my present and former colleagues at the University of Potsdam, whose suggestions, ideas and generally inspiring research have truly fostered my own work. In particular, I would like to thank Marta Wierzba for her help in improving my questionnaires and Doreen Georgi for lots of discussions concerning relative clauses. Many thanks are due to Martin Salzmann, Radek Šimík, Boban Arsenijević, Craig Thiersch, Andreas

Schmidt, Mira Grubic, Anne Mucha, Agata Renans, Flavia Adani, and Joseph DeVeaugh-Geiss for all their questions and suggestions during these years. I would also like to thank Claudius Klose, Jana Häussler, Frank Kügler, Anja Gollrad, Suse Genzel, Maria Balbach, Maja Stegenwallner-Schütz, Nikos Engonopoulos, Thuan Tran, Henry Zamchang Fominyam and Mary Amaechi for their various roles in making this time truly motivating and fun. I also owe many thanks to Jutta Boethke and Elke Pigorsch for their excellent support in administration during my time in the SFB. And, of course, I am truly indebted to Ines Mauer, who had the task of administering my own project.

I would like to thank my students of the seminars "The syntax of comparative constructions" and "Diachronic syntax", whose original and intelligent questions have been inspirational for my research.

Outside of Potsdam, I owe many thanks to my project cooperation partners for inspiring discussions and their useful suggestions concerning various parts of my research: Ellen Brandner (Konstanz/Stuttgart), Katalin É. Kiss (Budapest), Marco Coniglio (Berlin/Göttingen), Agnes Jäger (Köln), Marlies Kluck (Groningen), Svetlana Petrova (Wuppertal) and Helmut Weiß (Frankfurt). I am highly grateful to Jason Merchant for an inspiriting discussion on comparatives at ZAS.

My work has benefited substantially from the comments of anonymous reviewers I received for my papers and conference abstracts submitted during my doctoral project. I also owe many thanks to the audiences of various conferences I attended while I was working on this book, of which I would like to mention the following: "Linguistic Evidence" in 2014 in Tübingen (and Alexander Dröge and Ankelie Schippers in particular), "Third Cambridge Comparative Syntax Conference" in 2014 in Cambridge (and Ian Roberts and Georg Höhn in particular), "16th Diachronic Generative Syntax Conference" in 2014 in Budapest (and Beatrice Santorini and István Kenesei in particular), "12th International Conference on the Structure of Hungarian" in 2015 in Leiden (and Marcel den Dikken in particular), 17th Diachronic Generative Syntax Conference in 2015 in Reykjavík (and Roland Hinterhölzl, Jim Wood and Anthony Kroch in particular), "Budapest Linguistics Conference" in 2015 in Budapest (and Moreno Mitrović, Mojmír Dočekal and Kerstin Hoge in particular), "Categories in Grammar – Criteria and Limitations" in 2015 in Berlin (and Horst Simon and Christian Forche in particular), "12th International Conference on Greek Linguistics" in 2015 in Berlin, "SaRDiS 2015: Saarbrücker Runder Tisch für Dialektsyntax" in 2015 in Saarbrücken (and Augustin Speyer and Oliver Schallert in particular), "11th European Conference on the Formal Description of Slavic Languages" in 2015 in Potsdam (and Željko Bošković and Sergey Avrutin in particular), the workshop "The Grammatical Realization of Polarity. Theoretical and Experimental Approaches" of the "38th Annual Conference of the German Linguistics Society" in 2016 in Konstanz, the "39th Generative Linguistics in the Old World" in 2016 in Göttingen (and Gereon Müller and Jeroen van Craenenbroeck in particular), "Budapest–Potsdam–Lund Linguistics Colloquium" in 2016 in Budapest (and Gunlög Josefsson and Lars-Olof Delsing in particular), "Potsdam Summer School in Historical Linguistics 2016: Word Order Variation and Change: Diachronic Insights into Germanic Diversity" in 2016 in Potsdam (and Theresa Biberauer in particular), "Generative Grammatik des Südens 42" in 2016 in Leipzig (and Hubert Haider and Philipp Weisser in particular), "SaRDiS 2016: Saarbrücker Runder Tisch für Dialektsyntax" in 2016 in Saarbrücken (and Ellen Brandner and Göz Kaufmann in particular), "12th European Conference on the Formal Description of Slavic Languages" in 2016 in Berlin (and Jiri Kaspar, Teodora Radeva-Bork and Roland Meyer in particular), "Equative Constructions" in 2016 in Cologne (and Doris Penka in particular).

I owe many thanks to my informants for their valuable judgements. Many of them have been mentioned above; here I would like to add that I am highly grateful for Łukasz Jędrzejowski and Marta Ruda for their help with the Polish data. I am highly grateful to all my informants for completing my cross-Germanic survey: here I would also like to thank Ida Larsson for her help in finding Norwegian informants and Jóhannes Gísli Jónsson for his help in finding Icelandic informants.

Finally, I would like to thank my friends and my family for their support. In particular, many thanks go to my parents for their love and encouragement ever since I was born and for being the fun people they are. And of course lots of thanks are due to Ralf for everything, such as sharing my passion for photographing Berlin, and generally for making each and every day of my life wonderful. This book is dedicated to him.

1 Introduction

1.1 Aims and scope

The core problem to be dealt with in this book is the syntax of comparatives, that is, the structure of sentences that express comparison. As far as the notion of syntactic structure is concerned, I will basically adopt a minimalist framework (cf. for instance Chomsky 2001; 2004; 2008) and, in line with the principles of mainstream generative grammar, I assume that the derivation of structures is constrained by economy, and the number of structural layers, derivational steps and additional mechanisms is as small as possible. This means that although I adopt the view that various functional layers and mechanisms can be associated with these layers, I will keep them to a minimum and will not venture to introduce new ones unless there seems to be ample reason to do so.

Regarding the focus on comparative structures in particular, even though comparatives seem to be a very specific domain of research within syntax, the derivation of their structure raises questions of far more general interest, and providing meaningful answers to these questions may also have a bearing on our understanding of syntactic mechanisms, regarding, for instance, the functional left periphery of clauses, clause-typing, or various ellipsis processes.

It is very probably this diversity of problems that led to a significant interest in comparatives in generative frameworks already in the 1970s, most notably in Bresnan (1973; 1975), followed by various analyses with more or less shared concerns: for example, Corver (1993; 1997), Izvorski (1995), Lechner (1999; 2004), Kennedy (1997; 1999; 2002), Kennedy & Merchant (1997; 2000), and more recently Reglero (2006). I will strongly rely on these previous findings and especially the questions raised by them. While many questions have been answered by previous accounts, there are several others that have remained unresolved and have not received an adequate explanation which would hold cross-linguistically as well. Moreover, any proposal should follow from general principles of the grammar rather than by applying construction-specific mechanisms. The aim of this book is to provide such an analysis and to enable a better understanding of comparative clause formation.

In the following, I will briefly provide an overview of the structure of comparatives, to be followed by the concise outline of the problems to be dealt with in this book.

1.2 The structure of comparatives

In any human language, there are various means of expressing comparison between entities (or properties), and structures traditionally referred to as comparatives constitute only a subset of these possibilities. Consider the examples in (1):

(1)   a.   Mary was indeed furious when she saw that you had broken her vase. But you should have seen her mother!
      b.   Mary is tall but Susan is very tall.
      c.   Mary is faster than Susan.

In (1a), comparison is only implied: the first sentence makes it explicit that Mary was furious to a certain degree but the second sentence contains no explicit reference to a degree, yet it implies that the degree to which Mary's mother was furious exceeds the degree to which Mary was furious. In (1b), both the degree to which Mary is tall and the degree to which Susan is tall are explicitly referred to: without any further specification, it is understood that on a scale of height, the degree to which Mary is tall is greater than what is contextually taken to be average and that the degree to which Susan is tall is considerably greater than the average. Hence, the degrees of tallness are explicitly referred to, even if they remain vague; however, the comparison between the two degrees is not made explicit, but the relation of the two degrees can be inferred. Finally, (1c) exhibits a canonical comparative structure, which expresses that the degree to which Mary is fast exceeds the degree to which Susan is fast.

The present book aims at analysing syntactic comparative constructions, that is, the type represented by (1c) above. The sentence in (1c) shows the most important elements of comparative constructions: in this case, the degrees of speed of two entities are compared. The reference value of comparison is expressed by *faster* in the matrix clause (*Mary is faster*) and it consists of a gradable predicate (*fast*) and a comparative degree marker (*-er*). The standard value of comparison (that is, to which something else is compared) is expressed by the subordinate clause (*than Susan*) and is introduced by the complementiser *than*, which also serves as the standard marker.

There are some important remarks to be made here. First, in (1c), the comparative degree marker is a bound morpheme attached to the gradable predicate; however, this is not an available option for all adjectives in English and very often a periphrastic structure is used, when *-er* is present in the form of *more*, as in (2):

(2)   Mary is more pretentious than Susan.

Languages differ in terms of whether they allow both kinds of comparative degree marking and some languages (such as German) allow only the morphological way of comparative adjective formation, while others (such as Italian) have the periphrastic way by default.

Second, in (1c) the standard value of comparison is introduced by the complementiser *than* and the string *than Susan* is underlyingly a clause. This is explicitly shown by examples like (3) that contain a finite verb as well:

(3)   Mary is faster than Susan is.

Since the clause can be recovered, comparatives formed with *than* are invariably clausal. However, languages also differ with respect to the distribution of whether they have clausal and/or phrasal comparison. For instance, Hungarian has both clausal comparatives, introduced by *mint* 'than/as' and phrasal comparatives, see (4), where the standard value is expressed by an inherently Case-marked DP:

(4)   Mari magasabb Zsuzsánál.
      Mary taller   Susan.ADE
      'Mary is taller than Susan.'

In this case, the DP *Zsuzsánál* is inherently marked for adessive case and there is no clause that could be recovered. As my primary concern in this book is the structure of comparative subclauses, I will not be dealing with instances of phrasal comparison more than necessary: that is, I will briefly include them in the discussion when the arguments of the degree morpheme are considered and will relate them to subordinate clauses in this respect, but apart from this, they fall outside the scope of the present investigation.

It is also important to mention that degree constructions denote a larger set of structures than comparatives, within which one can distinguish between two major types, see (5): comparatives expressing equality, as shown in (5a), and comparatives expressing inequality, as in (5b) and (5c):

(5) a. Mary is as diligent as Susan.

   b. Mary is more diligent than Susan.

   c. Mary is less diligent than Susan.

In (5a), the degree to which Mary is diligent is the same as the degree to which Susan is diligent; by contrast, in (5b) and (5c) the degrees are different, such that the degree to which Mary is diligent is higher in (5b) and lower in (5c). As can be seen, the comparative subclause is introduced by *as* in (5a) and by *than* in both (5b) and (5c). The present book aims at providing an analysis for comparatives expressing inequality and more precisely for ones of the type given in (5b); nevertheless, the analysis has relevant conclusions for all types but I will not venture to discuss further differences here. The choice regarding (5b) is not arbitrary, though: this is the type that encompasses all comparative-related issues to some extent and the relevant literature has also mostly discussed this type.

1.3 The problems to be discussed

To start with, Chapter 2 will discuss the structure of degree expressions, with the aim of providing a unified analysis that relates the structure of comparatives to that of other (absolute and superlative) degrees. Naturally, a number of questions arise concerning the general structure of degree phrases, of which I will select only the ones that are relevant for the present book. The importance of comparatives in this respect is that they tend to contain a number of elements overtly that clearly indicate the presence of various functional layers, presenting a challenge for previous analyses, but at the same time indicating certain ways in which the syntactic structure of degree adjectives can best be captured.

One such problem is the presence of the degree morpheme itself, which becomes obvious when comparing the sentences in (5):

(6) a. Mary is **tall**.

   b. Mary is **taller** than Peter.

The contrast between (6a) and (6b) is that while the very same lexical adjective (*tall*) appears in both cases, in (6b) there is an additional degree morpheme (*-er*). The fact that the degree marker is syntactically separate from the adjective is more clearly indicated by periphrastic comparatives such as (7):

(7) Mary is **more intelligent** than John.

In (7), the comparative degree is marked by *more*; Chapter 2 will account for the difference and the relatedness of structures like (6b) and (7), showing that the same functional layers are present and the head element in the degree expression is *-er* in both cases.

Second, the relation between the comparative degree marker and the comparative subclause must also be explained as the type of the subclause seems to be defined by the comparative marker in the matrix clause:

(8) a. Mary is **taller** [than John].
     b. * Mary is **taller** [as John].
     c. * Mary is **as tall** [than John].
     d. Mary is **as tall** [as John].

As shown by the examples in (8), if the degree expression in the matrix clause contains the morpheme *-er*, then the subclause must be introduced by *than*; conversely, a degree expression with *as* in the matrix clause requires a subclause introduced by *as*. These selectional restrictions are obviously not dependent on the lexical adjective, which is invariably *tall*. I will show in Chapter 2 that the comparative subclause is one argument of the degree head, the other being the lexical AP itself; consequently, there are restrictions that hold between the degree head and the subclause but there are none that would hold between the AP and the subclause.

Even though my main concern is not the argument structure of adjectives, it should be mentioned that adjectives may have arguments of their own:

(9) Mary is proud [of her husband].

In cases like (9), the adjective (*proud*) takes a PP (*of her husband*) as its complement; this must also be accounted for, especially in relation to the subclauses indicated in (8), which are not directly introduced by the adjective itself but are nevertheless obligatory. Chapter 2 will argue that PP complements of adjectives are indeed complements of the adjective head but may appear in a right-dislocated position due to the nature of cyclic spellout to PF.

The structure adopted for degree expressions will be used when accounting for Comparative Deletion in Chapter 3, which constitutes the core part of the book. My aim here is to reduce the cross-linguistic differences attested in connection with Comparative Deletion to minimal differences in the relevant operators. I intend to show that Comparative Deletion is merely a surface phenomenon and hence does not have to be treated as a parameter distinguishing between languages; instead, I will adopt a feature-based account that can handle language-internal variation as well. I will argue that the difference is ultimately not between individual languages but rather between overt operators that do and covert operators that do not trigger Comparative Deletion. To my knowledge, this claim is radically new in the literature and hopefully it may account for several phenomena that have been unexplained so far. This chapter will also present data that has not been discussed in the literature, including non-standard English, German and Dutch patterns, as well as Hungarian and Slavic (mostly Czech) data.

The phenomenon of Comparative Deletion traditionally denotes the absence of an adjectival or nominal expression from the comparative subclause, as indicated in the following examples:

(10) a. Ralph is more qualified than Jason is ~~x qualified~~.
      b. Ralph has more qualifications than Jason has ~~x many qualifications~~.
      c. Ralph has better qualifications than Jason has ~~x good qualifications~~.

In the sentences above, x denotes a certain degree or quantity as to which a certain entity is qualified, good, etc. This is an operator that has no phonological content. In (10a), an adjectival expression is deleted: this type is referred to as the predicative comparative since the quantified adjectival expression functions as a predicate in the subclause. By contrast, in both (10b) and (10c) a nominal expression is deleted; structures like (10b) are nominal comparatives, where a nominal expression bears quantification, while (10c) is an attributive comparative, where the quantified adjectival expression is an attributive modifier within a nominal expression.

Therefore, one of the most important questions to be answered in connection with Comparative Deletion is how to account for the fact that different constituents seem to be deleted by Comparative Deletion. Moreover, this deletion process seems to be obligatory to the extent that the presence of the quantified expressions in (10) would lead to ungrammatical constructions; therefore, a proper analysis of Comparative Deletion must also address the issue why this process seems to be obligatory. I will argue that the site of Comparative Deletion is not the one indicated in (10) but a left-peripheral, [Spec,CP] position. The reason why the strings indicated as deleted elements in (10) cannot be overt is that they are lower copies of a moved constituent and are regularly eliminated.

The role of information structure underlying Comparative Deletion has to be taken into consideration as well. In subcomparative structures, an adjectival or nominal element may be left overt in the subclause; as opposed to the examples in (10), these elements are not logically identical to an antecedent in the matrix clause:

(11) a. The table is longer than the desk is **wide**.

b. Ralph has more books than Jason has **manuscripts**.

c. Ralph wrote a longer book than Jason did **a manuscript**.

I will show in Chapter 3 that movement takes place even in these cases, and hence the higher copy is regularly eliminated; the reason why the lower copies are realised overtly is that they are contrastive. My analysis will thus crucially differ from those (for example Kennedy 2002) that try to capture the surface dissimilarity between (10) and (11) on the basis of whether *wh*-movement takes place overtly, as in (10), or covertly, as in (11). I assume that syntactic movement triggered by a [+wh] or a [+rel] feature cannot be sensitive to the information structural properties of the lexical XP (AP/NP) that moves together with the operator for independent reasons (that is, the non-extractability of the operator from the functional projections containing these lexical elements).

Given that deletion in the [Spec,CP] position takes place if the operator is zero, it can be expected that visible operators can remain overt in this position. Though this option is not available in Standard English, substandard dialects may allow configurations such as (12) below:

(12) % Ralph is more qualified than **how qualified** Jason is.

Naturally, an analysis of Comparative Deletion must also address the question of how examples such as (12) relate to the ones given in (10) or (11); I will argue that all of these constructions involve the movement of the quantified expression, but the higher copy is not elided in (12) since the overtness requirement on left-peripheral elements is satisfied.

Apart from varieties of English that allow instances like (12), in some languages full degree expressions can be regularly attested at the left periphery of the subclause, as in the examples in (13) from Hungarian (cf. Kenesei 1992):

(13) a. Mari magasabb, mint **amilyen magas** Péter.
      Mary taller   than how   tall   Peter
      'Mary is taller than Peter.'

b. Marinak   több   macskája   van, mint **ahány**   **macskája**
Mary.DAT more cat.POSS.3SG is   than how.many cat.POSS.3SG
Péternek van.
Peter.DAT is

'Mary has more cats than Peter has.'

c. Marinak   nagyobb macskája   van, mint **amilyen nagy macskája**
Mary.DAT bigger   cat.POSS.3SG is   than how   big   cat.POSS.3SG
Péternek van.
Peter.DAT is

'Mary has a bigger cat than Peter has.'

As can be seen, Hungarian allows the overt presence of the degree elements, which again shows that Comparative Deletion must be subject to (parametric) variation. I will argue that this variation can be accounted for by the Overtness Requirement: Hungarian has overt operators while Standard English does not, and therefore the overt presence of lexical elements in a [Spec,CP] position is available in Hungarian, just as in the case of non-standard varieties of English.

Strongly related to this, the question arises to what extent the internal structure of the degree expression plays a role and whether individual operators exhibit different behaviour in this respect. In Hungarian, there are two comparative operators, *amilyen* 'how' and *amennyire* 'how much'. The operator *amilyen* may appear together with the adjective, as in (13a), but it does not allow the stranding of the adjective, as shown in (14):

(14)   * Mari   magasabb, mint **amilyen** Péter **magas.**
      Mary taller   than how   Peter tall

'Mary is taller than Peter.'

On the other hand, Hungarian has another operator, *amennyire* 'how much', which allows both options for the adjective, as shown in (15):

(15)   a. Mari   magasabb, mint **amennyire magas** Péter.
         Mary taller   than how.much tall   Peter

'Mary is taller than Peter.'

b. Mari   magasabb, mint **amennyire** Péter **magas.**
   Mary taller   than how.much Peter tall

'Mary is taller than Peter.'

In addition, as shown in (16), Hungarian also seems to require the presence of some operator if the adjective is overt (note, however, that it is allowed for the adjective and the operator to be non-overt at the same time):

(16)   a. Mari magasabb, mint (*magas) Péter.
            Mary taller   than   tall   Peter

            'Mary is taller than Peter.'

       b. Mari magasabb, mint Péter (*magas).
            Mary taller   than Peter   tall

            'Mary is taller than Peter.'

I will show in Chapter 3 that Hungarian lacks a covert operator, and that the difference between *amilyen* and *amennyire* is due to the fact that they occupy different positions in the extended degree expression, based on the findings concerning the structure of degree expressions in Chapter 2. Hence, my analysis of Comparative Deletion is based on the assumption that languages differ with respect to the presence/absence of the operator in a more intricate way than one that could be formulated on a +/– basis.

Following these lines of thought, Chapter 4 will address a special instance of Comparative Deletion, which is traditionally referred to in the literature as Attributive Comparative Deletion. I will show that Attributive Comparative Deletion can only be understood as a descriptive term indicating a phenomenon that is a result of the interaction of more general syntactic processes, and therefore there is no reason to postulate any special mechanism underlying Attributive Comparative Deletion in the grammar. By eliminating such a mechanism, it is possible to achieve a unified analysis of all types of comparatives. Chapter 4 will also show that Attributive Comparative Deletion is not a universal phenomenon: its appearance in English can be conditioned by independent, more general rules and the absence of such restrictions may lead to the absence of Attributive Comparative Deletion in other languages. In this respect, novel data from German and Hungarian will be presented and discussed.

Attributive Comparative Deletion refers to a peculiar phenomenon that involves the obligatory deletion of the quantified AP and the lexical verb from the comparative subclause, if the quantified AP functions as an attribute within a nominal expression. Consider the examples in (17):

(17)   a.   Ralph bought a bigger cat than George did ~~buy~~ a ~~big~~ cat flap.

      b.   Ralph bought a bigger cat than George ~~bought~~ a ~~big~~ cat flap.

      c. *Ralph bought a bigger cat than George bought a ~~big~~ cat flap.

    d. * Ralph bought a bigger cat than George bought a big cat flap.

    e. * Ralph bought a bigger cat than George ~~bought~~ a big cat flap.

    f. * Ralph bought a bigger cat than George did ~~buy~~ a big cat flap.

As can be seen, both the adjective (*big*) and the lexical verb (*buy*) have to be eliminated from the comparative subclause: this is possible either by eliminating the tensed lexical verb, as in (17b) or by deleting the lexical verb and leaving the tense-bearing auxiliary *do* intact, as in (17a). Note that both the verb and the adjective have to be deleted, as indicated by the ungrammaticality of the sentences in (17c)–(17f).

The obligatory elimination of the adjective is not directly related to the fact that it is GIVEN; the overt presence of the attributive adjective is ungrammatical even if it is different from its matrix clausal counterpart, as shown in (18):

(18)   a. *Ralph bought a bigger cat than George ~~bought~~ a wide cat flap.

        b. *Ralph bought a bigger cat than George did ~~buy~~ a wide cat flap.

It seems that the elimination of the adjective from the particular position is obligatory. On the other hand, note that the deletion of the lexical verb is required only if part of the DP is overt; if the entire DP is eliminated, as in (19), the lexical verb can remain:

(19)   Ralph bought a bigger cat than George bought ~~a big cat~~.

There are a number of questions that arise in connection with these phenomena. First, it has to be explained why the adjective has to be deleted and cannot appear overtly even if it is contrastive. Second, one has to account for the fact that the deletion of the adjective happens alongside with the deletion of the lexical verb: this is interesting especially because in structures like (17a) and (17b) the verb and the lexical verb do not even seem to be adjacent.

In line with Kennedy & Merchant (2000), Chapter 4 will show that the quantified adjectival phrase moves to a left-peripheral position within the extended nominal expression and hence appears as the leftmost element within that nominal expression, which results in its adjacency to the lexical verb at PF. I will argue that the unacceptability of the lexical AP in this position is due to a violation of the Overtness Requirement: this position within the nominal expression is essentially an operator position, and therefore lexical material is licensed to appear there only if the operator is visible, the condition of which is not met in the case of the comparative operator. The ellipsis mechanism effectively eliminating the AP is VP-ellipsis, which necessarily affects the lexical verb; contrary to

Kennedy & Merchant (2000), who claim that the rest of the nominal expression undergoes rightward movement, I will argue that the overtness of the F-marked DP (*a cat flap*) in (17a) and (17b) is possible because ellipsis proceeds in a strict left to right fashion at PF and F-marked constituents may stop ellipsis.

In this way, Attributive Comparative Deletion will be sufficiently linked to Comparative Deletion, as the deletion of the higher copy takes place even in cases like (17a) and (17b); furthermore, the PF-uninterpretability underlying both phenomena follows from the same kind of constraint, that is, the overtness requirement. On the other hand, VP-ellipsis is not a construction-specific mechanism either, and there is no reason to suppose a special process underlying Attributive Comparative Deletion.

The analysis of Attributive Comparative Deletion will also take cross-linguistic differences into consideration. For instance, in languages like Hungarian the full string may be visible in the subclause:

(20) Rudolf   nagyobb macskát vett,   mint amilyen széles macskaajtót
      Rudolph bigger   cat.ACC bought.3SG than how   wide cat.flap.ACC
      Miklós vett.
      Mike   bought.3SG
      'Rudolph bought a bigger cat then Mike did a cat flap.'

I will show that the acceptability of (20) in Hungarian follows from the fact that the comparative operator is overt in Hungarian and hence no Comparative Deletion is attested at all; on the other hand, the quantified adjective does not undergo movement to the left periphery within the nominal expression either.

On the other hand, there are languages, such as German, that do not permit Attributive Comparative Deletion, even if they have zero comparative operators:

(21) *Ralf   hat eine   größere   Wohnung als   Michael ein   Haus.
       Ralph has a.ACC.F bigger.ACC.F flat   than Michael a.ACC.N house
      'Ralph has a bigger flat than Michael a house.'

I will show that the unacceptability of (21) stems chiefly from the fact that the VP (as all vP layers) is head-final in German and therefore VP-ellipsis is not attested; furthermore, the German nominal expression does not allow the kind of inversion (that is, the movement of the quantified AP to a left-peripheral position) that can be observed in English. In this way, my analysis of Attributive Comparative Deletion accounts for cross-linguistic variation, apart from providing an explanation for the English data.

Regarding the mechanisms underlying the phenomenon of Comparative Deletion and that of Attributive Comparative Deletion, it seems that the Overtness Requirement regulates the realisation of the higher copy, while the realisation of the lower copy is essentially tied to the lexical XP being contrastive. In Chapter 5, I will address the question why some languages cannot realise contrastive lower copies either.

As far as the higher copy is concerned, the Overtness Requirement on left-peripheral elements is crucial, since this states that overt lexical material is licensed in an operator position only if the operator itself is overt. Hence, there are four logical possibilities, depending on whether the operator moves on its own, and whether the operator is overt or not. If the operator is able to strand a lexical AP or NP (or there is no lexical XP base-generated together with the operator at all), the lexical XP is spelt out in its base position, and the overtness of the operator is immaterial, as is the information structural status of the lexical XP. If an overt operator takes the lexical XP along to the [Spec,CP] position, the lexical XP is licensed irrespective of its information structural status. However, if a phonologically zero operator takes the lexical XP to the clausal left periphery, the entire phrase in [Spec,CP] has to be deleted in order to avoid a violation of the Overtness Requirement. In this case, the lower copy of the movement chain (in the base position) is realised overtly if it is contrastive. This leads to an asymmetry between contrastive and non-contrastive XPs: in the case of the latter, the absence of any overt copy results in the surface phenomenon traditionally referred to as Comparative Deletion. The realisation of contrastive XPs, on the other hand, appears to be straightforward.

Using data mainly from Slavic, Chapter 5 will demonstrate that the availability of the lower copy for overt realisation is not universal. Again, the discussion relies on new data that have not been discussed so far but the existence of which is crucial in understanding the idiosyncratic properties of the Standard English pattern. Consider the data in (22) from Polish:

(22) a. * Maria jest wyższa niż Karol   jest **wysoki**.
         Mary is taller   than Charles is   tall
      'Mary is taller than Charles.'
   b. */?? Stół jest dłuższy niż   biuro jest **szerokie**.
          desk is   longer   than office is   wide
      'The desk is longer than the office is wide.'

While the ungrammaticality of (22a) is expected on the basis of the English pattern, the question arises why Polish lacks predicative subcomparatives in the

English way, that is, why (22b) is ungrammatical. As will be shown, Polish is not unique in this respect: Czech shows the same distribution. I will argue that the realisation of the lower copy is dependent on more general properties of movement chains in a certain language, which results in a difference between English and Polish. In particular, I will show that the difference between English and Polish in this respect lies chiefly in the availability of multiple *wh*-fronting in Polish. As demonstrated by Bošković (2002), *wh*-elements have to undergo fronting in multiple *wh*-fronting languages independently of an active [wh] feature on C: that is, while the first moved *wh*-constituent checks off the [wh] feature on C and thus undergoes ordinary *wh*-movement, the further *wh*-elements merely undergo obligatory fronting. I assume that this is because these elements are equipped with an EDGE feature. Bošković (2002) shows that apparent exceptions to the fronting requirement are relatively rare and they are subject to certain conditions; further, these instances do not involve the lack of fronting but rather the realisation of a lower copy of a movement chain. I argue that since these requirements are absent from comparative constructions, it follows naturally that the realisation of a contrastive lower copy is not possible in these languages.

Finally, apart from issues directly related to the structure of degree expressions and the functional left periphery of comparative subclauses, the present book also aims at accounting for optional ellipsis processes that play a crucial role in the derivation of typical comparative subclauses. These issues will be discussed in Chapter 6.

In English predicative structures, see (23), this involves the elimination of the copula from structures such as (23b), as opposed to the one given in (23a):

(23) a. Ralph is more enthusiastic than Jason is.
      b. Ralph is more enthusiastic than Jason.

In nominal comparatives, see (24), the lexical verb may be deleted:

(24) a. Ralph bought more houses than Michael bought flats.
      b. Ralph bought more houses than Michael did flats.
      c. Ralph bought more houses than Michael did.
      d. Ralph bought more houses than Michael.

Verb deletion may result in a subclause without any verbal element, as in (24d), or the tense morpheme may be carried by the dummy auxiliary, as in (24b) and (24c). In addition, depending on whether the object contains a contrastive noun or not, the object nominal expression remains overt, as in (24a) and (24b), or it does not appear overtly, as in (24c) and (24d). A very similar pattern arises in attributive comparatives, as shown in (25):

(25) a. Ralph bought a bigger house than Michael did a flat.
      b. Ralph bought a bigger house than Michael did.
      c. Ralph bought a bigger house than Michael.

The main question here is whether the deletion of the lexical verb is merely the deletion of the verbal head or whether this involves VP-ellipsis; in the latter case, the possibility of having overt objects (or parts of objects) must be accounted for. Developing the analysis given in Chapter 4, in Chapter 6 I will argue that gapping is an instance of VP-ellipsis, which proceeds in a left-to-right fashion at PF and the starting point of it is an [E] feature on a functional v head, in line with Merchant (2001), and the endpoint of ellipsis is a contrastive phrase, if there is any. I will also show that since the [E] feature can be present on a C head as well, the derivation of comparative subclauses at PF may involve ellipsis starting from an [E] feature either on a C or a v head. Since the final string may be ambiguous, one of the central questions is whether a uniform kind of ellipsis mechanism may account for these ambiguities; this will be shown to be possible.

On the other hand, the fact that reduced comparative subclauses also exist in Hungarian raises yet another question, which is how languages with exclusively overt comparative operators may show the elimination of the entire degree expression, given that there is no Comparative Deletion in these languages. For instance, predicative comparatives in Hungarian show the pattern in (26):

(26) a. Mari magasabb volt,   mint **amilyen magas** Péter **volt**.
         Mary taller   was.3SG than how   tall   Peter was.3SG
         'Mary was taller than Peter.'
      b. Mari magasabb volt,   mint Péter.
         Mary taller   was.3SG than Peter
         'Mary was taller than Peter.'

As can be seen, in (26a) the subclause contains all the elements overtly, while the degree expression and the verb are absent from (26b). The same phenomenon can be observed in nominal comparatives, see (27):

(27) a. Mari több macskát vett,   mint **ahány**   **macskát** Péter
          Mary more cat.ACC bought.3SG than how.many cat.ACC   Peter
          vett.
          bought.3SG
          'Mary bought more cats than Peter did.'

      b. Mari több macskát vett,   mint Péter.
          Mary more cat.ACC bought.3SG than Peter
          'Mary bought more cats than Peter did.'

Finally, the same is true for attributive comparatives, as shown in (28):

(28) a. Mari nagyobb macskát vett,   mint **amilyen nagy macskát**
          Mary bigger   cat.ACC bought.3SG than how   big   cat.ACC
          Péter **vett**.
          Peter bought.3SG
          'Mary bought a bigger cat than Peter did.'

      b. Mari nagyobb macskát vett,   mint Péter.
          Mary bigger   cat.ACC bought.3SG than Peter
          'Mary bought a bigger cat than Peter did.'

In all of these cases it is true that the sentences of a given pair have the same meaning. The question is whether the deletion of the degree expression is independent from that of the verb or not. As I will show in Chapter 6, using novel and systematically tested data, these are not two independent processes since the verb cannot be overt in the absence of an overt degree expression. I will argue that this is the case because it is ungrammatical to have an operator in its base position in Hungarian, but since there is no separate mechanism that would eliminate the degree expression, a more general ellipsis process has to apply, which is essentially VP-ellipsis. The ellipsis mechanism is fairly similar to the one attested in English and the differences will be linked to the slightly different internal structure of the functional layers in the two languages. Otherwise ellipsis is carried out by an [E] feature on the leftmost functional head in Hungarian too.

I will argue that the difference between English and Hungarian in terms of gapping effects is chiefly a result of the different prosody in the two languages: while the Intonational Phrase is right-headed in English, it is left-headed in Hungarian. As a consequence, while contrastive elements are located at the right edge of the ellipsis domain in English, in Hungarian they are to the left of the functional head hosting the [E] feature or are themselves located in that head and consequently not part of the ellipsis domain either. Chapter 6 will show that since there is strong directionality in terms of ellipsis, in that it proceeds in a strict left-to-right fashion, this kind of ellipsis works only in head-initial phrases since the ellipsis domain (the complement) has to follow the head hosting the [E] feature. This accounts for why German does not have VP-ellipsis the way English has it: the German VP and all vP layers are head-final, while in English all VP projections are head-initial. Cross-linguistic differences concerning optional ellipsis processes can thus also be reduced to more general properties that hold in individual languages, and hence ellipsis processes in comparatives are not construction-specific.

2 The structure of degree expressions

2.1 Introduction

In this chapter, I provide a unified analysis of degree expressions that relates the structure of comparatives to that of other – absolute and superlative – degrees. Naturally, there arise a number of questions concerning the general structure of degree phrases, of which I will select only the ones that are relevant for the present work. Since my analysis is strongly built on the results of previous accounts, I will first give a short overview of the relevant literature, showing the problematic points thereof that I intend to eliminate in my approach. Again, the literature concerning the syntax of degree expressions is far greater than the selected examples presented here but I restrict myself to discussing those analyses that bear crucial significance for the understanding of comparatives.

2.2 Earlier accounts

2.2.1 The problems to be discussed

When considering the general structure of degree expressions, comparatives are especially interesting to consider because they contain a number of overt elements that clearly indicate the presence of various functional layers, presenting a challenge for previous analyses.

The very first problem is the appearance of the degree morpheme itself. Consider the examples in (1):

(1) a. Mary is **tall**.
     b. Mary is **taller** than John.

By comparing (1a) and (1b), it should be obvious that while it is the very same lexical adjective (*tall*) that appears in both cases, in (1b) there is an additional degree morpheme (that is, *-er*). The fact that the degree marker is syntactically separate from the adjective is more clearly indicated by periphrastic comparatives such as (2):

(2)   Mary is **more intelligent** than John.

In (2), the comparative degree is marked by *more*; a sound analysis for the structure of degree expressions must also account for the difference and the relatedness of structures like (1b) and (2).

Moreover, the relation between the comparative degree marker and the comparative subclause must also be explained as the type of the subclause seems to be defined by the comparative marker in the matrix clause:

(3)   a.   Mary is **taller** [than John].
      b.   * Mary is **taller** [as John].
      c.   * Mary is **as tall** [than John].
      d.   Mary is **as tall** [as John].

As can be seen, if the degree expression in the matrix clause contains the morpheme -*er*, then the subclause must be introduced by *than*; conversely, a degree expression with *as* in the matrix clause requires a subclause introduced by *as*. These selectional restrictions are obviously not dependent on the lexical adjective, which is *tall* in all of the examples in (3).

Last but not least, adjectives may have arguments of their own. Consider:

(4)   Mary is proud [of her husband].

The adjective *proud* takes the PP as its complement; this must also be accounted for, especially in relation to the subclauses indicated in (3), which are not directly introduced by the adjective itself but are nevertheless obligatory.

2.2.2 *Much*-deletion – Bresnan (1973)

I will start the overview with Bresnan's landmark paper, which opened the discussion on comparative constructions by taking into account a large number of phenomena not even considered before. The most important contribution of Bresnan (1973) is probably the separation of functional heads (Det and Q in her analysis, Deg and Q in later analyses), which makes it possible to explain why certain degree-like elements behave differently; moreover, the role of *much* is also addressed, which is crucial in terms of the structure of comparatives.

One of the most important observations is that *more* is a composite of *much* and the degree morpheme -*er*, hence in a way the comparative form of *much*. This is immediately shown by the paradigm of degree expressions. Consider the following examples (taken from Bresnan 1973: 277, exx. 4 and 5):

(5) a. as / too / that / so **much** bread

b. as / too / that / so **little** bread

c. as / too / that / so **many** people

d. as / too / that / so **few** people

As can be seen, all degree elements (i.e., *as*, *too*, *that* and *so*) combine with either *much*, *little*, *many* or *few*. Likewise with *-er*, we find all four forms as shown in (6), cf. Bresnan (1973: 277, exx. 4, 5 and 7):

(6) a. -er **much** bread → **more** bread

b. -er **little** bread → **less** bread

c. -er **many** people → **more** people

d. -er **few** people → **fewer** people

Naturally, there must be rules in the grammar for the changes from combinations such as *-er much* into *more*: these are partly syntactic rules and partly suppletion rules that belong to the level of morphology (Bresnan 1973: 279).

The structure of degree expressions can be drawn up as given in (7), according to Bresnan (1973: 277, ex. 6):

(7)

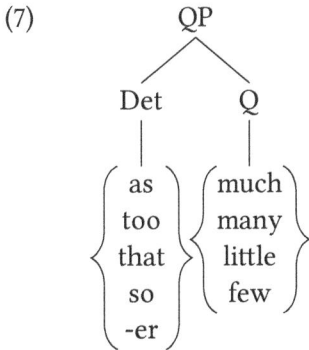

Degree expressions like *as much* are QPs, though Bresnan (1973: 277) admits that the label "is merely a temporary convenience". The head of the QP is occupied by the elements *much*, *many*, *little* and *few*, while the degree elements – including the comparative *-er* – are determiners in the specifier. Admittedly, the analysis has the advantage of ruling out certain impossible configurations such as **too more*: the Det position cannot be filled by *too* and *-er* at the same time (Bresnan 1973: 277), which would not be predicted by an analysis taking elements like *more* as atomic.

Let us now turn to cases where degree elements are followed by a lexical adjective (or adverb) and not a noun. The paradigm given in (5) does not seem to hold there, as the data in (8) indicate (see Bresnan 1973: 278, exx. 8 and 9):

(8) a.   Mary is **more** intelligent.
     b. * Mary is **so much** intelligent.
     c.   Mary speaks **more** cogently.
     d. * Mary speaks **so much** cogently.

The data above show the following problem: apparently, the sequence of a degree element (e.g., *so*) and *much* before an adjective or an adverb is not permitted, as indicated by the ungrammaticality of (8b) and (8d). However, *more* is acceptable in that position, as in (8a) and (8c). Therefore, if one maintains the idea that *more* is made up of -*er* and *much* in the same way as, for example, *so much* is constructed, then there are obviously conflicting requirements here.

Bresnan (1973: 278) mentions two logical possibilities that may account for this: either *more* does not derive from -*er* + *much* when preceding adjectives and adverbs, or it is deleted if it directly precedes an adjective or an adverb. Arguing for the latter, she provides an additional rule in the form of *Much*-deletion, given below (Bresnan 1973: 278, ex. 10):

(9) much → Ø / [..._____ A]$_{AP}$
     where A(P) = Adjective or Adverb (Phrase)

The fact that -*er much* becomes *more* is not merely a morphological matter: the syntax accounts for the word order change from the initial -*er much* into *much -er*, and morphology substitutes this latter form with *more*. According to Bresnan (1973: 279, ex. 20), the syntactic derivation is the following:

(10) a.   QP   ⟹   b.   QP

```
(10)  a.     QP        ⟹     b.      QP
            /\                       /\
          /    \                   /    \
        Det    Q                 Det    Q
         |     |                  |     /\
        -er  much                 Ø  much+er
```

By way of cliticisation, -*er* is attached to *much*, ultimately resulting in *more*. The point is that *much* will not be adjacent to the adjective following the original string -*er much*. The item -*er* will act as an intervener and consequently the rule given in (9) does not – and could not – apply. This is straightforward in the case of analytic comparatives (such as *more intelligent*) but requires extra rules for accommodating morphological comparatives (such as *taller*). Bresnan (1973: 279) assumes that *taller* is in fact underlyingly *more tall*, and is derived by separate rules for simple comparatives: first, *much-er tall* becomes *much-er taller*, and subsequently *much-er* is deleted, leaving *taller* as the final result. As far as the exact mechanism behind this is concerned, it is crucially missing from the analysis.

Turning back to the syntax of degree expressions, (10) shows that the core idea is to treat *much* or *many* as a Q head, which takes a Det degree item as a specifier. If a degree expression is modified by another one, this is achieved via adjunction. Consider the following example (Bresnan 1973: 290, ex. 132a):

(11)   I have **as many too many** marbles as you.

Here the degree expression *too many* is modified by *as many*. As shown in (12), the latter is left-adjoined to the former (Bresnan 1973: 290, ex. 131):

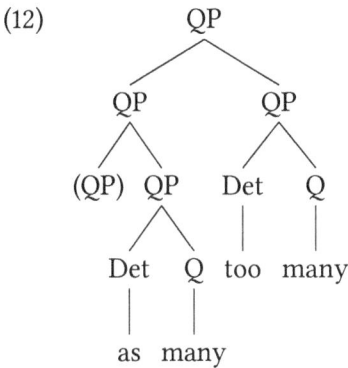

(12)

```
                QP
            ┌────────┐
          QP          QP
        ┌────┐      ┌────┐
     (QP)  QP     Det    Q
          ┌────┐    |    |
        Det    Q   too  many
         |     |
        as   many
```

A QP can be modified by another QP in a recursive way: additional QPs are adjoined in the same fashion. If there is also a lexical adjective (or adverb), the QP is left-adjoined to it (Bresnan 1973: 294, ex. 147):

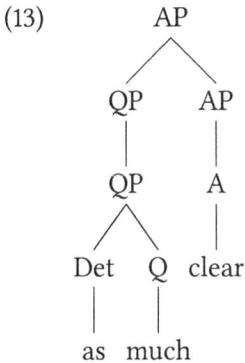

(13)

```
              AP
          ┌───────┐
        QP         AP
        |          |
        QP          A
      ┌────┐        |
    Det    Q      clear
     |     |
    as   much
```

The representation in (13) shows the underlying structure: *much*-deletion will later eliminate *much*, which is immediately followed by an adjective, ultimately giving the grammatical string *as clear*. The same would be true if the adjective had an adverbial modifier (e.g., *as much utterly stupid* → *as utterly stupid*, see Bresnan 1973: 294).

As for the comparative subclause, Bresnan (1973: 318–319) notes that it may originate in the Det (dominating the *-er* or the *as* head); however, how this is precisely achieved is not described. In the final structure, the comparative subclause ends in an extraposed position, as shown in (14) for the string *taller than my mother is tall*, see Bresnan (1973: 319, ex. 251):

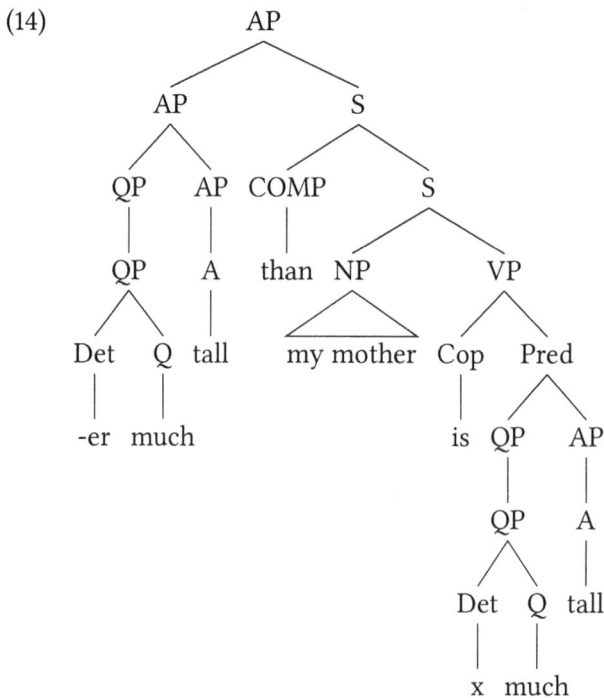

(14)

```
                          AP
                    ┌──────┴──────┐
                   AP             S
                 ┌──┴──┐      ┌───┴────┐
               QP    AP    COMP        S
                │     │      │      ┌───┴───┐
               QP     A     than   NP      VP
              ┌─┴─┐   │    ┌──┴──┐  ┌──┴──┐
            Det   Q  tall  my mother Cop  Pred
             │    │              │    ┌───┴───┐
            -er  much           is   QP      AP
                                      │       │
                                     QP       A
                                   ┌──┴─┐      │
                                  Det   Q     tall
                                   │    │
                                   x   much
```

As can be seen, the subclause is ultimately an adjunct to the entire AP, though it should be base-generated where the Det is located.

Though the analysis admittedly has advantages, it raises a number of problems as well. First of all, the structural representation can obviously not be maintained in a minimalist framework, especially as far as the Det is concerned. If elements like *-er* are indeed to be treated as heads and not as phrase-sized constituents, they should not be located in a specifier. This immediately raises the question of where degree items are located with respect to the AP and the QP; that is, which projection dominates which. If the degree item is indeed a head, rather than a phrase, it is highly unlikely that it would be dominated by the AP, unless extra movement processes are involved.

It is likewise problematic to relate QPs to each other by way of adjunction. It is true that QP modifiers are to a large extent recursive but certain restrictions seem to hold on their order, for instance, while *as many too many (marbles)* is grammatical, **too many as many (marbles)* is not.

Moreover, the very mechanism of *much*-deletion is highly questionable. It is credible that the formation of *more* before adjectives and adverbs should not differ from how it is formed before nouns. However, by merely considering the logical possibilities, this leaves us two alternative options and not just one, as Bresnan (1973) would imply. The first option is *much*-deletion before adjectives and adverbs. The second option is *much*-insertion elsewhere. The former option has two main problems: first, it is not clear why *much* should be inserted even when it lacks the syntactic function of a dummy and does not bear any semantic role. Second, the rule of *much*-deletion is highly arbitrary (cf. also Corver 1997; Jackendoff 1977; Brame 1986) and does not follow from any general constraint. It is therefore a rather circuitous way of defining the morphological difference between adjectives that form their comparative degrees with *much* and those that do not.

Last but not least, the position of the comparative subclause also raises at least two major questions. On the one hand, it remains unexplained how it is base-generated under the Det node. On the other hand, the extraposition of the clause to the right is also dubious, primarily because it seems to be obligatory rightward movement, in addition to the fact that rightward movement in itself is problematic. As there is very little said about the position of the comparative subclause, it is not surprising that the issue is not discussed in relation to PP arguments of adjectives, which should also be accommodated in the structure.

2.2.3 A DP-shell for comparatives – Izvorski (1995)

Let us now turn to the analysis of Izvorski (1995), who markedly builds on the semantics of comparative structures with respect to the formation of the syntactic structure. The importance of this study lies fundamentally in the fact that it aims at providing a unified syntactic representation for degree expressions, which will also play a crucial part in later analyses. By way of adopting a DP-shell analysis, Izvorski (1995) intends to provide a unified structure for predicative and nominal structures, which is desirable in the sense that the degree expression itself should not be different depending on whether it is a predicate or base-generated within a nominal expression.

According to Izvorski (1995: 107–118), the elements *more, less* and *as* are of the category Det, and they are heads of the DP they introduce. In this way, DPs have in fact two DP layers (hence the DP-shell), in the same way as double object constructions have VP-shells, cf. Larson (1988). It has to be mentioned that the label D for degree items is fundamentally used as a convenient syntactic notation and is therefore not intended to imply that all degree expressions would be nominal (Izvorski 1995: 111–119): they could also be of the category Deg, as for Abney (1987) and Corver (1990).

According to Izvorski (1995: 107–118, see especially ex. 23), the general structure of comparatives is the following:

(15)

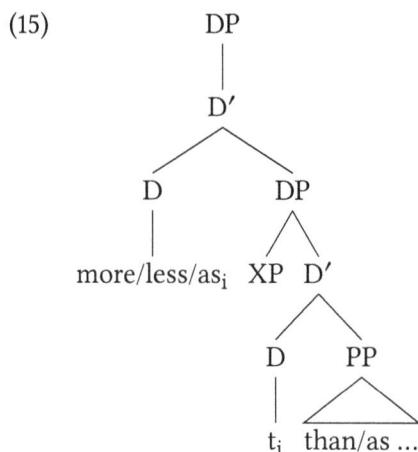

The XP stands for the lexical projection – a bare AP or NP – in the structure; in this way, there is no syntactic difference between predicative (e.g. *more intelligent than ...* and nominal (e.g. *more cats than ...*) comparatives, other than the category of the XP itself.

As Izvorski (1995: 109–119) points out, the analysis has the advantage of both directly relating the degree element – that is, *more, less* or *as* – to the comparative complement (here: the PP) and at the same time accounting for their discontinuity in the surface structure. Yet, this immediately raises the problem of distributional differences, as degree expressions containing an AP and those containing an NP clearly do not behave in the same way syntactically. Izvorski (1995: 111–120) overcomes this by saying that D is underspecified for the relevant (nominal or adjectival/adverbial) features; hence, it can take either of them into its (lower) specifier. Via specifier–head agreement, the XP is in turn responsible for specifying these features on the D head; finally, the movement of the D to the higher D position causes the features to be present on the entire DP.

This analysis clearly eliminates some of the problems that I mentioned in connection with Bresnan (1973), such as the treatment of Det as a specifier, the mechanism of *much*-deletion or the connection between the comparative subclause and the degree head. However, new ones arise as well, in particular the treatment of *more* and *less* as atomic: apart from the fact that there seems to be ample evidence in favour of analysing *more* as *much* + -*er*, Izvorski's proposal crucially leaves unexplained how simple morphological comparatives (e.g. *taller*) are formed.

In addition, the way to overcome distributional differences is ad hoc and does not take into account that there might be differences in terms of modification, too. As a matter of fact, the issue of modification is altogether missing from Izvorski's analysis (consider examples such as (11) above). The same applies to the position of arguments, especially the PP arguments of adjectives.

Moreover, while the account in Izvorski (1995) is general enough in the sense that it covers (or intends to cover) the structure of both predicative and nominal comparatives, it fails to say anything about attributive comparatives (e.g., *a more intelligent dog than ...*). As has been said, the XP is either a bare AP or a bare NP. It is not clear how an NP containing an attribute could be accommodated in the structure, especially because in these cases the comparative degree is associated primarily with the lexical AP and not with the entire NP, which becomes even more evident when considering attributive comparatives containing a morphological degree form (e.g. *a bigger dog than ...*), where the degree morpheme -*er* is clearly marked on the adjective.

Last but not least, the treatment of the subclause is highly questionable: apart from the fact that Izvorski (1995) analyses it as a PP, an issue I intend to address later on, there seems to be a problem in terms of extraposition, too. At first glance, the kind of extraposition proposed by Bresnan (1973) seems to be fortunately eliminated by Izvorski (1995): it is the degree element that moves away from the subclause. However, it has to be noted that the position given in (15) cannot be the final one. Consider the examples in (16):

(16) a. Brenda is **more enthusiastic** now [than she used to be].

  b. **More students** like Brenda's classes [than George's].

As can be seen, the bracketed comparative subclauses are separated by intervening material not only from the degree element *more* but also from the lexical AP (*enthusiastic*) or NP (*students*). Therefore, its final position cannot be within the degree expression, that is, the DP in Izvorski's analysis.

2.2.4 *Much*-support – Corver (1997)

Let us now turn to the analysis presented by Corver (1997), which is a landmark paper in terms of functional projections in the extended AP, primarily because it makes an important distinction between determiner-like and quantifier-like degree items in a more explicit way than Bresnan (1973) did. In addition, Corver (1997) adopts a functional head approach instead of a lexical head approach, which conforms to the general assumption that it is functional projections that dominate lexical ones and not vice versa. Last but not least, by claiming that the presence of *much* is due to insertion, Corver (1997) presents a theoretically more adequate treatment of *much* than the one given by Bresnan (1973), which included an extra deletion operation from the structures without a visible *much*.

Relying on Bresnan (1973), Corver (1997: 120–123) starts from the split degree hypothesis; that is, the idea that there should be a difference between quantifier-like degree items (QPs) and determiner-like degree items (DegPs). According to this, the general structure of degree expressions should be the following:

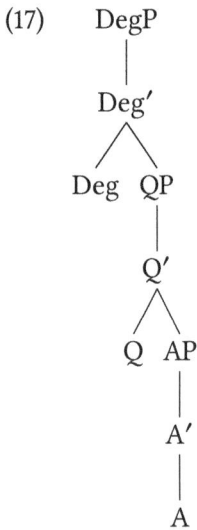

(17)   DegP
         |
        Deg′
        /\
     Deg QP
           |
           Q′
          /\
         Q AP
             |
             A′
             |
             A

Contrary to Bresnan (1973), however, Corver (1997: 122–123) treats the items *more* and *less* as atomic, in the sense that they are claimed to be base-generated as such – similarly to *enough* or the dummy quantifier *much* – and not as the results of syntactic derivation.

Note that the structure proposed by Bresnan (1973), as given in (13), is crucially different from the one shown in (17). The former is a lexical head approach, in that the entire degree expression is headed by the lexical A head, whereas the latter is a functional head approach, where the AP is dominated by functional layers in the degree expression.

There are reasons to believe that this is indeed the case. First, as pointed out by Corver (1997: 124–125), the syntactic derivation of morphological comparatives (e.g. *taller*) would be problematic if the bound *-er* morpheme were located in the specifier of the AP. In order to derive *taller*, either *-er* would have to move rightward or the adjective would have to move to its own specifier – in both cases, general constraints on movement would be violated. By contrast, under the functional head approach the adjective head can move up to the functional head *-er*. Note that this is a problem only if one assumes that the derivation of the final string *taller* from the underlying *-er tall* is carried out in syntax; as will be shown later on, this is not necessarily the case.

Second, the lexical head approach would face severe problems in connection with differences like (18), see Corver (1997: 125, exx. 16c and 17c):

(18) a. *How$_i$ do you think he is [t_i dependent on his sister]?
      b. **How heavily**$_i$ do you think he is [t_i dependent on his sister]?

As can be seen, it is grammatical to extract a phrase such as *how heavily* from within the degree expression, while the extraction of *how* is banned. The difference could not be explained under the lexical head approach, where *how* and *how heavily* would both be phrase-sized specifiers (QPs) within an AP. In Corver's approach, however, only the latter qualifies as a phrase-sized constituent: *how* in itself is a functional head above the AP and therefore it is straightforward that it cannot move out on its own.

Third, Corver (1997: 125, ex. 18) also calls attention to an interesting extraction paradigm, given in (19):

(19) a. ? **How many IQ-points**$_i$ is John [t_i less smart (than Bill)]?
      b. * **How many IQ-points less**$_i$ is John [t_i smart (than Bill)]?
      c. [**How many IQ-points less smart** (than Bill)] is John?

As pointed out by Corver (1997: 125–126), the lexical head approach would have to face the problem of extracting phrases from a specifier position both in (19a) and (19b), though the latter case is clearly ungrammatical. The functional head approach can handle this too: in (19a), a degree expression (*how many IQ-points*) is moved out of a specifier position from within the degree expression headed by *less*; by contrast, (19b) exhibits the movement of non-constituents, that is, of a phrase-sized specifier and the functional head. Naturally, the movement of the entire degree expression headed by *less* is again grammatical, see (19c).

Returning to the problem concerning the status of *much*, it has to be mentioned that Corver (1997: 123) makes a crucial distinction between the lexical quantifier *much* and the functional dummy quantifier *much*. An example of the first one is given in (20) below (based on Corver 1997: 121, ex. 5):

(20)   She is **too much too tall**.

In this case, the element *much* is claimed to be located in a specifier position of the extended AP projection (Corver 1997: 123). By contrast, dummy *much* is a Q head in the extended AP and is found in examples such as (21) below, see Corver (1997: 123, ex. 11):

(21)   John is fond of Sue. Maybe **too much so**.

The appearance of dummy *much* is, according to Corver (1997: 123), due to last resort insertion as the adjective in these cases does not move up to the Q head position. In other words, syntax crucially derives the structure without *much* and insertion happens only if necessary: this is exactly the opposite of what Bresnan (1973) claimed; that is, that the syntactic derivation by default contains *much* and a later rule may delete it. As was mentioned at the end of §2.2.2, the possibility of inserting dummy *much* is in fact logically plausible, even though Bresnan (1973) does not take it into consideration. In a way, Corver (1997) seems to answer one of the most compelling questions that arise in connection with the analysis given by Bresnan (1973).

Moreover, Corver (1997: 126–128) provides evidence for the existence of the QP-layer, which was only rather intuitively proposed by Bresnan (1973). Consider the following examples in (22) below (Corver 1997: 126, exx. 20a and 21a):

(22)   a. John seems fond of Mary, and Bill seems so too.
       b. John is fond of Mary. Bill seems [much less so].

Both cases are instances of *so*-pronominalisation: *so* replaces the entire AP *fond of Mary* and, as Corver (1997: 126) argues, not merely the adjective *fond* and not the entire degree expression either, as indicated by the fact that in (22b) *so* appears in a degree expression headed by *less*. This could still be accommodated in a system using only a DegP above the AP; but consider the data given in (23), taken from Corver (1997: 127, exx. 23a and 24a):

(23)   a. John is fond of Mary. *Maybe he is [too so].
       b. John is fond of Mary. Maybe he is [too **much** so].

As can be seen, the string *too so* is not grammatical: *much* has to be inserted into the structure. This can be handled relatively well if one assumes a structure like (17), where the Deg head would be *too*, the Q head *much* and the element *so* would occupy the position of the AP, see Corver (1997: 127–128).

Contrary to Bresnan (1973), Corver (1997: 128–129) argues that the Q head position is underlyingly empty and the insertion of *much* is only a last resort option: the insertion of *much* in all cases would violate general principles of economy. In this way, *much*-support is similar to *do*-support in the extended verbal domain, as described by Chomsky (1991); see Corver (1997: 129).

As for the position of modifiers, Corver (1997: 154–161) argues that they are located in the specifier position of the QP. Consider:

(24) [$_{QP}$ extremely *e* [$_{AP}$ poisonous]]

Under this approach, modifiers such as *extremely* are located in the [Spec,QP]; the Q head is empty. By contrast, though modifiers like *well* or *far* are likewise located in [Spec,QP], they attract the adjective head to move up to the Q head, see Corver (1997: 160):

(25) [$_{QP}$ far different$_i$ [$_{AP}$ t_i from the others]]

Corver (1997: 160), in line with Larson (1987), assumes that the morpheme *-ly* is a case-marking element and that the AP needs to be assigned Case. Hence, while in (24) the morpheme *-ly* can assign Case to the AP in situ, in (25) there is no *-ly* morpheme and the AP can get Case only via movement to the specifier of the QP.

Although Corver's analysis is in many respects attractive, it still raises certain problems. The most evident one is perhaps the treatment of modifiers. It is not clear why the AP should be assigned Case at all, and how case assignment can be linked to the *-ly* morpheme. More importantly, the distinction between elements like *far* and ones like *extremely* is not as simple as it may seem on the basis of Corver (1997). Consider the examples in (26):

(26) a. * Mary is **far tall**.
      b. Mary is **far taller** (than Agatha).
      c. Mary is **very/extremely tall**.
      d. * Mary is **very/extremely taller** (than Agatha).

The data above show that the modifiers *far* and *extremely* do not appear in the same constructions. While *extremely* appears regularly with the absolute degree (e.g. *tall*), and therefore patterns with *very, far* normally occurs when the degree expression is comparative (e.g. *taller*). The exceptional case is actually the one that Corver (1997) uses for his analysis, namely the possibility of *far different*; I will return to the question of why *different* patterns with comparative degree expressions rather than absolute ones later, but the basic claim will be that *different* is inherently comparative.

At any rate, there seems to be a crucial distinction among modifiers in terms of which degree they co-occur with. This difference remains unobserved and hence unexplained by Corver (1997). On the other hand, the fact that modifiers cannot be classified on the basis of whether they have the *-ly* ending or not is reinforced by the example of *very*, which behaves like *extremely* but could hardly be treated as a *-ly* adverb.

Furthermore, there is also a structural problem in connection with the status of modifiers in the analysis of Corver (1997). As shown in (24) and (25), the modifiers in question are located in the specifier of the QP, which – on the basis of the structure given in (17) – correctly predicts that these elements have to precede the AP and, if applicable, dummy *much*. However, the same structure in (17) would require Deg heads to precede these modifiers, which is clearly not the case, as shown by *far taller* in (26b) and by *far more intelligent* in (27):

(27) Mary is **far more intelligent** than Agatha.

These data explicitly show that the structure of degree expressions cannot be the one given in (17) or at least additional mechanisms would have to be taken into consideration.

Apart from the problem of how modifiers are treated by Corver (1997), the position of the comparative subclause itself is not even addressed, with respect to the matrix clausal degree expression and, possibly, arguments of adjectives. Assuming that the subclause is closely related to the Deg head, it is not clear how it ultimately appears in a clause-final position and how it is base-generated next to the Deg head in the first place. The specifier of the DegP seems to be a possible position but as Corver (1997) himself does not mention this possibility, I will refrain from speculating about it here.

2.2.5 The QP–DegP analysis – Lechner (1999; 2004)

Before turning to my proposal, let me briefly discuss the analysis provided by Lechner (2004), a revised version of Lechner (1999), which answers some of the questions that emerged in connection with the previous accounts mentioned

here and which provides important insights concerning the actual relations between the various functional projections. This study is important first and fore-
most because it reconsiders the syntactic relationship between the AP and the
Deg head, in that it reflects the semantics of the Deg head much better than
previous analyses.

Lechner (2004: 22) partially adopts the functional AP-hypothesis; that is, that
the AP is embedded under a functional projection, the DegP, cf. Abney (1987),
Bresnan (1973), Corver (1990; 1993; 1997), and Kennedy (1999). However, Lechner (2004: 22–23) assigns a different structure to the DegP, in that he proposes
that the AP is base-generated in the specifier position of the DegP and not as
a complement, in this respect recalling the proposal made by Izvorski (1995). At
the same time, the complement position serves to accommodate the comparative
subclause.

The structure – using the DegP in a string such as *Mary is younger than Peter
is* – is shown below (see Lechner 2004: 22, ex. 45):

(28)

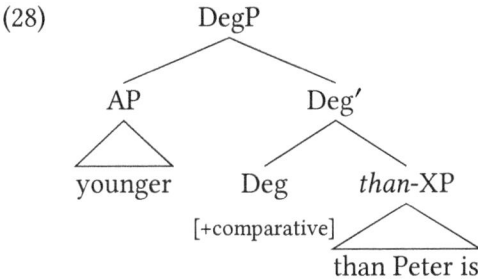

An advantage of assuming that the AP is in the specifier of the DegP is that in
this way, they can enter into a specifier–head relationship, and the [+compara-
tive] Deg head can check off the features of the AP. Note that Lechner (2004:
23) claims that comparative morphology is base-generated directly on the A
head, and therefore a string like *younger* cannot be syntactically decomposed
into *young* and the degree morpheme *-er*, contrary to Bresnan (1973), but in line
with Izvorski (1995) and Corver (1997). As a matter of fact, Lechner (2004: 23) assumes that *-er* morphology manifests a reflex of feature checking: this, however,
selectively surfaces only on certain A heads, namely ones that are monosyllabic
or bisyllabic. Hence, in the case of periphrastic forms (e.g., *more intelligent*), the
feature is claimed to be spelt out on Deg, resulting in the string *more + A*.

This raises a rather compelling question in connection with periphrastic structures, namely that if the comparative feature is spelt out on Deg in the form of
more, then, according to the representation in (28), the string should actually be A

+ *more*, e.g. **intelligent more*, which is clearly not the case. Lechner (2004) leaves the derivation of the grammatical order unexplained. However, Lechner (1999: 25) originally proposed that in periphrastic comparatives the DegP is embedded under a QP. Thus, for a string like *more intelligent than Peter is*, the structure in (28) should be modified in the way given in (29):

(29)

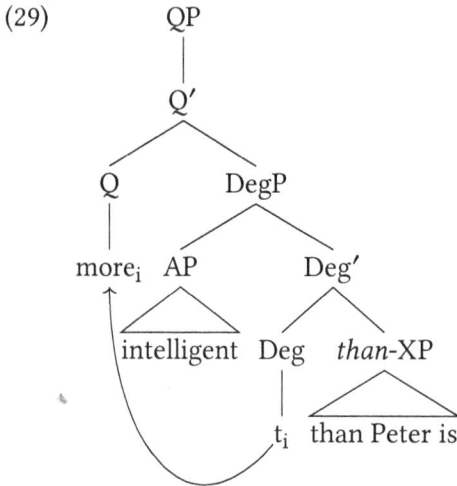

As can be seen, if there is a QP layer above DegP, *more* can move up to the Q head position, thus resulting in the grammatical word order.

One advantage of the analysis given in (28), as Lechner (2004: 23) argues, is "the dissociation of the surface position of *-er* from the location of its interpretation". The problem of not separating these two becomes obvious when considering the *unhappier* Bracketing Paradox, see Beard (1991), Pesetsky (1985) and Sproat (1992). This paradox lies in the observation that *unhappier* seems to be subject to two conflicting requirements. On the one hand, morpho-phonological rules would assign the following bracketing to the string (see Lechner 2004: 23, ex. 47a):

(30) [un [happier]]

The reason behind this is that *-er* may only be attached to an A head that maximally consists of two syllables, hence it must be attached prior to *un-*. However, this seems to produce the interpretation 'not happier' instead of 'more unhappy'. On the other hand, in order to derive the correct interpretation, the bracketing should be the one given in (31), see Lechner (2004: 23, ex. 47b):

(31)   [[unhappy] er]

Note that in this case the morpho-phonological rules mentioned in connection with (30) are violated.

In order to overcome this problem, Lechner (2004: 23) proposes that the correct bracketing is the one in (30), but the interpretation of *-er* is not directly associated with its base position: it is a manifest of feature-checking, which involves the entire AP (*unhappy*).

With respect to the location of adjectival arguments, Lechner (2004: 26) makes use of some German data exhibiting such constructions to provide additional evidence for the structure he attributes to nominal comparatives. According to his analysis, the PP argument of an adjective is a complement of the adjectival head and it may be subject to right dislocation. Consider (Lechner 2004: 26, ex. 51):

(32)   a.   weil Hans [pp auf seinen   Hund] stolz ist
             since Hans   of his.M.ACC dog   proud is

             'since Hans is proud of his dog'

       b.   weil Hans stolz   ist [pp auf seinen   Hund]
             since Hans proud is   of his.M.ACC dog

             'since Hans is proud of his dog'

According to Lechner (2004: 26), the underlying order is the one indicated in (32a), building on the assumption that the AP is head-final; for such views, see for instance Haider & Rosengren (1998). As will be discussed later, taking such a stance is problematic not only in terms of maintaining a universal directionality of headedness (cf. Kayne 1994) but also because it may rather be the case that the German AP is in fact head-initial. Nevertheless, taking up the argumentation of Lechner (2004), (32b) is claimed to exhibit right dislocation of the PP argument. However, if the AP is an attribute in a nominal expression, see (33),dislocation is not possible (Lechner 2004: 26, ex. 54):

(33)   a.   weil Hans eine   [pp auf ihren   Hund] stolze   Frau
             since Hans a.F.ACC   of her.M.ACC dog   proud.F.ACC woman
             getroffen hat
             meet.PTCP has

             'since Hans met a woman proud of her dog'

b. * weil Hans eine   stolze   Frau   getroffen hat [PP auf
    since Hans a.F.ACC proud.F.ACC woman meet.PTCP has   of
    ihren   Hund]
    her.M.ACC dog
    'since Hans met a woman proud of her dog'

As can be seen, the extraposition of the PP is ungrammatical; this leads Lechner (2004: 27) to conclude that extraposition is not permitted from a DegP that is an attribute within a nominal expression. The same is not true for the comparative subclause: this can apparently be extraposed. Lechner (1999; 2004) introduces a special mechanism for it, by way of which the (original) comparative subclause ends in such a position that it is coordinated with the (original) matrix clause. Since this is clearly a kind of syntactic process that would go against standard minimalist assumptions and also a problematic proposal inasmuch as comparatives can hardly be considered coordinated structures (see Bacskai-Atkari 2010a), I will not present this part of Lechner's analysis here.

Even if one disregards the problems related to the movement of the comparative subclause, further ones arise in connection with the analysis given by Lechner (1999; 2004). First, the treatment of *more* is highly disputable as it does not take into consideration that it is built up of *much* and the degree morpheme. It is therefore also not straightforward how strings like *as many (books)* should be analysed, where *as many* obviously cannot be considered atomic.

Second, the status of the QP is not clear either. Though on the basis of Lechner (1999) it ought to be generated in periphrastic structures, neither Lechner (1999) nor Lechner (2004) assume its presence in morphological comparatives. It appears that these contain merely DegP projections. On the one hand, this is a problem for a unified analysis of degree expressions as the maximal projections would be different, that is, either a QP or a DegP, without even implying any syntactic difference. More importantly, the absence of a QP layer leaves the question of where modifiers are located unanswered.

Last but not least, the treatment of PP arguments is far from being uncontroversial, especially because Lechner (2004) takes it for granted that the AP is head-final and the PP underlyingly precedes the A head. The opposing view is quite substantially present in the literature; see for instance Webelhuth (1992). However, there are serious problems with Lechner's examples as well in the sense that the data as such are misleading. Consider:

(34) a. [PP Auf seinen   Hund] sollte   Hans stolz   sein.
           of his.M.ACC dog   should.COND.3SG Hans proud be

      'Hans should be proud of his dog.'

      b. % [PP Auf seinen   Hund] stolz sollte   Hans sein.
            of   his.M.ACC dog   proud should.COND.3SG Hans be

      'Hans should be proud of his dog.'

      c. Stolz [PP auf seinen   Hund] sollte   Hans sein.
          proud   of his.M.ACC dog   should.COND.3SG Hans be

      'Hans should be proud of his dog.'

The data show the possible movement patterns of APs containing PP complements in main clauses. The most typical order is the one in (34a), where only the
PP moves to a position preceding the verb *sollte*. However, it is also possible to
move the entire degree expression. In that case, the natural order is A + PP, as
in (34c). If the PP precedes the A head, as in (34b), the clause is not accepted by
all speakers, and speakers who allow it remarked that the adjective *stolz* 'proud'
must be stressed, which indicates that the position of the adjective on the right
is most probably due to information structural requirements (and is therefore
not a neutral order). This is already problematic for Lechner (2004: 26), but the
problem only increases with the speakers who do not accept (34b) at all, while
Lechner (2004) would predict (34b) to be the unmarked case.

The apparent contradiction between (32) and (34) can be explained if we consider some basic facts about German clause structure. In simple terms, subclauses
show the underlying word order SOV, the VP (and the TP) being head-final
(Haider 1985: 34), whereas in main clauses the inflected verb moves to the topmost C (see Fanselow 2004: 30, following den Besten 1989, Richter & Sailer 1998:
133–134). The moved verb comes second in the clause; it tolerates only one preceding constituent. This condition is satisfied in (34c), where the A head precedes
the PP complement; however, in (34b) the word order is either the result of moving two constituents before the verb (ungrammatical) or of the PP moving into a
position above the AP (speaker-dependent), which is tolerated normally (by all
speakers) only if the AP is contained within a nominal expression, as in (33b).

I will return to the question of why degree expressions differ in predicative and
in attributive structures – for now, suffice it to say that the core problem concerning the data provided by Lechner (2004) is that they only seemingly support his
claim, but the desired word orders arise merely because he uses subclauses.

Apart from (34), the possibility of intervening modifiers also indicates that the
order PP + A head cannot be the underlying one. Consider the examples in (35):

(35)   a.   Lisa ist (wirklich) stolz [pp auf ihren   Mann].
            Liz is   really   proud   of her.M.ACC husband
            'Liz is (really) proud of her husband.'

       b.   Lisa ist [pp auf ihren   Mann]   (wirklich) stolz.
            Liz is   of her.M.ACC husband really   proud
            'Liz is (really) proud of her husband.'

In (35a), the adjective *stolz* takes a PP complement and may optionally be modified by an adverb such as *wirklich* 'really'. In (35b), the adjective and the PP
complement appear in the reverse order; since the adverb *wirklich* can intervene
between the two, it is obviously not the underlying order. This raises the question
of where modifiers could be located in the analysis provided by Lechner (2004),
indicating that his structural representation is far from complete.

2.3 Towards the analysis

In this section, I will present my analysis for degree expressions, which may provide a better explanation for the problems mentioned above. I will chiefly concentrate on the comparative degree, but absolute and superlative constructions
will also be shown to fit into the representation. I adopt the proposal of Lechner
(2004) that the AP and the CP are arguments of the degree head. The AP and the
CP establish a predicative relationship within the DegP, which is in this respect
similar to the Relator Phrase of den Dikken (2006) in its function. Consider the
representation for the string *far more interesting than the first one*:

(36)

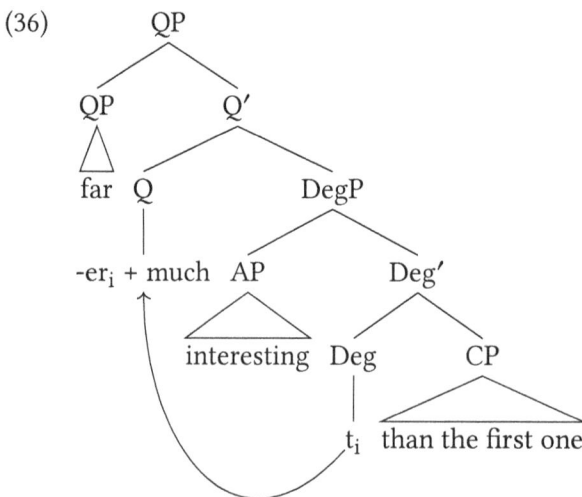

As can be seen, there are two major layers that constitute a degree expression: the DegP and the QP. Since arguments for the DegP and the QP have already been put forward in the literature, as described in the previous section, I will mention only additional arguments that support the analysis given in (36).

First, let us consider the DegP. The Deg head imposes selectional restrictions on its complement: in absolute constructions – in English – it can be expressed by a PP headed by *for*, in comparatives it is a CP headed by *than* and in superlatives it is a PP headed by *of*:

(37)   a. Mary is tall [PP for a schoolgirl].

        b. Mary is taller [CP than her classmates].

        c. Mary is the tallest [PP of the girls].

The structure is invariably the one given in (36); in absolute constructions like (37a), the Deg head takes a PP complement (*for a schoolgirl*) and the Deg head itself is a zero; in superlatives like (37c), the Deg head takes a PP complement (*of the girls*) and is filled by *-est*.

It is important to note that selectional restrictions concern the relevant degree features rather than the syntactic category of the complements. For instance, a superlative degree morpheme selects a complement with a superlative feature – since the P head *of* may be equipped with this feature, it is an *of*-PP that ultimately appears as the superlative complement. However, there are languages that allow the realisation of one degree complement by categorically different XPs. Consider the data in (38) from Italian:

(38)   a. Raulo è più   alto [CP che Alessandro].
           Ralph is more tall.M   that Alexander
           'Ralph is taller than Alexander.'

        b. Raulo è più   alto [PP di Alessandro].
           Ralph is more tall.M   of Alexander
           'Ralph is taller than Alexander.'

As can be seen, in Italian the comparative complement can either be a clause introduced by *che* 'that' or a PP headed by *di* 'of'; in both cases, the comparative degree head is *più* 'more'. In Hungarian, as shown in (39), there is a choice between a CP and a DP with inherent (adessive) case (cf. Wunderlich 2001):

(39)   a. Lujza magasabb volt,   [CP mint Mari].
           Louise taller   was.3SG   than Mary
           'Louise was taller than Mary.'

b. Lujza magasabb volt   [DP Marinál].
   Louise taller   was.3SG   Mary.ADE
   'Louise was taller than Mary.'

In both constructions, the DegP is headed by the morpheme *-bb* '-er'. Apparently, Russian[1] displays the same kind of variation:

(40) a. Ona vyše [NP svoix   odnoklassnikov].
         she taller   her.GEN.PL classmates.GEN
         'She is taller than her classmates.'

      b. Ona vyše [CP čem eë odnoklassniki].
         she taller   than her classmates.NOM
         'She is taller than her classmates.'

In the matrix clause, the degree expression is *vyše* 'taller', which contains the comparative morpheme *-eje* '-er'; the comparative complement is either a CP or a nominal expression marked for the genitive case.

In Russian, adjectives can regularly appear both in morphological and periphrastic constructions. However, only the clausal comparative complement is allowed with periphrastic comparatives:

(41) a. * Ona boleje vysokaja [NP svoix   odnoklassnikov].
           she more tall.F   her.GEN.PL classmates.GEN
           'She is taller than her classmates.'

      b. Ona boleje vysokaja [CP čem eë odnoklassniki].
         she more tall.F   than her classmates
         'She is taller than her classmates.'

As should be obvious, the ungrammaticality of (41a) cannot be the result of the mere fact that the degree expression is comparative since in that case (40a) should also be ruled out. There are two crucial differences between the degree expressions in (40) and the ones in (41): the degree head itself, which is *-eje* in (40) and *boleje* in (41), and the form of the adjective, that is, while *vyše* is not inflected for gender, *vysokaja* is. This latter difference has the prediction that, since attributes have to agree with their nouns in gender in Russian, morphological comparative degree expressions will never be attributes and, consequently,

---

[1]I owe many thanks to Maria Shkapa for her indispensable help with the Russian data.

the inherently case-marked NP comparative complement will not appear in attributive comparatives either. This prediction is in fact borne out.

On the other hand, it should be obvious that the Deg head imposes restrictions on both its specifier and its complement. It selects for complements headed by certain elements and it agrees with the AP, which may be manifest in diverse features; for instance, it may select exclusively for APs that are in a predicative form. I will address this issue later on; for the time being, suffice it to say that the way the degree head imposes restrictions on its arguments suggests that features independent from the degree property are also involved.

Returning now to the examples given in (37), it is worth mentioning that although the DegP proposed here does bear some resemblance to the Relator Phrase of den Dikken (2006), the treatment of the PP in (37a) highlights a crucial difference from his analysis. According to den Dikken (2006: 63), in structures such as *big for a butterfly*, the AP *big* is located in the specifier position of an RP, the DP *a butterfly* is the complement and the R head itself is *for* – using the DegP analysis, this would translate *for* as a Deg head. By contrast, I propose that the complement position of the Deg head is occupied by the PP *for a butterfly*, which leaves the Deg headed by a zero relator, that is, the absolute degree morpheme. The advantage is that this way, the complement may act as one constituent, irrespectively of whether it is a PP (like *for a butterfly*) or a CP (like *than the first one*). Separating the CP from its complementiser head *than* would clearly be problematic; the same is true for the PP, as shown in (42). The PP may actually be moved on its own, as shown in (42a), in the same way as the PP argument in superlatives, as in (42b):

(42) a. [PP For an adult], he is tiny.
      b. [PP Of all the girls], she is the most beautiful.

Of course, there are further restrictions on which phrases may actually undergo movement; that is, while the fact that a given string may undergo movement on its own seems indicative of that string being a phrase, it is not true that all phrases may undergo movement. This largely has to do with whether the complements of the Deg head are phrasal (smaller than a clause) or clausal. As for English, the PP complements in absolute and superlative constructions may move, while the CP in comparatives cannot. In Hungarian, there are two types of comparative complements: CPs and case-marked DPs. While CPs cannot move out, case-marked DPs can:

(43) a. * [CP Mint Péter]ᵢ magasabb voltam tᵢ.
            than Peter   taller   was.1SG
         'I was taller than Peter.'

b. [DP Péternél]$_i$ magasabb voltam t_i.
    Peter.ADE taller   was.1SG

'I was taller than Peter.'

Since both (43a) and (43b) are comparative structures, the difference with respect to extraposition is the result of having different syntactic categories, and not of having different degrees.

Note that the difference indicated in (43) is truly a result of a difference in the syntactic categories and is independent from the fact that (43a) contains ellipsis: the non-elided counterpart of (43a) would equally be ungrammatical. Consider the examples in (44):

(44) * [CP Mint Péter volt]$_i$ magasabb voltam t_i.
          than Peter was.3SG taller   was.1SG

      'I was taller than Peter.'

On the other hand, there are languages that tolerate the fronting of an elliptical clausal comparative complement. Consider the example in (45) from German (see Bacskai-Atkari 2014b on *als*-clauses being elliptical and not phrasal in German):

(45) [CP Als Peter] war   ich größer.
          than Peter was.1SG I   taller

      'I was taller than Peter.'

Returning now to the structure in (36), it can be seen that the AP moves up to the specifier of the DegP in order to agree with the degree head. One argument in favour of such an agreement is that in this way certain illicit configurations may be ruled out. Consider:

(46) a. * Liz is more pregnant than Mary.

      b. * This instalment is more impossible than the previous one.

The ill-formedness of the constructions in (46) stems from the comparative use of *pregnant* and *impossible*: pregnant and *impossible* are non-gradable adjectives, and hence cannot agree with a comparative degree head. I assume that with non-gradable adjectives, a DegP (and QP) layer is regularly not projected, since a Deg head cannot license a non-gradable AP in its specifier. Exceptions are non-gradable adjectives used as gradable ones in a given context that licenses a gradable interpretation: a sentence like (46a) may be licensed exceptionally in a

context to mean that Liz is more visibly pregnant than Mary, or that her preg-
nancy is more advanced than that of Mary.[2]

Another case where there is clearly agreement involved between the AP and
the Deg head is Icelandic. In Icelandic, as in other Scandinavian languages, the
adjective has to agree in gender with the noun it qualifies, both, when the adjective is a predicate and when it is an attribute. In addition, in Icelandic there
is gender agreement between the AP and the Deg head, as demonstrated by the
examples in (47):

(47)   a.   rík-ur
            rich-M
            'rich'

       b.   rík-ast-ur
            rich-SUPERLATIVE.M-M
            'richest'

       c.   * rík-ust-ur
            rich-SUPERLATIVE.F-M
            'richest'

In (47a), the adjective *rík* 'rich' takes a masculine ending *-ur*, forming the absolute adjective *ríkur*. In (47b), in order to form the superlative, the superlative
masculine morpheme *-ast* is added to the stem *rík*, and is followed by the regular
masculine ending *-ur*, resulting in the final form *ríkastur*. The reason why *ríkustur*
in (47c) is ungrammatical is that it contains the superlative feminine morphemes
-ust instead of the masculine one. Thus, in Icelandic there is not only agreement
between the full QP and the noun but also within the DegP. Note that in other
Scandinavian languages, such as Danish, there is agreement only between the
QP and the noun; however, the Danish comparative morpheme will invariably
remain *-(e)re*, irrespectively of gender.

Let us now examine the QP layer, which is invariably present on top of a degree
expression. In (36), it is headed by *much*, and the specifier may accommodate a
QP modifier such as *far*; the QP is obviously necessary for accommodating both
of these elements, as was argued for in the previous section. I also adopt the view
expressed by Corver (1997) that *much* is present in periphrastic structures in a

---

[2]Note that since these adjectives are non-gradable, they do not tolerate degree modifiers either,
e.g. *very pregnant*, *quite impossible*. This is in line with the claim that the Deg head has to
agree both with the AP and with QP modifiers, if any.

similar way as other dummy elements (e.g., *do*) enter the derivation, hence there is no need to stipulate any additional process such as *much*-deletion.

Periphrastic comparatives and superlatives are formed in the way given in (36): the Deg head *-er/-est* moves up to the Q head filled by *much* and the merge of *much* and *-er/-est* gives *more/most* (cf. Bresnan 1973; Corver 1997; Beck 2011; Kántor 2008a). Head adjunction results in the order *-er much* (or *-est much*) in syntax, due to Kayne's Linear Correspondence Axiom (Kayne 1994), see also the Mirror Principle of Baker (1985; 1988). It is the result of morphological merge at the PF interface that *-er/-est* is attached to *much*, which follows it.

This becomes even more important in the case of morphological comparatives, where there is no *much*. Here the Deg head *-er/-est* is still moved to a zero Q head in syntax and the degree morpheme undergoes morphological merge with the AP at PF, as argued for by Kántor (2010: 45–51). This is reinforced by the existence of irregular (suppletive) forms, such as *better*, which are formed by merging *-er* with *good*: this form obviously cannot be the result of simple syntactic merge of the two elements. Moreover, as Kántor (2010: 49–51) argues, the variation in possible forms in the case of complex adjectives can only be explained by attributing the mechanism to PF. For instance, an adjective like *good-looking* may have its comparative form either as *better-looking* or as *more good-looking*, the former being a clear indication of the fact that the *-er* is not attached to the AP (*good-looking*) in syntax but to the adjective itself in PF.[3]

Last but not least, the QP modifier is located in the specifier because it has to agree with the Q head (which is here *much*). As was mentioned in connection with the analysis given by Corver (1997), there are selectional restrictions as to which modifier can appear together with which degree, as illustrated in (48):

(48)   a. Mary is **very tall** / *****far tall**.

       b. Mary is *****very taller** / **far taller**.

As can be seen, the QP *very* can appear in absolute constructions but not in comparatives. By contrast, *far* is compatible with the comparative degree but not with the absolute. Due to this, the QP modifiers are clearly not adjuncts; therefore, the analysis based on specifier–head agreement can explain the restrictions better than one treating them as adjuncts, as was done for instance in Bresnan (1973) and Corver (1997).

---

[3]Note that it is the idiosyncratic property of (compound) adjectives whether they count as morphologically transparent or not. Whereas morphologically transparent ones (e.g. *well-paid* or *long-lasting*) tend to have both forms (e.g. *better-paid* and *more well-paid*, or *longer-lasting* and *more long-lasting*), the ones that are not transparent (e.g. *easy-going* or *hard-working*) can only be formed with *more* (e.g. *more easy-going* and not *easier-going*, or *more hard-working* but not *harder-working*).

Since the possibility of certain modifiers is merely dependent on the relevant degree features (and not, for instance, on the presence or absence of the ending *-ly*, as was proposed by Corver 1997), it is not inexplicable that strings such as *far different* should exist, even though there is no overt *-er* morpheme present. Since, as was mentioned before, *far* normally co-occurs with the comparative degree, the way to overcome this problem is to say that the adjective *different* inherently expresses comparison and therefore may be equipped with an inherent [+compr] feature, which agrees with a comparative Deg head. In fact, this is supported by the fact that in certain (American) dialects degree expressions with *different* typically take a *than*-clause instead of a PP, as in (49):

(49)   University life is **different** than I expected.

It is therefore preferable to analyse the relationship between QP modifiers and degree expressions as one determined by agreement between the modifier and the degree head moving to Q, rather than one depending on the *-ly* morpheme.

The analysis presented so far also has the advantage of treating morphological and periphrastic comparatives in a unified way, by assuming that the appearance of *much* in periphrastic comparatives is due to regular dummy insertion and not the lack of a stipulated deletion rule. The two remaining questions are therefore the role of the DegP other than marking the degree itself and how it may account for phenomena related to PP arguments of adjectives, and the mechanisms behind the extraposition of the comparative subclause.

2.4 Predicative and attributive adjectives

One important question regarding the analysis presented above is how it can account for the differences between predicative and attributive adjectives. There are adjectives that are inherently predicative; consider the examples in (50):

(50)   a.   The girl was **afraid**.
      b.   * I saw an **afraid** girl.

As can be seen, the adjective *afraid*, which is inherently predicative, can appear as a sentential predicate, as in (50a), but cannot be an attribute within a nominal expression, as demonstrated by the ungrammaticality of (50b). Similar adjectives include *alive, asleep* or *ill* in English.

On the other hand, there are inherently non-predicative adjectives too, such as *main* in (51):

(51)   a. *The reason is **main**.

      b. That is the **main** reason.

Contrary to *afraid*, the adjective *main* cannot function as a sentential predicate, as shown in (51a), but may be an attribute, as in (51b). It is interesting to note that most attributive-only adjectives are also non-gradable, e.g. *main, northern, mere, previous* or *utter*. However, this is by no means a necessity, as demonstrated by the examples in (52):

(52)   a. It is a **more recent** theory than the traditional transmission model.

      b. As he drinks, he gets into a **more drunken** state.

In fact, gradability and the choice between predicative and attributive uses are two independent properties which allow for six logical combinations: gradability is clearly binary and independently from this, adjectives may be predicative-only, attributive-only and may allow both options. Examples are given in Table 2.1.

Table 2.1: The classification of adjectives.

	predicative-only	attributive-only	both
gradable	*afraid*	*drunken*	*tall*
non-gradable	*alive*	*main*	*pregnant*

This strongly suggests that apart from the fact that a Deg head may appear only with a gradable adjective, there are also further features to be considered.

It has to be mentioned that there are considerable cross-linguistic differences as to which adjectives qualify as predicative-only or attributive-only. In Russian, for instance, all the adjectives mentioned above can be both predicative and attributive. Consider the examples in (53).

(53)   a. Eto **glavnyj** vokzal.
         this.N main   railway.station
         'This is the main railway station.'

      b. Etot vokzal   **glavnyj**.
         this.M railway.station main
         'This railway station is the main one.'

As can be seen, the adjective *glavnyj* 'main' can appear both as a predicate and as an attribute, contrary to English *main*. This shows that although there are general syntactic and semantic properties that play a crucial role in determining whether a given adjective can be predicative and/or attributive, and which hold across languages, there are also important cross-linguistic differences, and individual lexical items may be idiosyncratic, too.

The fact that there are idiosyncratic properties to be considered as well is indicated by the existence of synonyms that behave differently, in spite of there being no differences in their morphological structure. Such a pair is *ill* and *sick* in English: while *sick* may act both as a predicate and as an attribute, *ill* is licensed only in a predicative position. Apart from such unpredictable properties, however, there are of course certain semantic and syntactic properties that make restrictions predictable. As pointed out by Kenesei (2014), relational adjectives tend not to occur in attributive positions (cf. Bally 1944, McNally & Boleda 2004 and Fradin 2007, among others). This has an interesting morphosyntactic correlation in Hungarian, where the denominal adjective-forming suffix *-i* produces relational adjectives; therefore, as can be expected, adjectives formed with this suffix tend not to be allowed in attributive positions. Still, although most relational adjectives are attributive-only, there are ones that can function as predicates, e.g., *English*. Another semantic class that is known to be attributive-only is that of evaluative adjectives such as *damned*. I cannot examine these issues in detail here; however, it is important to bear in mind that there are several factors that determine whether a given adjective is predicative or attributive, including both semantic and syntactic features and cross-linguistic differences.

I propose that the difference between predicative-only and attributive-only adjectives can be formalised with the help of features that are independent from gradability.[4] First, let us consider the following examples:

---

[4]Since the aim of the present discussion is to provide an adequate analysis for the structure of degree expressions, I do not venture into a detailed examination of a feature-based categorisation of adjectives and will restrict myself to a basic distinction between predicative and non-predicative adjectives, which should suffice for the purpose of analysing degree expressions. As discussed by Fradin (2007), there are several criteria that have to be considered when examining the distribution of adjectives, including the syntactic position that they can take, gradability, and whether the adjective is denominal. These factors also interact with one another. Moreover, Fradin (2007) points out that, at least in languages that allow or even prefer postnominal modification, such as French, the distinction between a prenominal and a postnominal adjectival modifier is also crucial. Again, this is a problem I am not going to address, especially because the postnominal appearance of adjectives in the languages under scrutiny is rather due to the presence of a reduced relative clause and not to true rightward attachment of the QP modifier. Finally, I am not going to deal with the issue of category shift, that is, when an adjective can be assigned two different feature matrices depending on the noun it modifies, e.g., *osseux* 'bony' is gradable in constructions such as *visage osseux* 'bony face' but not in ones such as *tuberculose osseuse* 'bone tuberculosis', see Fradin (2007: 84–85).

(54)   a.   Mary is pregnant.

        b.   Mary is a pregnant woman.

        c.   Mary is tall.

        d.   Mary is a tall woman.

The respective semantic representations of the adjectives in (54) are given in (55) below:

(55)   a.   PREGNANT(x)

        b. $\exists$x[WOMAN(x)&PREGNANT(x)]]

        c. $\exists$d[TALL(x,d)]

        d. $\exists$x[WOMAN(x)&$\exists$d[TALL(x,d)]]

As can be seen, the difference between non-gradable adjectives like *pregnant* in (55a) and (55b) and gradable adjectives like *tall* in (55c) and (55d) is that the former simply denote sets of entities (x) that have a certain property, while gradable adjectives denote an ordered set of entities along the degrees (d) of an implied scale (see Kennedy & McNally 2005; Cresswell 1976; Heim 2000; Kennedy 1999). A gradable adjective equipped with a relevant syntactic feature, call it [+deg], contains information in its semantics with respect to a degree variable that quantifies over it; this is translated into syntax in such a way that the [+deg] feature must be checked against a Deg head. Non-gradable adjectives, on the other hand, are [−deg] and cannot enter into an agreement relationship with a Deg head; consequently, these adjectives are not supposed to be located within a DegP (and hence a QP).

On the other hand, there is a distinction between predicative and attributive adjectives: the latter do not take an individual but a variable (x), which is in turn taken by another predicate, both predicates being in the scope of the existential quantifier. Syntactically, this difference should be the presence of a feature that can be checked off against a noun, call it [+nom]. Attributive-only adjectives are inherently [+nom] and if they do not appear in an attributive position, this feature cannot be checked off by agreement. By contrast, predicative-only adjectives are inherently [−nom] and if they appear as attributes, there is a feature mismatch with the noun head, which causes ungrammaticality.

Adjectives that can be both predicates and attributes allow for both [+nom] and [−nom]. This may be manifest in distinct forms between the two uses; that is, in certain languages (such as German) there are inflected forms in the attributive position that overtly show agreement, while this is not so in predicative uses.

Since non-gradable adjectives can also be both [+nom] and [−nom], it should be clear that the choice is primarily not encoded in the Deg head, but rather on the AP itself: in the case of APs without a DegP projection, this syntactic information cannot be introduced elsewhere.

Naturally, in the case of gradable adjectives these features percolate up within the QP. First, the [±nom] feature of the AP percolates up to the DegP via specifier–head agreement (cf. Yoon 2001; Ortiz de Urbina 1993; Horvath 1997). Second, the movement of the Deg head to the Q head assures the percolation of the feature to the Q head. Hence a [+nom] QP can and must enter into a further agreement relationship with a nominal head.

Feature percolation is summarised in the diagram in (56):

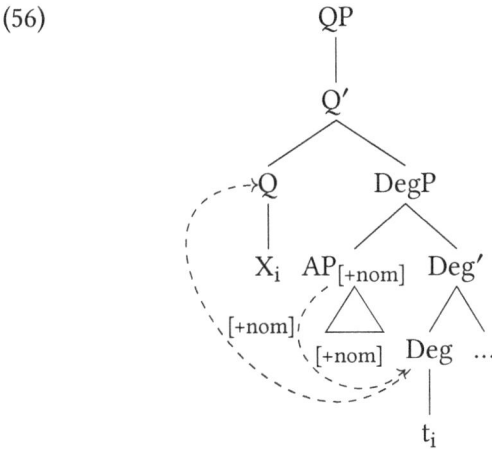

(56)

```
                        QP
                        |
                        Q'
                       / \
              - ->Q       DegP
             /    |       /  \
            /   Xᵢ  AP[+nom]  Deg'
         [+nom]     /\       / \
            \      /  \  [+nom] Deg  ...
             \    [+nom]        |
              ` - - - - - - ->  tᵢ
```

Predicative QPs can function as predicates in the clause or as postnominal modifiers and the Deg head is equipped with a [−nom] feature. Attributive QPs, by contrast, are modifiers of NPs and the Deg head is equipped with a [+nom] feature.

In the cases I have looked at so far, it was invariably the AP that defined the [±nom] nature of the degree expression, the Deg head itself being underspecified for this feature. However, it is possible that certain Deg heads are inherently [+nom] or [−nom]. This is the case of the Russian comparative head *-eje* as given in (41), which appears exclusively as a predicate: it takes a [−nom] AP in its specifier, uninflected for gender, and can never appear as an attribute. On the other hand, superlative constructions seem to be universally attributive-only (cf. Matushansky 2008, based on Heim 1999) and therefore it is justifiable that superlative Deg heads are inherently [+nom].

I do not wish to elaborate on the syntax and the semantics of superlatives here and to present an account for why superlatives are inherently [+nom] in particular. Note that the obligatory presence[5] of the definite article in superlatives is due to the presence of a nominal projection and is not required by the QP itself, as indicated by (57):

(57) This hypothesis is */??(the) best.

As indicated, the definite article *the* cannot be left out without affecting the grammaticality of the clause; still, there is no overt noun required. This is not the case for absolute and comparative adjectives such as (58a) and (58b):

(58) a. This hypothesis is **the good *(one)**.
      b. This hypothesis is **the better *(one)**.

In (58), there has to be either an overt lexical noun or at least the proform *one*, otherwise the structure is ungrammatical. By contrast, in simple predicative structures the article is absent and so is the noun (or *one*):

(59) a. This hypothesis is **good**.
      b. This hypothesis is **better**.

Such constructions are not readily available for superlatives, however, as shown in (60):

(60) */??This hypothesis is **best**.

Note also that different languages may behave differently with respect to the obligatory overtness of the noun head. In Hungarian, for instance, no such requirement is attested. Consider:

(61) a. Ez az elmélet a jó.
         this the theory the good
         'This theory is the good one.'

---

[5]The picture is in fact somewhat more complex in this respect, and the article may be omitted in certain cases, see Heim (1999) and Croitor & Giurgea (2016: 423–426) for discussion. Note, however, that definite DPs do not always require an overt definite article either, and the fact that the article does not always occur when a superlative is present reinforces the assumption that the article is not part of the degree phrase.

    b. Ez az elmélet **a**   **jobb**.
        this the theory the better

        'This theory is the better one.'

    c. Ez az elmélet **a**   **legjobb**.
        this the theory the best

        'This theory is the best one.'

As can be seen, all the cases in (61) involve the sequence of an overt definite article and an adjective but there is no phonologically visible noun head. I will not examine why this option is available for the absolute and the comparative degrees in Hungarian but not in English. What is important to note is that in the absence of a nominal projection, the superlative is not possible in Hungarian either:

(62)   a.   Ez az elmélet **jó**.
          this the theory good

          'This theory is good.'

       b.   Ez az elmélet **jobb**.
          this the theory better

          'This theory is better.'

       c. *Ez az elmélet **legjobb**.
          this the theory best

          'This theory is the best.'

In structures such as (62), there is no covert noun head and the QP functions as a predicate in the clause. This is possible with the absolute and the comparative degree, as in (62a) and (62b), respectively, but since the superlative degree is licensed only if there is a noun head in the structure, (62c) is not grammatical.

One of the obvious advantages of the analysis presented so far is that it provides a unified approach that covers both predicative and attributive structures. Recall that this was precisely one of the chief concerns expressed by Izvorski (1995). However, her analysis was shown to be problematic for several reasons. Contrary to her assumptions, I claim that the inner syntactic structure of degree expressions is the same in both cases, but the features determining whether the entire QP may function as a predicate or an attribute are indeed QP-internal.

2.5 Arguments of adjectives

Providing a formal account for the differences between predicative and attributive adjectives becomes especially important when considering arguments of adjectives. Recall that certain adjectives are known to have arguments of their own, as shown in (63):

(63)   a. Liz is proud [pp of her husband].

          b. Mary is afraid [pp of snakes].

In the examples above, the adjectives *proud* and *afraid* take the bracketed PPs as their arguments. However, adjectives with PP complements are not allowed in an attributive position, as shown in (64):

(64)   a. * Liz is a proud [pp of her husband] woman.

          b. Liz is a proud woman.

          c. Liz is a woman proud [pp of her husband].

As demonstrated by the data above, the appearance of *proud* with its PP complement is ungrammatical in the attributive position, as shown in (64a), despite the fact that *proud* can otherwise appear in this position, as shown in (64b). It is of course possible to have the adjective together with its PP argument in a postnominal position, as in (64c).

The same pattern can be observed in the case of inherently predicative-only adjectives, see (65):

(65)   a. * Mary is an afraid [pp of snakes] girl.

          b. Mary is a girl afraid [pp of snakes].

The ungrammaticality of (65a) is expected since the appearance of the adjective *afraid* in an attributive position would be ungrammatical anyway; again, the postnominal position leads to an acceptable construction, as in (65b). It seems that the ungrammaticality of (65a) is truly due to a problem with the particular position.

The explanation for this relies on the observation that PPs are invariably [−nom] in English. This is straightforward as they cannot be attributes. Consider the examples in (66):

(66)   a. The ladder is [pp behind the house].

          b. * The [pp behind the house] ladder is green.

          c. The ladder [pp behind the house] is green.

As can be seen, the PP *behind the house* can naturally appear in a predicative position but is excluded as the attribute of the noun *ladder*, as shown in (66b). However, it is grammatical for the PP to appear post-nominally, as in (66c).

One apparent counterexample is the case of *inside*, which can appear as an attribute, see (67):

(67)   a.   The robbery was an inside job.

      b.   He was keen to get an inside look.

However, *inside* in these cases is an adjective and not a preposition. The availability of *inside* as an adjective is demonstrated by the possibility of comparative and superlative forms, see (68):

(68)   a.   The trip gave us a more inside look at the area.

      b.   The guide promised to give us the most inside look at the area.

The question arises whether PPs could function as attributes at all. Interestingly, Hungarian postpositional phrases seem to allow this. Consider the examples in (69):

(69)   a.   A   létra   [pp a   ház   mögött] van.
          the ladder   the house behind is.

          'The ladder is behind the house.'

      b.   *A   [pp ház   mögött] létra   zöld.
          the   house behind ladder green

          'The ladder behind the house is green.'

In (69a), the PP *a ház mögött* 'behind the house', headed by the postposition *mögött* 'behind', is in a predicative position. By contrast, in (69b) it appears as an attribute within the nominal expression, and the result is ungrammatical. The only possibility for the PP to appear in an attributive position is when it is embedded in a phrase headed by the suffix *-i*:[6]

---

[6]Note that the suffix *-i* is attached to the entire PP, not only to the P head. As pointed out by Kenesei (1995: 163), the *-i* suffix derives an AP from the PP but the attachment of this suffix to a bare P head would be ungrammatical, as shown in (i):

(i)   *a   mögött-i   létra
    the behind-AFF ladder

    'the ladder behind'

(70)　A　[$_{XP}$ [$_{PP}$ ház　mögött] -i]　létra　zöld.
　　　　the　　　　house behind　AFF ladder green
　　　'The ladder behind the house is green.'

I will not venture to examine the exact status of the suffix -*i* here; suffice it to say that PPs in themselves cannot function as attributes in Hungarian either. In any case, the point is that in English, there is no construction such as (70) available for PPs either, and therefore PPs in English are never attributive in nature.

The problem regarding the position of attributive APs taking PP complements is also indicated by German word order differences (cf. Haider 1985: 202), as was partly discussed in connection with Lechner (1999; 2004). Consider the examples in (71):

(71)　a.　Lisa ist (wirklich) stolz [$_{PP}$ auf ihren　　Mann.]
　　　　　Liz　is　really　　proud　　of her.M.ACC husband
　　　　　'Liz is (really) proud of her husband.'

　　　b.　Lisa ist [$_{PP}$ auf ihren　　Mann] (wirklich) stolz.
　　　　　Liz　is　　of her.M.ACC husband really　　proud
　　　　　'Liz is (really) proud of her husband.'

　　　c.　Die [$_{PP}$ auf ihren　　Mann] stolze Frau　ist Lisa.
　　　　　the.F　of her.M.ACC husband proud.F woman is　Liz
　　　　　'The woman proud of her husband is Liz.'

　　　d.　* Die　stolze　[$_{PP}$ auf ihren　　Mann] Frau　ist Lisa.
　　　　　the.F proud.F　of her.M.ACC husband woman is　Liz
　　　　　'The woman proud of her husband is Liz.'

In (71a), the adjective *stolz* 'proud' takes a PP complement and may optionally be modified by an adverb such as *wirklich* 'really'. In (71b), the adjective and the PP complement appear in the reverse order. Recall that since the adverb *wirklich* can intervene between the two, it is obviously not the underlying order. This is crucial because while in predicative structures both orders converge, in the case of attributive adjectives only the inverse order, that is, where the PP has moved

---

The reason for this is that the P head must have a complement and cannot stand on its own. If the -*i* suffix were attached to the P head directly, however, then the string *mögötti* would be an adjective as such and should be allowed to appear as a modifier. Since this is not the case, it should be clear that the suffix -*i* is attached to the entire PP.

to the left, is grammatical, as in (71c), and the adjective taking its PP complement in its base position leads to ungrammaticality, as in (71d).

The reason for all this is that head-complement agreement between the adjective and its PP complement rules out a feature mismatch between the head and the PP. This makes two important predictions. First, inherently [+nom] adjectives do not take PP complements. Second, adjectives that otherwise allow both for [+nom] and [−nom] may take a PP complement, but if the QP functions as an attribute, the PP has to escape from this position prior to PF transfer. This is possible in German, where the PP can be moved to the left. Therefore, the lower copy (the complement of the adjective head) can be deleted. In English, by contrast, there is no such movement available; as a consequence, PPs cannot be taken by attributive adjectives.

The fact that the behaviour of PP arguments is directly linked to the structure of degree expressions by way of applying the same features renders an optimal explanation for the interrelated phenomena considered here.

2.6 Phases and deletion

It seems that PP arguments, while not available as complements of adjectives in attributive constructions, may appear together with adjectives in predicative positions without causing further problems for the analysis. However, this is not exactly the case, as the PP complement is apparently not adjacent to the adjective head:

(72) a. Liz is proud enough [pp of her husband].

   b. * Liz is proud [pp of her husband] enough.

Although the PP *of her husband* is clearly the argument of the adjective *proud*, it is ungrammatical for it to remain adjacent to the head, as shown by (72b). The only grammatical configuration is the one shown in (72a), where *enough* seems to intervene between the two. Note that the same would be true for a Deg head such as *-er*:

(73) Liz is prouder [pp of her husband] than Mary is.

In (73), the adjective *proud*, which moves up to the specifier of the DegP, is again not adjacent to its original complement PP.

Though it may be tempting to analyse constructions like (72a) as the results of rightward movement of the PP, the phenomenon can actually be explained by phase theory. Phases are derived syntactic objects, which are transferred to the interfaces as such (Chomsky 2008: 9). Therefore, phases may be spelt out separately. However, there are two important rules to be observed here. First, the phases spelt out the earliest will appear last in the PF order; and second, phases that are already spelt out become opaque, that is, invisible for syntax (Chomsky 2001; 2004; 2008; Nissenbaum 2000; Svenonius 2004; Kántor 2008a).

To illustrate this, let us take the example of the CP complement in comparatives, as described by Kántor (2008a). Consider the examples in (74):

(74)   a.   * I saw a taller [$_{CP}$ than John] man.
       b.   I saw a taller man [$_{CP}$ than John].
       c.   I saw [$_{DP}$ a [$_{QP}$ taller [$_{CP}$ opaque]] man] [$_{CP}$ than John].

In (74a), the CP appears adjacent to *taller*, that is, in its base position as a complement within the QP modifying the NP *man*. The result is, however, ungrammatical: the well-formed configuration is shown in (74b), where the CP appears as the rightmost element. PF ordering is shown in (74c). The CP *than John*, as a phase, is spelt out first: hence its rightmost position in the linear structure. Since it is spelt out, it will appear as opaque in the syntactic structure in its base position (and will of course not be overt at PF either).

There are two observations to be made here. First, the order of spell-out is not completely independent from the order of merge. If a phase-sized XP is merged into the structure earlier than a phase-sized YP, and if the XP can be spelt out earlier than YP is merged, then XP will naturally be spelt out earlier than YP. Second, any XP can be spelt out only if it has checked off its uninterpretable features. This is crucial when dealing with cross-linguistic data. In Hungarian, for instance, relative clauses are embedded within a DP headed by a matrix pronominal element that is responsible for introducing the relative clause into the structure (cf. É. Kiss 2002: 243–248). It is a possible configuration that the CP is spelt out earlier but the DP, which can for instance be a focus, has features to be checked and cannot be spelt out. This is demonstrated in (75):

(75)   [$_{DP}$ Azt   [$_{CP}$ *opaque*]] felejtsd   el, [$_{CP}$ amiről
            that.ACC   forget.IMP.2SG off   what.REL.DEL
       beszéltünk]!
       talked.1PL
       'Forget what we talked about!'

Since the pronoun *azt* is focussed but the subclause itself is not, they naturally appear as disjoint elements in the linear structure. However, if the subclause is interpreted as a topic, see (76), it may move together with the rest of the DP (example from É. Kiss 2002: 244, ex. 40a):

(76) [DP Azt,   [CP amiről   beszéltünk,]] felejtsd   el!
          that.ACC   what.REL.DEL talked.1PL   forget.IMP.2SG off

'Forget what we talked about!'

I will not examine here the conditions on why and how subordinate CPs may not appear sentence-finally, as it would require a separate and thorough investigation on its own, especially because in several languages, such as Japanese, Korean, Chinese and Turkish, there are pre-nominal relative clauses, see Larson & Takahashi (2007).

Turning back to the seemingly extraposed PPs in structures like (72), the explanation relies on the assumption that PPs can be considered phases too (Lee-Schoenfeld 2007; Drummond et al. 2010; Gallego 2010; Fowlie 2010); consequently, they can be spelt out separately. Therefore, what happens in the case of (72) can be demonstrated as given in (77):

(77) Liz is proud [PP *opaque*] enough [PP of her husband].

The PP *of her husband*, being a phase, is spelt out first and it appears as the last element in the PF ordering. At the same time, it becomes opaque in its base position in the syntax.

It has to be stressed that this does not happen in an unrestricted way. The PP can be spelt out only if its features are checked off. As should be obvious, [−nom] features cannot be present in an attributive construction, hence a structure like (78) is ruled out:

(78) *Liz is a proud woman [PP of her husband].

From this, it follows that separate spell-out is not an escape hatch for ungrammatical configurations to converge, but is instead very strictly rule-governed.

A further restriction concerns ordering: the phase spelt out first appears last. This predicts that the order of a comparative subclause and a PP argument of an adjective is fixed, as shown in (79):

(79)   a.   Liz is prouder [PP of her husband] [CP than Mary is].

        b. * Liz is prouder [CP than Mary is] [PP of her husband].

Only the order in which the CP appears last converges. This is so because the CP is merged into the construction earlier than the PP, and therefore the CP has to be spelt out first.

This shows that though the ordering of various elements largely depends on the order of PF transfers, PF ordering is ultimately defined by syntax. The present analysis is fairly advantageous to previous ones that neither considered the difference between the base and the surface position of the comparative subclause, nor did they apply some kind of rightward movement. On the other hand, the apparent extraposition of comparative subclauses and PP arguments of adjectives can be handled in a similar way, without assuming that they would have the same or even similar positions in the syntax.

3 Comparative Deletion

3.1 Introduction

The aim of this chapter is to provide an account for Comparative Deletion and to reduce the cross-linguistic differences attested in connection with it to minimal feature differences in the relevant operators. On the one hand, the advantage of the proposal lies in the fact that Comparative Deletion does not have to be treated as a parameter distinguishing between languages that have it and ones that do not. On the other hand, the feature-based account is apt for handling language-internal variation as well, since the difference is ultimately not between individual languages but rather between operators that do or do not trigger Comparative Deletion. In order to see in what way my claim is radically new, I will first review some of the most important analyses concerning Comparative Deletion, also showing the problems that arise in connection with them and that they can be fully eliminated using the feature-based approach proposed here.

3.2 Earlier accounts

3.2.1 The problems to be discussed

The phenomenon of Comparative Deletion (CD) traditionally denotes the absence of an adjectival or nominal expression from the comparative subclause. Consider the following examples:

(1)   a.   Ralph is more qualified than Jason is ~~x qualified~~.
      b.   Ralph has more qualifications than Jason has ~~x many qualifications~~.
      c.   Ralph has better qualifications than Jason has ~~x good qualifications~~.

In all of the examples above, x denotes a certain degree or quantity as to which a certain entity is qualified, good, etc. (that is, the standard value). This is an operator that has no phonological content (cf., for example, Chomsky 1977). As can be seen, in (1a) an adjectival expression is deleted: this type is referred to as the predicative comparative since the quantified adjectival expression functions as a predicate in the subclause. By contrast, in both (1b) and (1c) a nominal expression is deleted; structures like (1b) are nominal comparatives, where a nominal expression bears quantification, while (1c) is an example of attributive comparatives, where the quantified adjectival expression is an attributive modifier within a nominal expression.

Therefore, one of the most important questions to be answered in connection with Comparative Deletion is how the fact that different constituents seem to be deleted by Comparative Deletion can be accounted for. Moreover, this deletion process seems to be obligatory inasmuch as the presence of the quantified expressions in (1) would lead to ungrammatical constructions; thus a proper analysis of Comparative Deletion must also address the issue of why it seems to be obligatory.

Additionally, the role of information structure underlying Comparative Deletion has to be taken into consideration as well. In subcomparative structures, an adjectival or nominal element may be left overt in the subclause; as opposed to the examples in (1), these elements are not logically identical to an antecedent in the matrix clause:

(2)　a.　The table is longer than the desk is **wide**.
　　　b.　Ralph has more books than Jason has **manuscripts**.
　　　c.　Ralph wrote a longer book than Jason did **a manuscript**.

The main question is of course whether such examples are to be treated as being exempt from Comparative Deletion or whether Comparative Deletion still applies in these cases.

Strongly connected to this, the exact site of Comparative Deletion has to be investigated, for which there are two main candidates: the base position of the quantified element, and an operator position in the left periphery of the subclause. Interestingly, it seems that an operator can in certain cases be visible even in English (cf. Chomsky 1977):

(3)　% Ralph is more qualified than **what** Jason is.

This raises the question of how examples such as (3) relate to the ones given in (1) in terms of Comparative Deletion; more specifically, whether constructions like (1) also involve the movement of the quantified expression and, on the other hand, whether Comparative Deletion takes place in (3) as well.

Moreover, apart from instances like (3), in some languages full degree expressions – i.e. when the degree element is combined with a lexical AP or an NP – can be attested at the left periphery of the subclause (cf. Kenesei 1992). The following examples are from Hungarian:

(4) a. Mari magasabb, mint **amilyen magas** Péter.
Mary taller   than how   tall   Peter
'Mary is taller than Peter.'

b. Marinak több macskája   van, mint **ahány   macskája**
Mary.DAT more cat.POSS.3SG is   than how.many cat.POSS.3SG
Péternek van.
Peter.DAT is
'Mary has more cats than Peter has.'

c. Marinak nagyobb macskája   van, mint **amilyen nagy macskája**
Mary.DAT bigger   cat.POSS.3SG is   than how   big cat.POSS.3SG
Péternek van.
Peter.DAT is
'Mary has a bigger cat than Peter has.'

As can be seen, Hungarian allows the overt presence of the degree elements, which shows that Comparative Deletion must be subject to parametric variation. The question is how this variation can be accounted for; that is, what licenses the overt presence of these elements in Hungarian but not in English. Conversely, a satisfactory answer to this question should also explain what underlies Comparative Deletion in English (and other languages that behave in the same way as English).

Strongly related to this, the question arises to what extent the internal structure of the degree expression plays a role and whether there is any difference among the individual operators. In Standard English, as shown in (2a), the adjective that remains overt in the subclause is found in its base position without an overt operator. The Hungarian operator *amilyen* 'how' may appear together with the adjective, as in (4a), though the adjective may not be stranded, as shown by the ungrammaticality of (5):

(5) * Mari magasabb, mint **amilyen** Péter **magas**.
Mary taller   than how   Peter tall
'Mary is taller than Peter.'

On the other hand, Hungarian has another operator, *amennyire* 'how much', see (6), which allows both options for the adjective.

(6)   a. Mari magasabb, mint **amennyire magas** Péter.
          Mary taller   than how.much tall   Peter

     'Mary is taller than Peter.'

    b. Mari magasabb, mint **amennyire** Péter **magas**.
          Mary taller   than how.much Peter tall

     'Mary is taller than Peter.'

Note that though the availability of (6b) with *amennyire* may at first sight suggest that it is a VP-modifier, it will be shown later on that such a claim could not be maintained and that *amennyire* is hence an operator within the extended degree expression.

In addition, it has to be mentioned that Hungarian requires the presence of some operator if the adjective is overt (note, however, that it is allowed for the adjective and the operator to be non-overt at the same time). This is illustrated by (7):

(7)   a. Mari magasabb, mint (***magas**) Péter.
          Mary taller   than   tall   Peter

     'Mary is taller than Peter.'

    b. Mari magasabb, mint Péter (***magas**).
          Mary taller   than Peter   tall

     'Mary is taller than Peter.'

Therefore, a sound analysis of Comparative Deletion must also take into account that languages differ with respect to the presence/absence of the operator in a more intricate way than one that could be formulated on a +/− basis.

In the following, I am going to present three approaches to Comparative Deletion. The first one is that of Bresnan (1973), which can be regarded as the first description and analysis of Comparative Deletion as such. Second, I am going to present the proposal made by Lechner (1999; 2004), which is interesting especially because it takes a deletion in situ approach, which is not typical for the literature on Comparative Deletion. Finally, I am going to deal with the analysis of Kennedy (2002), which adopts the more traditional view of *wh*-movement in comparative subclauses, strongly relying on the literature since Bresnan (1973) and at the same time approaching the question of Comparative Deletion in a more formalistic way than previous proposals.

3.2.2 Comparative Deletion and identity – Bresnan (1973)

Bresnan (1973: 316) assumes that something in the comparative subclause "is al-ways deleted under 'identity with' (nondistinctness from) the head". This oper-ation is referred to as Comparative Deletion (Bresnan 1973: 317). Consider the examples in (8), taken from Bresnan (1973: 316, ex. 242):

(8) a. I've never seen a man **taller** than my father.
   b. I've never seen **a taller man** than my father.
   c. I've never seen a man **taller** than my mother.
   d. I've never seen **a taller man** than my mother.

In both (8b) and (8d) the quantified nominal expression in the matrix clause is *a taller man*, which has a parallel in the subclause; the analysis by Bresnan (1973: 317, ex. 245) is as follows:

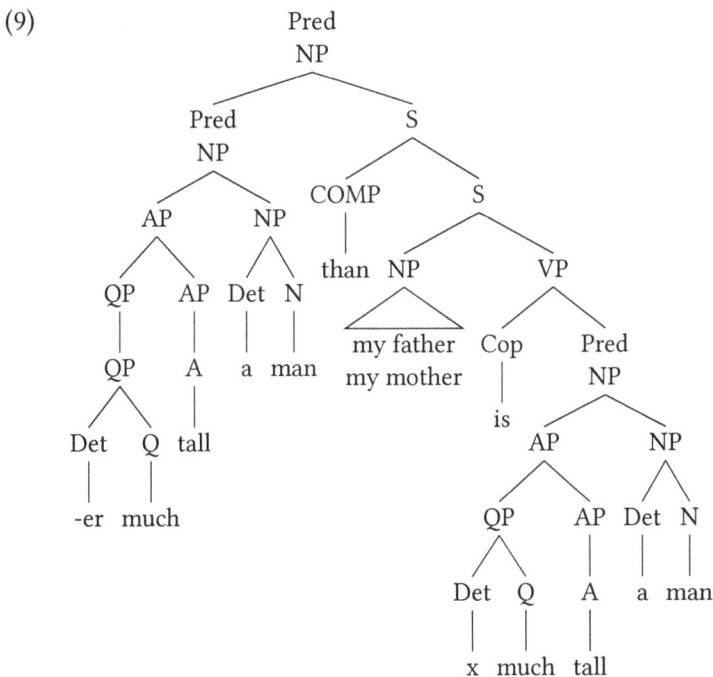

(9)

```
                              Pred
                              NP
                 _____/      _____
              Pred                               S
              NP                          ____/     \____
         ____/    \____              COMP              S
        AP            NP             |            ___/    \___
      _/  \_         _/ \_         than NP       VP
    QP      AP    Det   N        __/  _____    __/  \__
    |       |     |     |       my father  Cop      Pred
    QP      A     a    man      my mother   |        NP
  _/ \_     |                               is    __/    \__
Det   Q    tall                           AP         NP
 |    |                                 __/  \__     _/ \
-er  much                              QP      AP  Det  N
                                     _/ \_     |    |   |
                                   Det   Q     A    a  man
                                    |    |     |
                                    x  much  tall
```

Disregarding now the apparent word order problems (e.g. how the string *-er much tall a man* ultimately gives the surface string *a taller man*), the primary importance of the particular representation for Bresnan (1973) is that it explains why (8b) is unproblematic while (8d) is semantically awkward: the reconstructed (underlying) structure of the subclause contains the predicate *an x-much tall man* as a predicate, which is fully acceptable with a subject such as *my father* but is normally unavailable for a subject such as *my mother* since there is a gender mismatch in the latter case.

As for Comparative Deletion itself, what happens in a structure like (9) is that Comparative Deletion eliminates the predicate in the subclause, which in this case is an NP. By contrast, in structures such as (8a) and (8c) above, Bresnan (1973: 319, ex. 251) suggests that we have the following structure:

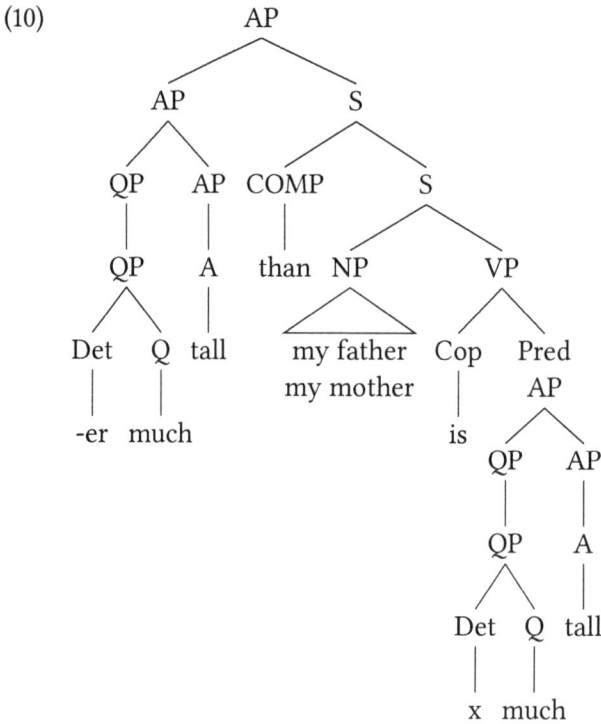

(10)

```
                              AP
                   ┌──────────┴──────────┐
                  AP                       S
              ┌────┴────┐          ┌───────┴───────┐
             QP    AP  COMP              S
              │     │    │          ┌────┴────┐
             QP     A  than  NP            VP
          ┌───┴──┐  │      ┌──┴──┐      ┌──┴──┐
        Det   Q  tall   my father  Cop   Pred
         │    │         my mother   │     AP
         │    │                     │   ┌──┴──┐
        -er  much                  is  QP     AP
                                        │      │
                                       QP      A
                                     ┌──┴──┐   │
                                    Det  Q   tall
                                     │   │
                                     x  much
```

As can be seen, in this case the degree expression in the subclause is a predicate on its own; consequently, the sentences in (8a) and (8c) are both felicitous because there is no gender mismatch in either case.

What happens in both (9) and (10) is that the predicate of the subclause is deleted under identity with its matrix clausal antecedent: crucially, this identity holds in terms of syntactic structure as well. Disregarding now the problem of how Comparative Deletion exactly deletes this material, the point of the argument is that deleted material must be recoverable, and it seems that the most straightforward way of recovering elided material is that a structurally identical string is reconstructed. This is crucially important when trying to account for certain mismatches. Consider the following examples (cf. Bresnan 1973: 320, ex. 254):

(11)   a. John wants to find **a better solution** than Christine did.

        b. John wants to find **a better solution** than Christine's.

In this case, both constructions are grammatical: the elided element in the subclause is the nominal expression *an x-much good solution*, which may occur both as the object of the verb, as in (11a), and as the predicate, as in (11b); cf. Bresnan (1973: 319–320). These cases correspond to the representation given in (9). By contrast, if the elided element has an antecedent that is not a nominal modifier, a construction like (11a) is ruled out:

(12)   a. *John wants to find a solution **better** than Christine did.

        b. John wants to find a solution **better** than Christine's.

As pointed out by Bresnan (1973: 320), the problem with (12a) is that the head of the comparative is an AP; that is, the degree expression in the matrix clause (*better*) is not an attribute but a predicate. Thus, the structure corresponds to the one in (10) and the degree expression in the subclause should also be a complement of the verb as such, which is ruled out in (12a): the AP cannot be the object of the verb.

Such differences also hold if the degree expression is a verbal modifier, as in (13) below (Bresnan 1973: 320, ex. 256):

(13)   a. Jack eats caviar **more** than he eats mush.

        b. Jack eats **more caviar** than he eats mush.

        c. Jack eats caviar **more** than he sleeps.

        d. *Jack eats **more caviar** than he sleeps.

As indicated, in the case of (13a) and (13c), the degree expression is *more*, which is a VP-modifier and as such is available in both constructions. By contrast, in (13b) and (13d) the degree expression is *more caviar*, which can have a corresponding element in the subclause in the former (i.e. *x-much mush*) but not in the latter: in (13d) there is no (reconstructed) nominal element in the subclause in which a degree element could appear as an attribute.

Similar examples could be cited but the basic assumption made by Bresnan (1973) should be clear now: Comparative Deletion eliminates something from the subclause that is in some way identical to its matrix clausal antecedent; this element may be a predicate AP, as in (9) and (12), a predicate NP, as in (10) and (11), the degree expression within a predicate NP, as in (13b), or a verbal modifier, as in (13a) and (13c).

Furthermore, there are instances where only part of a predicate AP is deleted, as in the following example (Bresnan 1973: 322, ex. 262):

(14)   The table is **longer** than the door is **wide**.

According to Bresnan (1973: 322–324), the clause given in (14) should have the structure given in (10): the predicate AP in the subclause is then *x-much wide*, and deletion affects the QP modifier *x-much* but leaves the adjective itself (*wide*) intact.

Although the observations made by Bresnan (1973) on the phenomenon of Comparative Deletion are crucially important, it has to be stressed that they can be regarded as a description of certain problems rather than the analysis thereof. First of all, it is left entirely unexplained what the mechanism of Comparative Deletion actually is: Bresnan (1973) convincingly shows that – in order to get the right interpretations – the elements undergoing Comparative Deletion have to be present in the structure at some point in the derivation but that they later also have to be eliminated in order to produce grammatical configurations. However, it is not clear why these elements cannot remain overt in the first place.

Second, Bresnan (1973) does not elaborate on how exactly the deletion process is carried out: it seems that the elements in question are elided in their base position (though the subclause itself is claimed to be extraposed) but it remains unaddressed how the mechanism of Comparative Deletion can detect what the deletion site in each case is. At this point, it seems that Comparative Deletion is assigned considerable power in the sense that it has the ability to actually decide how much of structure must and may be elided. Again, this is undesirable because it leads to circularity, that is, we know what Comparative Deletion has to elide on the basis of the data but then the data are claimed to be such precisely because Comparative Deletion applies in such a way. Therefore, instead of having a mechanism that can potentially elide anything, it would be desirable to have a well-defined rule or rather rules interacting with each other, which would operate in a more restricted way. In addition, a minimalist account should also clearly state which operations take place in overt syntax and which belong to PF.

Third, if one were to assume that Comparative Deletion takes place in the base position of the arguments, the question arises how to account for constructions that involve *wh*-movement even in English and to what extent evidence for *wh*-movement in any comparative subclause can be disregarded when trying to provide an explanation for Comparative Deletion. Strongly connected to this, the last problem with Bresnan (1973) is that she does not take cross-linguistic data into consideration: if Comparative Deletion is taken to be an obligatory operation, this very definition of Comparative Deletion proves to be untenable in the light of cross-linguistic data clearly contradicting the assumption that Comparative Deletion would always be obligatory in the way it seems to be in English.

3.2.3 Comparative Deletion and coordination – Lechner (1999; 2004)

As formulated by Lechner (2004: 9), the view concerning Comparative Deletion in the generative literature since Bresnan (1973; 1975; 1977) has been that Comparative Deletion is "an obligatory operation which removes the gradable property from the comparative complement (*than*-XP), accounting for the observation that comparatives in English and in related languages characteristically contain a gap which cannot be lexically filled."

Lechner (2004: 9) considers Comparative Deletion to be an instance of syntactic ellipsis and tries to account for it by way of the AP-Raising Hypothesis, contrary to Lerner & Pinkal (1992; 1995) and Kennedy (1997; 1999), who fundamentally build on the assumption that the ellipsis site is recovered at the semantic component. The chief argument against a fully semantics-based analysis stems from the fact that if Comparative Deletion is an LF operation, then "the principles which operate only on syntactic representations (overt syntax or LF)" should be "blind to the content of" Comparative Deletion (Lechner 2004: 14).

Lechner (2004: 14–21) presents two major arguments in favour of treating Comparative Deletion as a process operating in syntax: disjoint reference effects and ATB extraction. Examining first the issue of disjoint reference effects, let us consider the examples in (15) containing the adjective *proud* (Lechner 2004: 14, ex.20):

(15)   a.   Mary is prouder of John than Bill is _____ of Sally.
            (_____ = x-proud)
       b.   Mary is prouder of John than Bill is _____ .
            (_____ = x-proud of John)

As can be seen, the adjective *proud* may take a PP complement and deletion may affect either the adjective head alone or the adjective and the PP together (Lechner 2004: 14). As argued for by Lechner (2004: 15–16), based on similar analyses in coordination such as Jayaseelan (1990), Johnson (1997) and Lasnik (1995), in both cases the AP is eliminated by Comparative Deletion: the difference stems from the fact that in (15a) the PP moves out of the AP and is thus not affected by deletion.

The importance of this becomes straightforward when considering examples such as (16) below (Lechner 2004: 16, ex. 24):

(16)   * Mary is prouder of John$_i$ than he$_i$ is _____ .
          (_____ = x-proud of John$_i$)

As Lechner (2004: 16) argues, this example "lacks a reading in which *John* and *he* are construed as coreferential, attesting to a Principle C violation." Given that "Principle C is operative in syntax, the object PP accordingly has to be present at least by LF"; furthermore, because the PP is part of the site Comparative Deletion, one may conclude that the site "has been restored already during the syntactic computation, i.e. prior to semantics" (Lechner 2004: 16). In the light of this, consider the following example (Lechner 2004: 16, ex. 25):

(17)   Mary is prouder of John$_i$ than he$_i$ believes that I am _____ .
          (_____ = x-proud of John$_i$)

In this case the Principle C effect is obviated; what happens is that "Binding Theory treats the name inside" the site of Comparative Deletion "as a pronoun, and not as an R-expression" (Lechner 2004: 16). Thus, the reconstruction into site of Comparative Deletion "for Principle C is subject to *Vehicle Change* (in the sense of Fiengo & May 1994) from R-expressions to pronouns" (Lechner 2004: 16). As pointed out by Lechner (2004: 16, ex. 26), a similar difference between (16) and (17) can also be observed in coordination, as shown by (18):

(18)   a.   * Mary is proud of John$_i$ and he$_i$ is _____ , too.
                 (_____ = proud of John$_i$)
         b.   Mary is proud of John$_i$ and he$_i$ believes that I am _____ , too.
                 (_____ = proud of John$_i$)

Since *Vehicle Change* implies that there is material present in the syntax before LF, and since there is a strong resemblance to the kind of ellipsis observed in coordination, which is treated as syntactic deletion, there is reason to believe that Comparative Deletion is indeed an instance of syntactic deletion, too.

On the other hand, comparatives seem to allow ATB extraction, in structures such as (19) below (Lechner 2004: 19, ex. 35):

(19)   a person **who**$_i$ Mary is [more proud of t_i] than Peter is _____
       (_____ = x-proud of t_i)

As Lechner (2004: 19) notes, this might at first sight resemble parasitic gap constructions, such as (20), cf. Lechner (2004: 19, ex. 36):

(20)   **a book**$_i$ which you filed t_i [before reading t_i]

There is, however, a crucial difference between parasitic gap constructions and comparatives in that the former but not the latter tolerate asymmetric extraction out of the matrix clause (Lechner 2004: 19). Consider the example in (21), taken from Lechner (2004: 19, ex. 37):

(21)   **a book**$_i$ which you filed t_i [before reading the newspaper]

However, the same is not available in comparatives (see Lechner 2004: 19, ex. 38):

(22)   a.   * a person **who**$_i$ Mary is [more proud of t_i] than Peter is _____ of
             John$_k$
             (_____ = x-proud of t_k)
       b.   * a person **who**$_i$ Mary is [more proud of John] than Peter is _____
             (_____ = x-proud of t_i)

In this respect, comparatives seem to resemble coordination; consider the following examples (Lechner 2004: 19, exx. 39–40):

(23)   a.   a person **who**$_i$ [$_{IP}$ Mary is proud of t_i] and [$_{IP}$ Peter is proud of t_i]
       b.   * a person **who**$_i$ [$_{IP}$ Mary is proud of t_i] and [$_{IP}$ Peter is proud of
             John]
       c.   * a person **who**$_i$ [$_{IP}$ Mary is proud of John] and [$_{IP}$ Peter is proud of
             t_i]

In line with previous proposals (see Pinkham 1982; Napoli 1983; McCawley 1988; Moltmann 1992; Corver 1993), Lechner (2004), as well as Lechner (1999), builds his analysis on the apparent parallelism between coordination and comparative structures. What is relevant for us here is that in structures such as (23), extraction out of only one of the conjuncts, as in (23b) and (23c), is prohibited by the Coordinate Structure Constraint (CSC), which is syntactic in nature (Lechner 2004: 19–20). Thus, if there is a similar phenomenon observed in comparatives, as in (22), it is presumably also due to syntactic constraints. Furthermore, since these constraints have to apply to the degree expression in the subclause, the degree expression itself must be present in the syntactic derivation. It logically follows that Comparative Deletion involves some kind of syntactic deletion and is not merely an LF constraint (Lechner 2004: 21).

Lechner (2004: 38–50) proposes that Comparative Deletion is in fact AP-raising, which involves the overt movement of the AP in the subclause (located in the [Spec,DegP] position) to the matrix clause (likewise to the [Spec,DegP] position). In the case of nominal or attributive comparatives, the NP and the AP are treated as a single constituent undergoing the same movement, to the exclusion of the Deg head itself.

Therefore, for a string such as *Mary knows younger authors than Peter knows*, the representation would be as follows (based on Lechner 2004: 41, ex. 90):

(24)

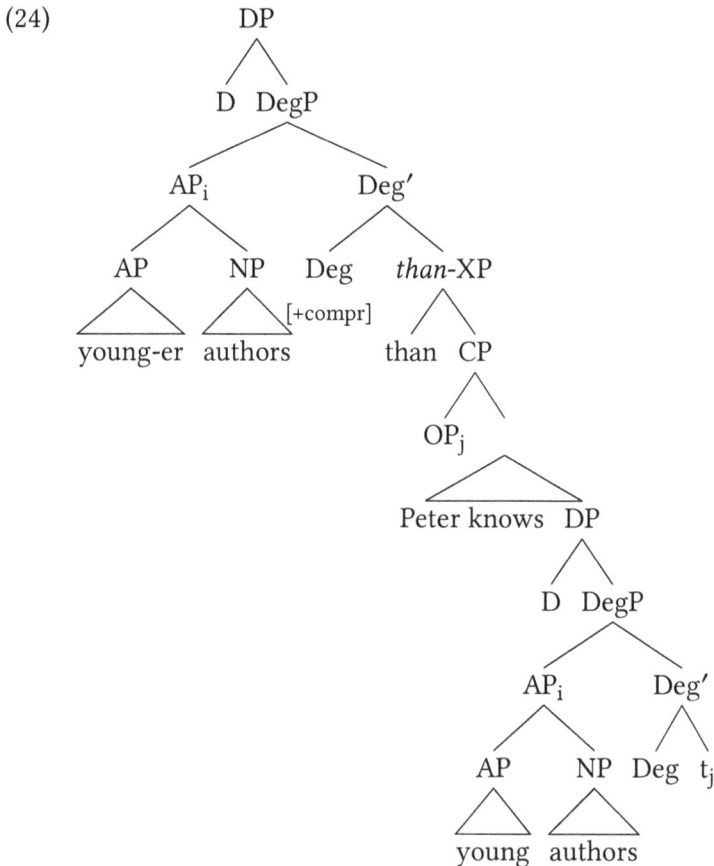

As can be seen in (24), AP-Raising constitutes the upward movement of the AP in the subclause to the matrix clause, from a [Spec,DegP] position into another [Spec,DegP] position (Lechner 2004: 40–41). This kind of movement is supposed to leave a semantically interpretable copy in its base position (in the subclause) and so both copies are claimed to be visible at LF (Lechner 2004: 42–43). The chief difference between the two DegP projections is that while the one in the matrix clause is equipped with a [+comparative] feature, the one in the subclause is not; consequently, only the higher DegP is interpreted as [+comparative], see Lechner (2004: 41). Note that the movement of the comparative operator to the [Spec,CP] position happens independently from AP-Raising (Lechner 2004: 41).

In other words, by separating the identity that holds between the two APs and the non-identity that is maintained between the two DegPs, the analysis aims at accounting for one of the most important issues in terms of comparatives; that is, how far identity is required to hold between the two degree expressions. Since the two Deg heads are clearly distinct from each other, there is nothing to require identity between them. However, as far as the APs are concerned, movement by definition ensures that these have to be identical since they are two copies of one and the same syntactic object. Movement itself is motivated by the presence of the [+comparative] feature on the Deg head in the matrix clause: this feature is claimed to be uninterpretable on the Deg head and it can be checked off by moving an AP to the specifier of the DegP.

Although certain points in the analysis may seem to be advantageous, it also raises a number of rather serious problems. First, it builds on a strong identity between the two APs and is therefore unable to account for subcomparative structures; that is, where the AP in the matrix clause differs from the one in the subclause, as in (2). One might suppose that in these cases there is an AP base-generated in the matrix clause and the [+comparative] feature of the Deg head can be checked off without the movement of the subclausal AP. In turn, the AP in the subclause would remain overt as it would not qualify as a lower copy. However, this also raises the question of why base-generation is not an available option even if the two APs are identical, especially as the fact that both copies are to be interpreted by LF at the same time seems to require an extra condition anyway; moreover, base-generation would in fact be more economical than movement. Strongly related to this, the syntactic motivation behind AP-Raising is unclear in itself.

Second, the analysis of degree expressions and of DPs containing degree expressions is problematic, as should be clear from the discussion in Chapter 2. I will return to the issue of where degree expressions are located within the DP in

Chapter 4; for the time being, suffice it to say that treating the NP as part of the AP is at least counterintuitive as the sequence of an AP and an NP is more likely to be treated as a nominal expression by syntax. More importantly, however, the representation in (24) fails to account for cases when the D head itself is filled by a determiner (e.g. *a younger author than Peter knows*): according to Lechner (2004), only the AP (containing the NP) moves out, which has two implications. On the one hand, the D head in the matrix clause should contain a base-generated determiner, which again raises the question of why there is no base-generation available for the entire AP. On the other hand, the D head in the matrix clause should be deleted by some stipulated deletion process targeting only this D head, which is obviously rather problematic. Alternatively, one may stipulate that the D head cannot be filled in the subclause but this idea is again refuted by subcomparative structures (e.g. in structures like *Mary wrote a longer poem than Peter did a play*).

Third, the analysis clearly fails to account for cases where Comparative Deletion does not seem to be obligatory, see the examples in (4) from Hungarian. In these cases the AP in the subclause does remain overt even if it is identical to its counterpart in the matrix clause: this would be ruled out by Lechner (2004), whose analysis predicts that the elimination of the lower AP happens regularly.

Moreover, there is a yet more serious problem, which is the separation of AP-movement from operator movement, at least in the form proposed by Lechner (2004). While in Standard English the separation of the zero operator from the AP may seem to be unproblematic, in languages such as Hungarian it is obvious that the operator can and in some cases must move together with the AP, provided that the AP is overtly present in the structure: see the examples in (4), (5), (6) and (7). This not only indicates that the structure of degree expressions adopted by Lechner (2004) is flawed but also that there is no separate AP-Raising as such: the AP either moves together with the operator (that is, as part of the entire QP, or as part of the entire DP containing such a QP), or it may stay in its base position.

This latter distinction points to a further gap in the theory presented by Lechner (2004), namely that comparative operators seem to differ with respect to whether they require overt APs and whether these APs may then be stranded or not. Since all of the problems enumerated here are crucial in terms of identifying what Comparative Deletion is, especially in cross-linguistic terms, it should be clear that Lechner (2004) fails to provide a sound explanation for Comparative Deletion, and hence an alternative should be sought.

3.2.4 Comparative Deletion and movement – Kennedy (2002)

Before turning to the discussion of my analysis for Comparative Deletion, let me briefly discuss one more proposal, namely that of Kennedy (2002), which is crucially important in that it acknowledges that there is movement in comparative subclauses and in that it builds the explanation on this fundamental assumption.

The core part of the analysis relies on the distinction between Comparative Deletion (CD) structures and Comparative Subdeletion (CSD) structures (Kennedy 2002: 553–554). The crucial difference between the two is that while in the case of Comparative Subdeletion "an amount or degree term must be omitted from the constituent that provides the point of comparison with the morphologically marked phrase in the matrix clause", in Comparative Deletion "the lexical content must be omitted from the compared constituent as well" (Kennedy 2002: 554).

Note, however, that even if the compared constituent is logically identical to its counterpart in the matrix clause, it may remain overt if it bears contrastive focus (Kennedy 2002: 555). Consider the example in (25), taken from Kennedy (2002: 555, ex. 5a), quoting Chomsky (1977):

(25)   A: This desk is **higher** than that one is **wide**.

      B: What is more, this desk is **higher** than that one is **HIGH**.

As noted by Kennedy (2002: 555), "most analyses of comparatives in English have hypothesized that CSD structures are basic, and that the omission of additional material in CD can be derived from general principles of redundancy reduction" (cf. for example Lees 1961). In other words, such views assume that Comparative Deletion and Comparative Subdeletion have different syntactic derivations, in that the former but not the latter involves a deletion process. Contrary to this, Kennedy (2002: 555–556) proposes that both structures involve the movement of the compared constituent to the lower [Spec,CP] position: however, while in Comparative Deletion structures this movement is overt, in Comparative Subdeletion it is claimed to be covert. Consequently, the two types are essentially identical at LF but differ at PF; that is, there is deletion taking place in the case of Comparative Deletion (Kennedy 2002: 556).

Evidence for there being movement in both structures comes from the fact that both constructions are ill-formed when the gap is within an extraction island (Kennedy 2002: 557–558, based on Ross 1967, Huddleston 1967, Chomsky 1977 and Postal 1998). This is indeed attested in various types of extraction islands (complex NP islands, Wh-islands, adjunct islands and sentential subjects); consider the examples in (26) involving complex NP islands (Kennedy 2002: 558, ex. 9):

(26)   a. *Michael has more scoring titles than Dennis is a guy who has.

     b. *Michael has more scoring titles than Dennis is a guy who has tattoos.

In both cases there is a complex NP in the comparative subclause (*a guy who has* and *a guy who has tattoos*); the sentences are ungrammatical precisely because movement of a degree expression takes place from within these complex NPs.

Apart from island sensitivity, both Comparative Deletion and Comparative Subdeletion constructions show crossover effects (Kennedy 2002: 558–559) and as far as the interpretation of these structures is concerned, they have the same type of truth conditions (Kennedy 2002: 559). Admittedly, there are some differences as well; most importantly, there seems to be a problem with extracting the DegP on its own in subcomparatives (Kennedy 2002: 563–564). Consider the examples in (27), taken from Kennedy (2002: 564, ex. 32):

(27)   a. Michael has more scoring titles than [$_{CP}$ Op Dennis has [$_{DP}$ ~~Op~~ tattoos]].

     b. The shapes are longer than [$_{CP}$ Op they are [$_{DegP}$ ~~Op~~ thick]].

As can be seen, the operator moves out on its own and the lower copy gets deleted; this is problematic, however, if the operator has actual phonological content, as then we clearly have violations of the Left Branch Constraint (in the sense of Ross 1967), as pointed out by Kennedy (2002: 564). Consider the example in (28), taken from Kennedy (2002: 564, ex. 33):

(28)   a. *How many does Dennis have [$_{DP}$ ~~how many tattoos~~]?

     b. *[$_{CP}$ How were the shapes [$_{DegP}$ ~~how thick~~]]?

The conclusion drawn by Kennedy (2002: 570) is that Comparative Deletion and Comparative Subdeletion "are the same in their basic syntactic properties"; that is, both involve "the same functional vocabulary and are subject to the same syntactic operations" but they "differ in the level of representation at which these operations apply". Therefore, while the two types "have structurally identical LF representations", they have "structurally distinct PF representations" (Kennedy 2002: 571).

As shown by Kennedy (2002: 571–574), Comparative Deletion and Comparative Subdeletion structures have essentially the same semantics, in addition to syntactic similarities (see above); "the comparative clause is interpreted as a description of a maximal amount, and supplies the standard of comparison for the comparative morpheme" (Kennedy 2002: 574). In either case, the compared constituent has to move at LF (or before) "because the quantificational force of the comparative clause (the maximality operator) is introduced by the degree morphology on the compared constituent, not by a higher operator" and hence "to generate the right interpretation of the comparative clause [...] the compared constituent must take scope over the rest of the clause" (Kennedy 2002: 574–575).

Note that in both types of comparatives the entire compared constituent is assumed to move; as pointed out by Kennedy (2002: 581–582), partial movement would in certain cases lead to Left Branch Constraint violations. Consider the examples in (29), taken from Kennedy (2002: 581, ex. 79):

(29) a. Michael has more scoring titles than Dennis has **(tattoos)**.
      b. Michael's hands are wider than your feet are **(long)**.

As can be seen, it is grammatical to have a DP or an AP in the comparative subclause without an overt degree marker, which may lead one to the conclusion that in such cases the degree operator moves out on its own. However, comparatives then should have an analogous structure to the questions in (30), which are ungrammatical (Kennedy 2002: 581, ex. 80):

(30) a. *How many** does Dennis have **tattoos**?
      b. *How (much)** are your feet **long**?

Instead, the claim made by Kennedy (2002) is that (sub)comparatives are analogous to the structures in (31), see Kennedy (2002: 581, ex. 81):

(31) a. **How many tattoos** does Dennis have?
      b. **How long** are your feet?

The claim that in subcomparatives the entire compared constituent moves implies for Kennedy (2002) that this movement is covert, since the overt copy of the compared constituent remains in its base position.

Essentially, Kennedy (2002: 582–583) claims that in the case of Comparative Deletion, that is, when the compared constituent is identical to its counterpart in the matrix clause, both movement and deletion take place, whereas in CSD neither deletion nor movement happens. In his analysis, this is formulated in an optimality-theoretic approach, in that deletion is claimed to be favourable to overt movement (Kennedy 2002: 583). Since I do not adopt the framework of optimality theory, I will not provide further details of his analysis here.

Instead, let me point out some problems that, despite the merits of the analysis given by Kennedy (2002), make it necessary to continue investigating the issues in question. First of all, while it is obvious that movement takes place in both Comparative Deletion and Comparative Subdeletion structures, it is not straightforward how syntax should decide on which degree expressions in the subclause have to move before spell-out and which cannot: taking identity as such into account would require semantic interpretation but movement, at least in the case of Comparative Deletion, takes place before that. Moreover, identity is not a satisfactory criterion in itself: as demonstrated by the grammaticality of examples like (25), the degree expression may remain overt even if it is identical to its matrix clausal counterpart.

This leads to the second problem, which is the following: while it is true that recoverability is a prerequisite for material to be deleted, it is certainly not true that recoverable material falls under obligatory deletion. Such a stance would be untenable in general but is also immediately refuted by languages such as Hungarian, where there is no obligatory Comparative Deletion. In other words, while Kennedy (2002: 554) notes that the requirement on the obligatory nature of Comparative Deletion "is important, as it distinguishes CD from other deletion operations in English, such as ellipsis, which is optional", his analysis clearly does not account for cross-linguistic variation.

Third, the distinction between Comparative Deletion and Comparative Subdeletion on the basis of whether they contain overt or covert movement is highly questionable, too. As demonstrated by languages lacking Comparative Deletion, such as Hungarian, the degree expression in the subclause moves up in both types of constructions to a [Spec,CP] position. Note that I assume that the two CP-layers in comparatives are available in Hungarian as well, the higher headed by complementisers and the specifier of the lower one hosting relative operators: see Kántor (2008b), Bacskai-Atkari (2010b). Consider the examples in (32):

(32) a. Mari magasabb, mint **amilyen magas** Péter.
        Mary taller   than how   tall   Peter
        'Mary is taller than Peter.'
    b. Az asztal hosszabb, mint **amilyen széles** az iroda.
        the table longer   than how   wide the office
        'The table is longer than the office is wide.'

On the other hand, in languages such as English, it is always the lower copy that remains overt, even if it happens to be identical to its matrix clausal counterpart, see (25). Therefore, the chief distinction seems to be one that holds between languages and not one that can be observed between the two constructions.

Fourth, the analysis presented by Kennedy (2002) does not consider examples which show that overt material below *than* may be overt in English as well: the overtness of *what* was shown in (3), but constructions with *how* are also possible in certain dialects, as demonstrated in (15):

(33)   a.   % Ralph is taller than **how tall** Peter is.

   b.   % The desk is longer than **how wide** the office is.

The overtness of *how tall* in (33a) and *how wide* in (33b) contradicts the assumption that movement to [Spec,CP] necessarily involves deletion in English; moreover, the availability of (33a) refutes the implied claim that only contrasted degree expressions may remain overt in the subclause.

In sum, it seems that the analysis provided by Kennedy (2002) does not take into consideration a number of phenomena that would be important for gaining a better understanding of how Comparative Deletion works; and, most importantly, it is not explained why it should take place at all when it does.

3.3 Constraints on deletion

In order to provide an account for Comparative Deletion, let me first briefly summarise the most important issues concerning deletion mechanisms in general. One such general constraint is that of GIVENness. Roughly speaking, elements can be GIVEN or focus-marked (F-marked), see Selkirk (1996; 2005); Schwarzschild (1999); Merchant (2001); Büring (2006). Consider the examples in (34):

(34)   a.   Ralph was reading a novel and Peter ~~was reading~~ an epic.

   b.   * Ralph was reading a novel and Peter ~~was writing~~ an epic.

The sentence in (34a) is grammatical: the elided verb in the second conjunct is *read*, which is GIVEN, and can be deleted. As opposed to this, in (34b) *write* is F-marked as *read* in the matrix clause is not a salient antecedent for it: consequently, it is ungrammatical to elide it. This is fundamentally a recoverability condition on deletion: a constituent α can be deleted iff α is e-GIVEN (ellipsis-GIVEN, see Merchant 2001: 38), hence α must have a salient antecedent in the discourse.

It is worth mentioning that optional deletion processes may save a given construction from ungrammaticality. This is true for sluicing, which, as shown by the grammaticality of (35a), is optional:

(35) a. They want to hire someone who speaks a Slavic language, but I don't
          remember who they want to hire.
      b. They want to hire someone who speaks a Slavic language, but I don't
          remember who ~~they want to hire~~.

Sluicing, as can be seen in (35b), deletes the string after a *wh*-pronoun (*who*)
that has moved to the [Spec,CP] position, which in this case has moved from
within the elided subclause (see Merchant 2001; van Craenenbroeck & Lipták
2006). Since (35a) is grammatical and in (35b) sluicing takes place regularly, the
sentences in (35) are fundamentally equivalent to each other.

The situation is different when the underlying structure is ungrammatical. The
examples in (36) contain island violations (based on Merchant 2001: 114, ex. 15):

(36) a. * They want to hire someone who speaks a Slavic language, but I
            don't remember which they want to hire someone [who speaks].
      b.   They want to hire someone who speaks a Slavic language, but I
            don't remember which ~~they want to hire someone [who speaks]~~.

In both cases, *which* moves up from within the subclause (*who speaks*), which is
a *wh*-island violation. In (36a), the sentence is therefore not grammatical, while
in (36b), where sluicing takes place, the result is fully grammatical. Obviously,
sluicing in this case not only deletes the subclause responsible for ungrammaticality but a larger chunk as well, since sluicing by definition can only delete the
entire complement of a functional head (C) equipped with an [E] feature. Since
in this case the fully overt construction is ill-formed, while sluicing deletes precisely the part causing ill-formedness at PF, only the sentence containing deletion
will converge out of the two options. Thus, optional deletion processes are able
to save structures from ungrammaticality, without having to suppose that these
processes would be obligatory. This conclusion will be important later when considering certain deletion mechanisms.

In the exact mechanism of sluicing, deletion itself takes place at PF; however,
deletion is licensed by an [E] feature inserted in syntax, see Merchant (2001). The
significance of this is partly that optional deletion processes can be handled in
the syntax: while the insertion of an [E] feature requiring deletion is optional
in the syntactic component, the presence or the absence of the feature contains
unequivocal information for PF in terms of whether deletion should take place.
This is because while the prohibition of deleting F-marked elements is an axiom,
GIVEN elements are not necessarily deleted. Hence GIVENness in itself is not unequivocal information for PF; in turn, PF is responsible for the linear structure
and does not produce syntactic and/or semantic features.

3.4 An analysis of Comparative Deletion

3.4.1 General considerations

Recall that, descriptively, Comparative Deletion (CD) is a process which elimi-nates the QP or the quantified DP from the subclause, if it is logically identical to its antecedent in the matrix clause (Bacskai-Atkari 2010b, Bacskai-Atkari 2012a) in examples such as (1), repeated here for the sake of convenience as (37):

(37)   a. Ralph is more qualified than Jason is ~~x-qualified~~.

   b. Ralph has more qualifications than Jason has ~~x-many qualifications~~.

   c. Ralph has better qualifications than Jason has ~~x-good qualifications~~.

Comparative subclauses exhibit regular operator movement (see Chomsky 1977, Kennedy 2002) to a [Spec,CP] position. This is illustrated in (38):

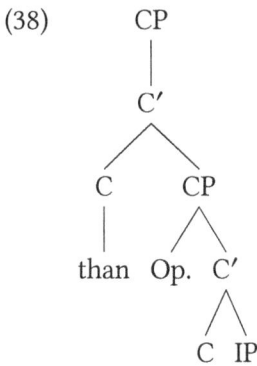

(38)

```
        CP
        |
        C′
       /  \
      C    CP
      |   /  \
    than Op.  C′
             /  \
            C    IP
```

As for the structure of the left periphery, I assume that the CP can be split (cf. Rizzi 1997: 297, Rizzi 1999: 1, Rizzi 2004: 237–238), even though I do not adopt a cartographic approach and the various CPs should rather be regarded as in-stances of an iterated CP. Rizzi's split CP is illustrated in (39):

(39)   [CP [TopP* [FocP [TopP* [CP]]]]]

Rizzi assumes that multiple TopPs and a designated FocP may appear between the two CP projections; however, this is irrelevant for the present analysis, and therefore I will neither include them in the representations, nor will I discuss possible arguments against a strict cartographic approach. Further, Rizzi (1997; 1999; 2004) attributes different functions to the two CPs: he assumes that the higher C head is responsible for the "illocutionary" Force of the clause, while the lower is responsible for Finiteness.

The term "illocutionary Force" is fundamentally used to cover clause types, that is, categories such as declarative, interrogative, relative, comparative, etc.; it is terminologically unfortunate to involve the concept of illocution since the kind of illocution discussed by Rizzi has little to do with how Austin (1962) and Searle (1969) introduced the term, the sentence types in question not being performative. In addition, the distinction between Force and Finiteness is problematic as well because, though the relative position of a given C head in a combination (that is, whether it is a lower or a higher one) is straightforward, it is hard to disentangle the various functions in cases where a single C head marks both. Due to these reasons, I will henceforth not mark the Force/Finiteness distinction.

3.4.2 Predicative versus attributive and nominal structures

Turning back to the representation given in (38), the complementiser head of the comparative subclause (*than*) occupies the higher C position, while the comparative operator (Op.) moves to the specifier of the lower CP.

In predicative structures, such as (37a), the QP containing the AP is headed by a phonologically empty operator (*x*), and the entire QP moves up to the specifier of the CP, where it is deleted. By contrast, in nominal and attributive structures, such as (37b) and (37c), respectively, the QP is an adjunct within the DP (Kennedy & Merchant 2000, Kántor 2008a) and thus the entire DP moves up and is deleted. This is because the QP cannot be extracted from the DP due to the DP-island constraint (cf. Kayne 1983, Ross 1986, Izvorski 1995: 217, Grebenyova 2004, Bošković 2005).

Movement in predicative structures is represented in (40), based on (37a):

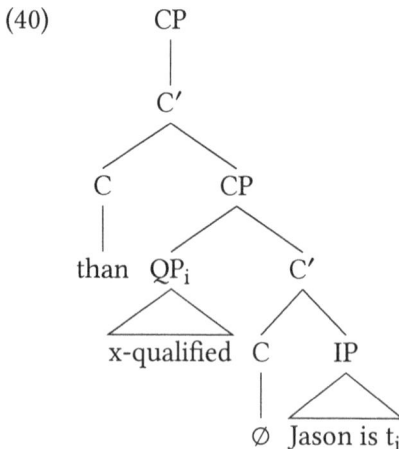

(40)

```
              CP
              |
              C'
            /    \
          C        CP
          |      /    \
        than  QP_i     C'
             /   \    /  \
       x-qualified  C    IP
                    |   /  \
                    Ø  Jason is t_i
```

Movement in attributive and nominal structures is represented in (41), based on the examples given in (37b) and (37c):

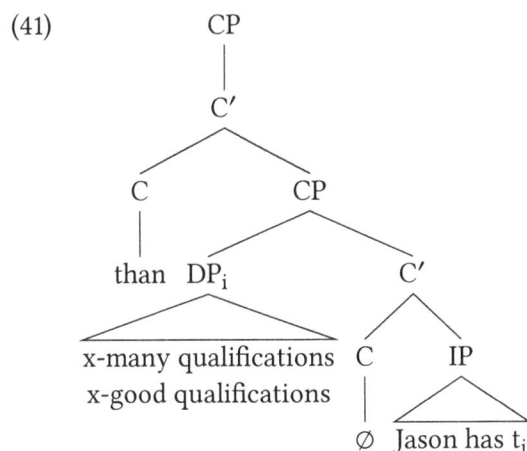

(41)

```
              CP
              |
              C'
          ╱      ╲
        C          CP
        |        ╱    ╲
     than  DPᵢ        C'
                     ╱  ╲
  ┌──────────────────┐  ╱  ╲
  x-many qualifications  C    IP
  x-good qualifications  |   ╱  ╲
                         Ø  Jason has tᵢ
```

All this can be derived from more general rules and is hence not specific for comparative subclauses, as similar phenomena can be observed in other constructions containing operators (cf. Kennedy & Merchant 1997: 7). Consider the examples given in (42):

(42) a. * **How** is Ralph **qualified**?
      b.   **How qualified** is Ralph?
      c. * **How big** did Ralph see **cats**?
      d.   **How big cats** did Ralph see?
      e. * **How many** did Ralph see **cats**?
      f.   **How many cats** did Ralph see?

As can be seen, the QP *how qualified* and the DP *how big cats* or *how many cats* can be moved only as a whole: neither the Q head may be extracted from the QP nor the QP from the DP. I will return to the issue later, also casting light upon how it varies cross-linguistically. At this point, suffice it to say that in cases such as (42a) and (42b) above the Q head cannot be extracted because then it would have to occupy a phrase position in the lower [Spec,CP] as a head. On the other hand, as I will show later, in some languages the quantifier may also be realised as a QP modifier within the QP heading the adjective in question, and it can in such cases be extracted, cf. Kántor (2008a). Similarly, the extraction of the QP out of the DP is highly dependent on the parametric settings of a given language:

while English, Bulgarian and Greek prohibit it, it is allowed in Polish and Czech (Kennedy & Merchant 2000); these questions will be addressed inChapter 4 in detail.

Turning back to comparative subclauses in English, it is important to investigate the issue of copies. In our case, there are only two copies to consider: the lower one in the base position of the QP or the DP and the higher one in the lower [Spec,CP] as a result of movement. The higher copy, as has already been seen, is deleted by Comparative Deletion; note that this is independent from whether the AP or NP is identical to the one in the matrix clause. The lower copy is regularly deleted by PF (cf. Bobaljik 2002, Chomsky 2008, Bošković & Nunes 2007: 44–48), which is possible because the QP or DP in question is e-GIVEN. The deletion processes taking place in (37) are shown in (43):

(43)   a.   Ralph is more qualified [$_{CP}$ than [$_{CP}$ ~~[$_{QP}$ x-qualified]~~ Jason is ~~[$_{QP}$ x-qualified]~~]].

   b.   Ralph has more qualifications [$_{CP}$ than [$_{CP}$ ~~[$_{DP}$ x-many qualifications]~~ Jason has ~~[$_{DP}$ x-many qualifications]~~]].

   c.   Ralph has better qualifications [$_{CP}$ than [$_{CP}$ ~~[$_{DP}$ x-good qualifications]~~ Jason has ~~[$_{DP}$ x-good qualifications]~~]].

As should be obvious, Comparative Deletion takes place in all structures, hence there is no difference between predicative and attributive/nominal constructions: the fact that the entire DP has to be eliminated in the latter is due to different, independent constraints.

One obvious advantage of this approach is that it accounts for the deletion of QPs and DPs without having to resort to extra mechanisms: Comparative Deletion takes place in the lower [Spec,CP] position and it deletes any material that is there. In turn, differences in terms of what phrases are found there arise simply out of movement constraints. I will return to the issue of why Comparative Deletion has to take place at all later, also accounting for the differences found between languages and varieties. At this point, suffice it to say that a movement analysis claiming that the entire QP or DP moves (and not only the operator) can successfully account for the elimination of both copies by assuming that Comparative Deletion obligatorily takes place in the lower [Spec,CP], eliding the higher copy, and that lower copies are regularly deleted at PF. Though it is a prerequisite that deleted material has to be e-GIVEN, the fact that obligatory deletion takes place is not directly linked to these elements being recoverable, contrary to Kennedy (2002): rather, it is associated with a syntactic position where it happens independently of whether the material there is e-GIVEN or not.

3.4.3 Comparative Subdeletion

The case of Comparative Subdeletion, as found in subcomparatives, may at first sight seem to be a counterexample for what has been established for Comparative Deletion. In these (predicative) structures, as was mentioned at the beginning of this chapter, the QP in the subclause remains overt:

(44)   The table is longer than the desk is **wide.**

However, even in such cases Comparative Deletion takes place regularly in the [Spec,CP] position: if Comparative Deletion did not occur, then the higher copy should remain (cf. Bacskai-Atkari 2010b). On the other hand, the lower copy cannot be eliminated since it is F-marked: it contrasts with the AP (*long*) in the matrix clause. As pointed out by Bošković & Nunes (2007: 48), lower copies may remain overt if the pronunciation of the higher copy would make the derivation crash at PF. Thus, the following happens in (44):

(45)   The table is longer [CP than [CP [QP x-wide]F the desk is [QP x-wide]F]].

As can be seen, the higher copy of the QP is deleted by Comparative Deletion exactly the same way as in (43a) and the two clauses differ in fact only with respect to whether the lower copy remains; however, this difference can be derived from recoverability. This all indicates that subcomparatives are not exceptional in terms of Comparative Deletion, and thus there is no separate Comparative Subdeletion process.

In this way, the relation between Comparative Deletion and Comparative Subdeletion can be easily handled, without having to resort to distinguishing the two on the basis of whether they include overt or covert movement, as was seen in connection with Kennedy (2002). Again, the role of information structure is not directly related to Comparative Deletion itself: Comparative Deletion is treated as a mechanical process eliminating material from the lower [Spec,CP] position and the fact that the lower copy of the QP can remain overt is due to F-marking.

Note that being F-marked is not identical to not being e-GIVEN; it is rather intended to express some kind of contrast. For instance, the QP *x-wide* in (45) is in contrast with the QP *longer* of the matrix clause. Also, this QP appears in a clause-final position, which is the canonical position for foci and/or contrasted elements in English: see Selkirk (1984; 1986), Nespor & Vogel (1986), McCarthy & Prince (1993). This QP expresses the main contrast involved in comparison and it follows logically that it appears in a position where it can bear main sentential stress.

As far as the overt lower copy of an e-GIVEN AP is concerned, it is usually ungrammatical because it should regularly be eliminated as a lower copy and it should not appear in a contrastive position. However, if there is a context in which it can be interpreted as a contrasted element even though it is GIVEN, it may remain overt: see also (25). The difference is illustrated in (46) below:

(46) a. ??/*The table is longer than the desk is **long**.

  b. A: The table is longer than the desk is wide.

    B: No, the table is longer than the desk is **LONG**.

In both cases the subclause contains an overt lower copy of the QP that is identical to the one in the matrix clause. However, in (46a) it should have been eliminated as there is no additional instruction for PF to preserve the lower copy. As opposed to this, (46b) is grammatical because the QP in question is contrasted: this contrast holds not with the QP in the matrix clause but with the one in the preceding sentence.

It can be concluded that subdeletion constructions also include Comparative Deletion in the regular way, and the fact that the lower copy remains overt stems from constraints independent from the mechanism of Comparative Deletion.

3.5 The structure of degree expressions revisited

3.5.1 On Hungarian operators

In order to understand the mechanism of Comparative Deletion, let us first consider a language where it does not operate. In Hungarian, as has been mentioned, the quantified AP may remain overt, that is, both the comparative operator and the lexical AP can be visible in the [Spec,CP] position. However, there are differences between the available operators in this respect.

The canonical comparative operator is *amilyen* 'how', which is shown in (47):

(47) a. Mari magasabb, mint **amilyen magas** Péter volt.
       Mary taller   than how   tall   Peter was.3SG

     'Mary is taller than Peter was.'

  b. * Mari magasabb, mint **amilyen** Péter volt   **magas**.
      Mary taller   than how   Peter was.3SG tall

     'Mary is taller than Peter was.'

As can be seen, the operator *amilyen* is inseparable from the lexical AP (*magas* 'tall'): it is grammatical to have them both overtly in the lower [Spec,CP] position, as in (47a), but the AP cannot be stranded and left behind in its base position, as in (47b).

Hungarian also has the operator *amennyire* 'how much': this can otherwise modify VPs and it may modify APs as well, though there is some variation among speakers with respect to the availability of this operator as an AP modifier. Still, if it appears in comparatives, it behaves differently from *amilyen*, as shown by (48):

(48)   a. Mari magasabb, mint **amennyire magas** Péter volt.
           Mary taller   than how.much tall   Peter was.3SG

           'Mary is taller than Peter was.'

       b. Mari magasabb, mint **amennyire** Péter volt   **magas.**
           Mary taller   than how.much Peter was.3SG tall

           'Mary is taller than Peter was.'

Unlike *amilyen*, *amennyire* may appear both together with the lexical AP in [Spec,CP], as in (48a), and it may also allow the stranding of the AP, as in (48b). Thus, *amennyire* is separable from the lexical AP.

There are reasons to believe that the operator *amennyire* in structures like (48) is indeed base-generated within the degree expression and is not a VP-modifier. First, if it were a VP-modifying operator, then it could not move together with the lexical AP to the lower [Spec,CP] position, as, for instance, in (48a), because then they would not form one constituent. Second, if an adverb modifies the verb, then the verb must be overt, whereas if the structure is simply predicative, the present-tense 3rd singular copula is not overt, as demonstrated by the pattern in (49):

(49)   a. Mari jól   *(van).
           Mary well is

           'Mary is well.'

       b. Mari fáradt (*van).
           Mary tired   is

           'Mary is tired.'

As far as comparatives containing *amennyire* are concerned, the copula *van* is not permitted to appear overtly in structures like (50):

(50) Mari magasabb, mint amennyire Péter (*van) magas.
Mary taller   than how.much Peter is   tall
'Mary is taller than Peter.'

If *amennyire* modified the verb, then the presence of *van* 'is' would be required, which is not the case, and therefore *amennyire* cannot be a VP-modifying adverb in comparative subclauses.

Before turning to the further examination of the difference between *amilyen* and *amennyire*, note that Hungarian has no zero comparative operators, and constructions like (51) are ungrammatical:

(51)   a.   * Mari magasabb, mint **magas** Péter volt.
           Mary taller   than tall   Peter was.3SG

           'Mary is taller than Peter was.'

   b.   * Mari magasabb, mint Péter volt   **magas**.
           Mary taller   than Peter was.3SG tall

           'Mary is taller than Peter was.'

As shown above, it is impossible to have an overt AP without an overt operator (i.e. one with actual phonological content) either in the [Spec,CP] or in its base position.

It has to be stressed that the differences between *amilyen* and *amennyire*, as well as the impossibility of zero operators, are not dependent on whether the AP is e-GIVEN or F-marked. The operator *amilyen* cannot be separated from F-marked APs either, as shown in (52):

(52)   a.   Az asztal hosszabb, mint **amilyen széles** az iroda.
           the desk longer   than how   wide   the office

           'The desk is longer than the office is wide.'

   b.   * Az asztal hosszabb, mint **amilyen** az iroda **széles**.
           the desk longer   than how   the office wide

           'The desk is longer than the office is wide.'

By contrast, *amennyire* tolerates both positions of the AP, as shown in (53):[1]

---

[1] Though the sentences marked as grammatical are all indeed grammatical, it must be mentioned that the degrees of acceptability may show individual differences, and there are structures that are clearly preferable. I will return to this question later on in the last section.

(53) a. Az asztal hosszabb, mint **amennyire széles** az iroda.
          the desk longer   than how.much wide the office

      'The desk is longer than the office is wide.'

      b. Az asztal hosszabb, mint **amennyire** az iroda **széles**.
          the desk longer   than how.much the office wide

      'The desk is longer than the office is wide.'

Finally, just as in (51), zero operators are not allowed with F-marked APs either, as shown in (54):

(54) a. *Az asztal hosszabb, mint **széles** az iroda.
          the desk longer   than wide the office

      'The desk is longer than the office is wide.'

      b. *Az asztal hosszabb, mint az iroda **széles**.
          the desk longer   than the office wide

      'The desk is longer than the office is wide.'

The data shown in this section clearly demonstrate that Hungarian has no Comparative Deletion. In addition, there seem to be two types of operators. On the one hand, *amilyen* is an operator that must move together with the AP: in this case, the higher copy of the entire degree expression is overt in the [Spec,CP] position, and the lower copy of the entire degree expression is deleted regularly. On the other hand, the operator *amennyire* can move out on its own; it is by no means obligatory for it to do so, and if it does not, it behaves exactly the same way as *amilyen*. However, if it moves out on its own, the higher copy of *amennyire* appears overtly in the [Spec,CP] position but without any AP there; in turn, the lower copy of *amennyire* is deleted regularly and the AP itself remains overt in situ.

The difference between the two types of operators is also attested in interrogative operators. As shown in (55), the operator *milyen* 'how' does not allow the stranding of the AP:

(55) a. **Milyen magas** volt   Péter?
          how   tall   was.3sɢ Peter

      'How tall was Peter?'

      b. ***Milyen** volt   Péter **magas**?
          how   was.3sɢ Peter tall

      'How tall was Peter?'

By contrast, as shown by (56), the operator *mennyire* 'how much' may be separated from the AP:[2]

(56)   a. **Mennyire magas** volt   Péter?
           how.much tall   was.3SG Peter

           'How tall was Peter?'

       b. **Mennyire** volt   Péter **magas**?
           how.much was.3SG Peter tall

           'How tall was Peter?'

As can be seen, the interrogative operators *milyen* and *mennyire* have exactly the same distributions as their relative operator counterparts, *amilyen* and *amennyire*, respectively. Since the difference seems to hold systematically, it presumably has to do with structural differences between the two types of operators.

3.5.2 Operator positions

In Chapter 2, I proposed a unified analysis for the structure of degree expressions, concentrating primarily on the degree expression in the matrix clause of comparatives expressing inequality. Recall that, for a string like *far more intelligent than Peter is*, the representation in (57) was established:

(57)

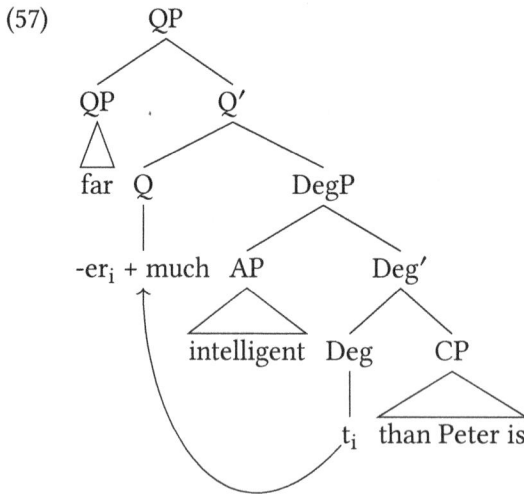

---

[2] Again, *mennyire* 'how much' is a degree element in the degree expression just like its relative counterpart *amennyire* 'how much' for exactly the same reasons.

Since this was and is intended to be a unified analysis for degree expressions, I claim that the same structure is present in subclausal QPs, too. This has two main aspects: the difference between operators that cannot be extracted and ones that cannot, and the availability of operators as proforms standing for the entire degree expression.

Let us first examine the general structure underlying degree expressions. This is given in (58), showing also the possible positions for operators (Op.):

(58)

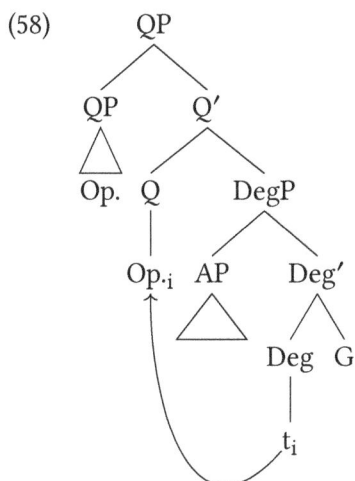

Recall that the DegP is headed by the degree head, which takes two arguments and which projects a QP layer. The arguments of the degree head are the lexical AP itself (cf. Lechner 2004) and the Grade argument (*G*), which expresses the standard value (cf. Lechner 2004). In matrix clausal degree expressions it is typically the subordinate clause itself but it may also remain covert if it is recoverable from the context. Consider:

(59)   A: Mary is as tall as Peter.
        B: No, she is taller.

In (59), the Grade argument of *taller* remains implicit as it is recoverable from the previous utterance. As far as the Grade argument of subclausal degree expressions is concerned, it is also implicit but it relates the degree in question to a certain point on a scale.

The QP layer, as was seen in Chapter 2, is projected above the DegP and the Deg head moves up to Q: the Q head itself is one of the possible positions for comparative operators. The specifier of the QP may host other QP modifiers; this is the other position that comparative operators may occupy. Note that these positions are operator positions inasmuch as they may host operators; however, it is not necessary for them to be filled by operators: for instance, in matrix clausal QPs such as (57), they obviously contain non-operator elements.

Accordingly, the degree expression in the subclause has a structure conforming to (58); *amilyen* is a Deg head, and it ultimately occupies the Q position:

(60)

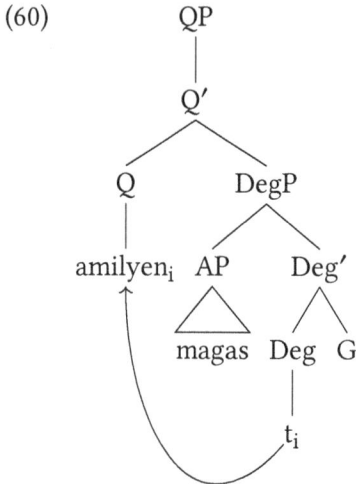

By contrast, *amennyire* is a QP modifier:

(61)

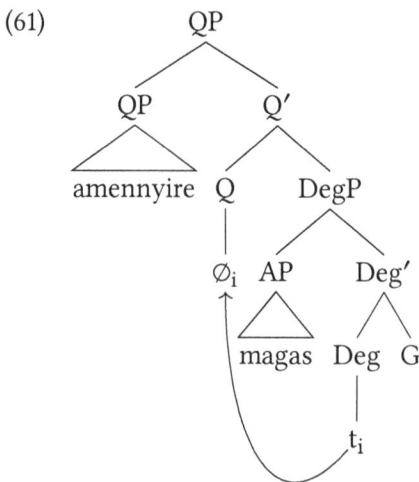

Note that this applies to cases where the operator *amennyire* is used together with an adjective. Interestingly, if it modifies an adverb, it seems to be a Deg head, hence conforming to the structure in (60):

(62) a. Mari jobban tudja a   verset,   mint **amennyire jól** Péter
          Mary better knows the poem.ACC than how.much well Peter
          tudja   a   verset.   ˙
          knows the poem.ACC
          'Mary knows the poem better than Peter does.'

      b. *Mari jobban tudja a   verset,   mint **amennyire** Péter tudja
          Mary better knows the poem.ACC than how.much Peter knows
          jól   a   verset.
          well the poem.ACC
          'Mary knows the poem better than Peter does.'

As can be seen, in these cases *amennyire* has to move together with the adverb, just as was seen for *amilyen* 'how' with adjectives, which suggests that *amennyire* has been grammaticalised into a Deg head with adverbs. Since the main focus here is not to provide an account for this difference, I will not venture to analyse this issue any further.

Due to the fact that both *amilyen* and *amennyire* are operators, they cannot be co-present: only one [+rel] operator is licensed in the clause, which then moves to a [Spec,CP] position and checks off the [+rel] feature there. The zero element in (61) is merely a degree marker, not an operator, and thus the operator in [Spec,QP] is necessary for the construction to survive.

The structural difference between *amilyen* and *amennyire* accounts for their different behaviour. While *amennyire* is a QP modifier that thus may be extracted out of the entire degree expression on its own, *amilyen* is the head of that degree expression itself, and therefore it cannot be extracted and naturally cannot move to the [Spec,CP] position (a phrase position) as a single head.

3.5.3 Proforms

Given the structural difference between individual operators described above, it is expected that further asymmetries should arise. This is indeed the case, as will be shown in connection with proforms. So far I have been dealing with degree expressions containing a lexical AP. However, this is not always necessary; for instance, *amilyen* 'how' may appear without a lexical AP, as shown in (63):

(63) Mari magasabb, mint **amilyen** Péter volt.
        Mary taller   than how   Peter was.3SG
        'Mary is taller than Peter was.'

This is in line with the representation given in (60) for *amilyen*: as a Deg head it may not require an overt AP to be present in the structure but may stand for the entire degree expression overtly.

The expectation is that *amennyire* 'how much' should behave differently in this respect, since the QP modifier then should be attached to a QP that has no phonological content. This is indeed the case, as demonstrated by the ungrammaticality of (64):

(64) * Mari magasabb, mint **amennyire** Péter volt.
          Mary taller   than how.much Peter was.3SG
          'Mary is taller than Peter was.'

As can be seen, *amennyire* is not allowed to appear as a comparative operator on its own: the reason behind this is that, conforming to the representation given in (61), *amennyire* is a QP modifier that should be attached to a QP with some phonological content. Since the co-presence of Q heads and QP modifiers is ruled out, the only way would be to have an overt lexical AP, which is not the case in the example (64).[3]

3.6 Operators in English

Having established all this, let us now return to English comparative operators. Altogether, there are three candidates: the zero, *how* and *what* (see Chomsky 1977 on treating *what* as an operator in comparatives).

---

[3] As was mentioned earlier, *amennyire* 'how much' seems to behave as a Deg head with adverbs but not with adjectives. If this is indeed so, then the expectation is that *amennyire* should be able to function as a proform with adverbs. Consider:

(i) Mari jobban tudja a   verset,   mint amennyire Péter tudja a   verset.
      Mary better knows the poem.ACC than how.much Peter knows the poem.ACC
      'Mary knows the poem better than Peter does.'

The grammaticality of (i) above shows that this is indeed so, and thus there is a difference that holds between *amennyire* as an adjectival modifier and *amennyire* as an adverbial modifier.

Let us start with the element *what*, which prohibits the co-presence of an overt AP in [Spec,CP] but not in its base position. This is demonstrated by (65):[4]

(65)   a.   % Mary is taller than **what** Peter is.
       b.   * Mary is taller than **what tall** Peter is.
       c.   * The desk is longer than **what wide** the office is.
       d.   % The desk is longer than **what** the office is **wide**.

As shown by (65), *what* may appear below *than*, at least in certain non-standard dialects of English. However, it is not allowed to co-occur with a lexical AP, as in (65b) and (65c). Yet it is possible to have an overt, contrastive AP in its base position, as in (65d). If *what* were an operator taking a lexical AP in [Spec,DegP], then (65b) and (65c) should be grammatical. On the other hand, if *what* were a proform operator never allowing the gradable predicate to be overt, then (65d) should be ruled out. Therefore, it seems that *what* in comparatives is actually a lower C head, and the comparative operator is zero, just as in Standard English (note that the presence of an operator is required by degree semantics). In fact, there are a number of languages allowing the lexicalisation of the lower C head in comparatives, as will be shown later on for German; see Bacskai-Atkari (2014a) on German and Hungarian, cf. Jäger (2010) on German, and Bacskai-Atkari (2016) on Slavic.

Turning now to *how*, it must be noted that *how* as a comparative operator again shows dialectal variation. Consider the examples in (66):

(66)   a.   % Mary is taller than **how tall** Peter is.
       b.   * Mary is taller than **how** Peter is **tall**.
       c.   * Mary is taller than **how** Peter is.
       d.   % The desk is longer than **how wide** the office is.
       e.   * The desk is longer than **how** the office is **wide**.

The only acceptable configurations with *how* as a comparative operator are given in (66a) and (66d). As indicated, these are completely well formed for some speakers, while for others they are ungrammatical. However, constructions such as (66b) and (66e), where the AP is stranded, are ungrammatical even for those who would accept (66a) and (66d), which suggests that *how* is a Deg head that cannot be extracted out of the degree expression. Unlike Hungarian *amilyen* 'how',

---

[4]I owe many thanks to Craig Thiersch for the discussion of the data with *what*.

how is a Deg head that requires the presence of an overt AP, as indicated by the ungrammaticality of (66c).

Note that whether a given Deg head may combine with a lexical AP is independent from whether the AP is e-GIVEN or not: Deg heads that must take APs take them in either case.

Finally, let us turn to the zero comparative operator, which is acceptable for all English speakers. This is a Deg head that cannot move out on its own. Observe the difference in (67):

(67) a. ??/* Mary is taller than Peter is **tall**.

    b. The desk is longer than the office is **wide**.

If the zero were a QP modifier, then it should be able to move out to the [Spec,CP] on its own and (67a) should be acceptable, just like (67b); however, (67a) is clearly unacceptable to an extent that cannot be attributed merely to the redundancy of the AP. On the other hand, the fact that the zero can co-occur with a lexical AP in cases such as (67b) implies that in canonical Comparative Deletion constructions, where an e-GIVEN AP is eliminated, there is indeed deletion at hand: as has been said, the Deg head imposes restrictions on the presence or the absence of any AP irrespectively of whether that AP is e-GIVEN or not.

3.7 Operators cross-linguistically

From the discussion above, it should be clear that comparative operators may differ from each other in two respects: overtness and extractability. Since these criteria are independent from each other, this leaves one with four logical possibilities for comparative operators. The operators I have dealt with so far (that is, the ones in English and Hungarian) can be grouped according to Table 3.1.

Table 3.1: Comparative operators in English and Hungarian

	overt	covert
Deg head	*how* (English) *amilyen* (Hungarian)	zero (English)
QP modifier	*amennyire* (Hungarian)	

The question is of course how operators from other languages fit into this scheme: more precisely, whether there are other overt QP modifier operators and whether there are covert QP modifier operators at all.

Let us first examine the case of Czech.[5] As shown in (68), Czech has the operator *jak* 'how' that may appear in interrogative clauses:

(68)   a. **Jak vysoký** je Karel?
           how tall   is Charles

           'How tall is Charles?'

      b. **Jak** je Karel **vysoký**?
           how is Charles tall

           'How tall is Charles?'

As indicated, *jak* can appear together with the AP, as in (68a), but the AP may also be stranded, as in (68b). This shows that *jak* is a QP modifier. Note that if *jak* were a VP-modifier and base-generated independently from the AP, then (68a) should not be possible because the AP would not undergo *wh*-movement in itself.

The expectation is that the same can be observed in comparative subclauses. This is indeed the case, as shown by (69):

(69)   a. ?? Marie je vyšší, než **jak vysoký** je Karel.
            Mary is taller than how tall   is Charles

           'Mary is taller than Charles.'

      b. ? Marie je vyšší, než **jak** je **vysoký** Karel.
          Mary is taller than how is tall   Charles

          'Mary is taller than Charles.'

      c. ?? Ten stůl je delší, než **jak široká** je ta kancelář.
           that desk is longer than how wide   is that office

          'The desk is longer than the office is wide.'

      d. Ten stůl je delší, než **jak** je ta kancelář **široká**.
          that desk is longer than how is that office   wide

          'The desk is longer than the office is wide.'

The slight markedness of the examples above stems from two factors: positional preferences (that is, the AP is preferably stranded instead of moving together with the operator as high as the [Spec,CP] position), and redundancy in

---

[5]For his indispensable help with the Czech data, I owe many thanks to Radek Šimík.

the case of an e-GIVEN AP. I will return to the positional preferences later; what is important here is that these are all possible structures, indicating that *jak* behaves in the same way as in interrogatives, in that it may be separated from the lexical AP.

On the other hand, Czech does not have a zero comparative operator. Consider the examples in (70):

(70)   a. * Marie je vyšší, než **vysoký** je Karel.
             Mary is taller than tall   is Charles

             'Mary is taller than Charles.'

     b. * Marie je vyšší, než je **vysoký** Karel.
             Mary is taller than is tall   Charles

             'Mary is taller than Charles.'

     c. * Ten stůl je delší, než **široká** je ta kancelář.
             that desk is longer than wide is that office

             'The desk is longer than the office is wide.'

     d. * Ten stůl je delší, než je ta   kancelář **široká**.
             that desk is longer than is that office   wide

             'The desk is longer than the office is wide.'

We can conclude that the comparative operator is invariably an overt QP modifier in Czech.

Let us now turn to Dutch,[6] where the interrogative operator *hoe* 'how' is nonseparable from the AP, as can be seen in (71):

(71)   a. **Hoe groot** is Jan?
             how tall   is John

             'How tall is John?'

     b. * **Hoe** is Jan **groot**?
             how is John tall

             'How tall is John?'

Since *hoe* does not allow the stranding of the AP, as demonstrated by (71b), it can be concluded that it is a Deg head. Accordingly, *hoe* as a comparative relative

---

[6]I owe many thanks to Jos Tellings for all his help with the Dutch data.

operator is also a Deg head (for speakers who find *hoe* acceptable as a comparative operator).[7] Consider the examples in (72):

(72) a. % Maria is groter dan **hoe groot** Jan   is.
          Mary is taller than how tall   John is

         'Mary is taller than John.'

    b. * Maria is groter dan **hoe** Jan   **groot** is.
          Mary is taller than how John tall   is

         'Mary is taller than John.'

    c. % De tafel is langer dan **hoe breed** het   kantoor is.
          the table is longer than how wide the.N office   is

         'The table is longer than the office is wide.'

    d. * De tafel is langer dan **hoe** het   kantoor **breed** is.
          the table is longer than how the.N office   wide is

         'The table is longer than the office is wide.'

In addition, it is worth mentioning that *hoe* cannot be a proform, as shown by the ungrammaticality of (73):

(73) * Maria is groter dan **hoe** Jan   is.
      Mary is taller than how John is

     'Mary is taller than John.'

Thus, *hoe* behaves in the same way as *how* does in English (that is, for speakers who accept it as a comparative operator).

In addition to *hoe*, Dutch also has a covert comparative operator; this, however, behaves differently from the zero operator observed in English.[8] Consider the examples in (74):

---

[7]Note that the acceptability of *hoe* 'how' in comparatives varies among dialects and speakers, similarly to what was attested for *how* in English. I conducted a short online survey in August–September 2013 with 70 native participants (many thanks go to Laura Bos and Marlies Kluck for their help in distributing the survey), in which informants were asked to rate sentences on a scale from 1 (bad) to 5 (good). The sentence given in (72a) here was accepted as fully grammatical (5) by 16% of the participants, while the sentence given in (72c) by 27%. This shows that even if *hoe* as a comparative operator is not acceptable for all speakers, its acceptability is still significant. Since my aim here is not to investigate comparatives in Dutch but rather to give a cross-linguistic survey, I will not venture to analyse and describe the results of the online survey here.

[8]Again, there is considerable variation among speakers but (74a) was judged by 10% to be fully acceptable (5) and by 21% to be acceptable (4) in the online survey mentioned before. On the other hand, (74b) was fully acceptable (5) for 81% and acceptable (4) for 11%.

(74)   a. ? Maria is groter dan Jan **groot** is.
           Mary is taller than John tall   is
           'Mary is taller than John.'

       b. De tafel is langer dan het   kantoor **breed** is.
           the table is longer than the.N office   wide is
           'The table is longer than the office is wide.'

If Dutch had no zero operator, then the sentences in (74) would be ungrammatical, as in Hungarian: see (51) and (54). On the other hand, if the Dutch zero operator were a Deg head like the one in English, then (74a) should be ungrammatical, which is not the case: though marked because of redundancy, (74a) is still acceptable, in contrast to (67a). This leaves only one option: namely that the zero operator in Dutch is a QP modifier. Of course, this also means that the AP may in principle move together with the operator to [Spec,CP]: in this case, just like in English, it is deleted by Comparative Deletion.

The same is true for the zero operator in German, as shown by (75):

(75)   a. ? Maria ist größer als   Johann **groß** ist.
           Mary is taller than John   tall is
           'Mary is taller than John.'

       b. Der Tisch ist länger als   das   Büro **breit** ist.
           the.M table is longer than the.N office wide is
           'The table is longer than the office is wide.'

Again, the markedness of (75a) is due to redundancy, as opposed to (67a) in English. Therefore, the AP is indeed available in a stranded position in German.

Note that the other logically possible candidate for the comparative operator in German is not available as an operator in comparative subclauses. The interrogative operator *wie* 'how' is a Deg head, as can be seen in (76):

(76)   a. **Wie groß** ist Johann?
           how tall   is John
           'How tall is John?'

       b. * **Wie** ist Johann **groß**?
           how is John   tall
           'How tall is John?'

This suggests that *wie* should appear together in the [Spec,CP] position in comparatives. However, this is not the case, as demonstrated by (77):

(77) a. * Maria ist größer als   **wie groß** Johann ist.
Mary is taller   than how tall   John   is
'Mary is taller than John.'

   b. * Der   Tisch ist länger als   **wie breit** das   Büro ist.
the.ᴍ table is longer than how wide the.ɴ office is
'The table is longer than the office is wide.'

The data indicate that *wie* is not a comparative operator in German: it is in fact a grammaticalised (lower) C head. The discussion of this question falls outside the scope of the present investigation; see the arguments in Bacskai-Atkari (2014a) and Bacskai-Atkari (2014c: 223–226), following Jäger (2010). What matters for us here is that German has only a zero QP modifier operator.

The same asymmetry can be observed in Italian, too (the discussion below applies to Northern dialects). Consider the examples in (78):

(78) a. **Quanto alta** è Maria?
how   tall.ꜰ is Mary
'How tall is Mary?'

   b. * **Quanto** è Maria **alta**?
how   is Mary tall.ꜰ
'How tall is Mary?'

As can be seen, *quanto* 'how' is also a Deg head, and the AP cannot be stranded. However, the grammatical interrogative configuration in (78a) has no matching counterpart in the comparative subclause, as demonstrated in (79):

(79) a. Maria è più   alta di quanto Giovanni sia   alto.
Mary is more tall.ꜰ of how   John   be.ꜱʙᴊᴠ.3ꜱɢ tall.ᴍ
'Mary is taller than John.'

   b. * Maria è più   alta di quanto alto   Giovanni sia.
Mary is more tall.ꜰ of how   tall.ᴍ John   be.ꜱʙᴊᴠ.3ꜱɢ
'Mary is taller than John.'

   c. La   tavola è più   lunga di quanto l'ufficio sia   largo.
the.ꜰ table is more long.ꜰ of how   the.office be.ꜱʙᴊᴠ.3ꜱɢ wide.ᴍ
'The table is longer than the desk is wide.'

   d. * La   tavola è più   lunga di quanto largo l'ufficio sia.
the.ꜰ table is more long.ꜰ of how   wide.ᴍ the.office be.ꜱʙᴊᴠ.3ꜱɢ
'The table is longer than the desk is wide.'

Again, the issue of grammaticalisation in Italian comparatives cannot be addressed here (see Bacskai-Atkari 2014a: 226–228, Bacskai-Atkari 2014c); what is important here is that *quanto* cannot be interpreted here as a Deg head, otherwise (79b) and (79d) should be grammatical and (79a) and (79c) should be ruled out. In other words, *quanto* is not the comparative operator. On the other hand, the grammaticality of (79a) and (79c), showing APs in their base positions, indicates that the degree expressions containing these APs have a QP modifier zero operator.

Naturally, several other languages could be examined in this respect; however, the point here is not to provide a fully-fledged comparative analysis of several languages but rather to show how overtness and extractability interact. This allows for an update in the representation shown in Table 3.1, given in Table 3.2.

Table 3.2: Comparative operators cross-linguistically

	overt	covert
Deg head	*how* (English) *amilyen* (Hungarian) *hoe* (Dutch)	zero (English)
QP modifier	*amennyire* (Hungarian) *jak* (Czech)	zero (German) zero (Dutch) zero (Italian)

As shown, there are indeed covert QP modifier operators and other types are also more widely attested. In addition, it has to be stressed that a given language may have several operators and these do not necessarily fall into the same slot.

While the availability of both an overt and a covert operator in a given language seems to be a straightforward option, the case of Hungarian with two overt operators seems to be special. The availability of these operators is also due to the fact that Hungarian developed a rich system of operators in Late Old Hungarian and Early Middle Hungarian, and there are several degree operators (cf. G. Varga 1992: 525, Bacskai-Atkari 2013b; 2014a). This means that at some point there were distinct operators for diverse functions, yet grammaticalisation processes may affect the system. For instance, VP-adverbs may grammaticalise into QP modifiers within degree expressions, and quantifiers may grammaticalise into degree heads (which seems to be a common process, cf. Doetjes 2008), and degree operators may also grammaticalise into C heads in comparative subclauses (but naturally not in interrogatives), as shown by Bacskai-Atkari (2014a), Bacskai-Atkari (2014c: 175–228). Still, the question arises whether Hungarian is unique in having both an overt Deg head operator and an overt QP modifier operator in interrogative and relative structures. Interestingly, Estonian exhibits a similar distinction between *kui* 'how' and *kuivõrd* 'how much' in interrogatives.[9] Consider the examples given in (80):

(80) a. **Kui pikk** on Peter?
          how tall   is Peter
          'How tall is Peter?'

      b. * **Kui** on Peter **pikk**?
             how is Peter tall
             'How tall is Peter?'

      c. **Kuivõrd   pikk** on Peter?
          how.much tall is Peter
          'How tall is Peter?'

      d. **Kuivõrd**   on Peter **pikk**?
          how.much is Peter tall
          'How tall is Peter?'

As can be seen, the operator *kui* is not separable from the lexical AP while the operator *kuivõrd* is, demonstrating essentially the same difference that holds between Hungarian *milyen* 'how' and *mennyire* 'how much'. As shown in (81), Polish shows the same phenomenon with the operators *jak* 'how' and *jaki* 'how' (cf. Borsley & Jaworska 1981: 81):

(81) a. **Jak wysoki** jest Karol?
          how tall   is   Charles
          'How tall is Charles?'

      b. * **Jak** jest Karol **wysoki**?
             how is   Charles tall
             'How tall is Charles?'

      c. **Jaki wysoki** jest Karol?
          how tall   is   Charles
          'How tall is Charles?'

---

[9] I owe many thanks to Nele Salveste for the data.

    d.   **Jaki** jest Karol   **wysoki?**
          how is   Charles tall
          'How tall is Charles?'

However, the same difference cannot be traced in comparative subclauses in either Estonian or Polish, since the interrogative operators in question are not available as comparative operators. Since the investigation of this issue would lead further than necessary here, I will leave this question open; what is important for us is that the availability of a Deg head operator and a QP modifier operator in degree expressions is attested in languages other than Hungarian, too.

3.8 The Overtness Requirement

Observing Table 3.2, the answer to Comparative Deletion is quite straightforward. Comparative Deletion, that is, the obligatory elimination of the quantified expression in the [Spec,CP] position, is always attested if the comparative operator is a covert Deg head (as in Standard English) and it may take place if the comparative operator is a covert QP modifier, provided that the lexical AP moves up together with the operator (e.g. in Dutch). That is, Comparative Deletion takes place if (and only if) there is a covert operator taking a lexical AP in the relevant [Spec,CP] position.

Essentially, then, Comparative Deletion takes place because otherwise a requirement on certain operator elements would be violated. I propose that this Overtness Requirement states that a phonologically visible lexical XP may appear in an operator position only if it appears together with a phonologically visible operator.

Let us elaborate on this in more detail. A QP or a DP containing a QP qualifies as [+rel] if there is a relative operator that either heads the QP or percolates this feature up to the DP. Phrases equipped with a [+rel] feature must move up to the [Spec,CP] position because of their [EDGE] feature: unlike, for instance, [+wh], there is no relative-in-situ (at least in the languages under scrutiny). However, in a [+rel] position only material that is overtly marked as [+rel] may appear overtly: in the case of a zero comparative operator, this condition is clearly not satisfied.

Note that, as far as the CP-domain is concerned, the overtness requirement is meant to capture the impossibility of lexical material without operators in CPs that are indeed operator positions, in this case [+rel]. German is known to have V2 in main clauses and this is generally attributed to the fact that the verb moves up to a C head and a phrase-sized constituent (most typically the subject) moves to the specifier of the same CP (see e.g. Fanselow 2004). In these cases, the presence of lexical phrases is allowed without an overt (relative) operator but this is so because these CPs are not [+rel] and the Overtness Requirement simply does not apply to them.

The overt realisation of lower copies does not have to face this problem, hence the grammaticality of subcomparatives in English. On the other hand, if the operator is overt, irrespectively of whether it has a lexical phrase alongside it, no deletion takes place. Similarly, if there is a zero operator that moves on its own, there is no need for deletion: all material in the [Spec,CP] is already covert.

The proposal, based on cross-linguistic data, is strongly built on the formal characteristics of comparative operators and does not try to link Comparative Deletion directly to the information-structural properties of the AP. In other words, defining Comparative Deletion as an operation eliminating the GIVEN AP would be fundamentally flawed as Comparative Deletion is essentially about the properties of the operator.

There are basically three independent factors here interacting with each other. First, the overtness of the operator defines whether Comparative Deletion is required to take place in [Spec,CP]. Second, the position of the operator in the degree expression decides whether the AP is separable or not. Third, the information-structural properties define the preferred position of the AP. I will return to the last criterion in the next section; for now, let us concentrate on the properties of operators.

There is considerable variation with respect to the acceptability of operators as comparative operators. In English, for instance, *how* is only marginally or dialectally acceptable, while the zero operator is fully grammatical. Naturally, any such candidate has to qualify as a degree element (either interpreted as the Deg head of the entire degree expression or as a QP modifier), otherwise it cannot be interpreted as a comparative operator.

In addition, a comparative operator is equipped with comparative and relative features, that is, [+compr] and [+rel]. The separation of [±compr] and [±rel] is justified: a feature matrix of these two binary features gives four logical possibilities, all of which are attested. Consider Table 3.3 showing examples from English.

The acceptability of individual elements as comparative operators fundamentally depends on whether they are equipped with both a [+rel] and a [+compr] feature. This may vary depending on the dialect and/or the speakers, hence the differences attested between dialects and individual speakers.

Table 3.3: The features [±compr] and [±rel]

	[+rel]	[−rel]
[+compr]	zero % *how*	*-er*
[−compr]	*which*	zero absolute degree marker

3.9 The role of information structure

Finally, let us briefly revisit the issue of information structure as attested in comparative clause formation. As has been established, Comparative Deletion is not the same as the elimination of a GIVEN AP. It is nevertheless true that once Comparative Deletion takes place in the relevant [Spec,CP] position, the lower copy of an e-GIVEN AP is preferably eliminated: that is, unless there is some contrast expressed by this AP, it undergoes deletion regularly as a lower copy, as in (67a), repeated here as (82):

(82)   ??/* Mary is taller than Peter is **tall**.

On the other hand, if there is no Comparative Deletion, then the APs may remain overt irrespectively of their information-structural status.

It is expected, though, that certain positional differences between e-GIVEN and F-marked APs may arise: more precisely, contrastive elements are expected to prefer contrast positions, while non-contrastive elements are presumably more likely to appear in neutral positions.

Naturally, the question makes sense only in the case of separable operators, that is, QP modifiers. If the operator is a Deg head, there is no choice in the positions for an overt AP: if the operator itself is overt, such as *how* in certain English dialects or *amilyen* in Hungarian, invariably the higher copy is realised - if the operator is zero, as in standard English, it is always the lower copy of the AP that is realised, the higher one being regularly deleted due to the Overtness Requirement. However, if the operator is separable, it is expected that GIVEN APs will typically appear in neutral positions and F-marked APs will appear in stress positions.

Let us first have a look at Czech, where the operator *jak* 'how' is a separable QP modifier. If it is combined with an e-GIVEN AP, the pattern in (83) arises:

(83) a. ?? Marie je vyšší, než **jak vysoký** je Karel.
        Mary is taller than how tall   is Charles

        'Mary is taller than Charles.'

    b. ? Marie je vyšší, než **jak** je **vysoký** Karel.
        Mary is taller than how is tall   Charles

        'Mary is taller than Charles.'

    c. # Marie je vyšší, než **jak** je Karel **vysoký**.
        Mary is taller than how is Charles tall

        'Mary is taller than Charles.'

The differences in the acceptability of these examples can be explained via considering the basic information structural properties of Czech clauses (Radek Šimík, p.c.). The most preferable position for a GIVEN AP is the one in (83b), where it is in a position for GIVEN elements; this is even preferable to the [Spec,CP] position, which is by definition not reserved for either GIVEN or F-marked elements. Finally, (83c) is infelicitous because the AP appears in the canonical contrast position, that is, clause-finally; however, in (83c) the AP does not carry contrast at all, and the main contrast is expressed by the DP *Karel*, which should appear clause-finally, as in (83a) and (83b).

Turning now to F-marked APs, the opposite pattern is attested, as illustrated in (84): the infelicitous configuration arises when the AP is clause-internal, not when it is clause-final.

(84) a. ?? Ten stůl je delší, než **jak široká** je ta   kancelář.
        that desk is longer than how wide   is that office

        'The desk is longer than the office is wide.'

    b. # Ten stůl je delší, než **jak** je **široká** ta   kancelář.
        that desk is longer than how is wide   that office

        'The desk is longer than the office is wide.'

    c. Ten stůl je delší, než **jak** je ta   kancelář **široká**.
        that desk is longer than wide is that office   wide

        'The desk is longer than the office is wide.'

Again, the [Spec,CP] position, which is not specified in terms of informational-structural content, is less preferred than the most natural one, which is the clause-final position (the canonical contrast position), as shown in (84c). Just as expected, the appearance of the F-marked AP in a position maintained for neutral elements is infelicitous, see (84b): since the main contrast is expressed by this AP, it should appear clause-finally, where it can bear sentential stress.

Similarly to Czech, Hungarian also shows a predictable correlation between the information-structural properties of the APs and their preferred positions; obviously, this is attested only in the case of *amennyire* 'how much', which is a QP modifier. Consider the following examples:

(85) a. Mari magasabb, mint **amennyire magas** Péter volt.
          Mary taller   than how.much tall   Peter was.3SG
          'Mary is taller than Peter was.'

      b. # Mari magasabb, mint **amennyire** Péter **magas** volt.
          Mary taller   than how.much Peter tall   was.3SG
          'Mary is taller than Peter was.'

      c. ?? Mari magasabb, mint **amennyire** Péter volt   **magas**.
          Mary taller   than how.much Peter was.3SG tall
          'Mary is taller than Peter was.'

As shown, GIVEN APs are preferably located in the [Spec,CP] position, as in (85a); note that this is an unmarked position in the sense that it is not reserved either for GIVEN or F-marked elements. Less typically, they can appear clause-finally, but this position would prefer either total de-accenting or secondary focus, hence the slight markedness of (85c); still, as this particular position is not a contrast position either, (85c) is possible. However, (85b) is infelicitous because *magas* 'tall' is located in the preverbal position, which is the canonical contrast position where focussed elements move (cf. Brody 1990; 1995, É. Kiss 2002).

On the other hand, the following pattern can be established for F-marked APs:

(86) a. ? A macska kövérebb, mint amennyire széles a   macskaajtó
          the cat   fatter   than how.much wide the cat.flap
          volt.
          was.3SG
          'The cat is fatter than the cat flap was wide.'

      b. A macska kövérebb, mint amennyire a   macskaajtó széles
          the cat   fatter   than how.much the cat.flap   wide
          volt.
          was.3SG
          'The cat is fatter than the cat flap was wide.'

   c. ? A   macska kövérebb, mint amennyire a   macskaajtó volt
      the cat   fatter   than how.much the cat.flap   was.3SG
      széles.
      wide

      'The cat is fatter than the cat flap was wide.'

The most preferred position is the preverbal contrast position in (86b) and the other two possibilities are less preferred, as shown by (86a) and (86c); this is so because the main contrast is expressed by the AP itself and therefore it should appear in the focus position. Note that, while there is a canonical contrast position, there is no canonical non-contrast position, as opposed to Czech: hence the asymmetry between the patterns in (85) and (86), in that an F-marked AP is not infelicitous even in the less preferred positions, contrary to what was attested in Czech.

Again, it has to be stressed that individual judgements may differ but for the vast majority of my informants (86b) was perfectly acceptable while the other two options were both marked, though to different degrees. It seems that once the contrastive AP is stranded, then it should appear in the preverbal position, as it expresses the main contrast involved in the comparison. Since this places a requirement on the AP to appear in the preverbal position but does not affect the position of the other elements, it should be possible to reverse the positions of the AP *széles* 'wide' and the DP *a macskaajtó* 'the cat flap' in (86a), which is indeed the case:

(87)   A   macska kövérebb, mint **amennyire széles** volt   a   macskaajtó.
      the cat   fatter   than how.much wide was.3SG the cat.flap

      'The cat is fatter than the cat flap was wide.'

In (87), the contrastive AP is in the focus position and since the postverbal position is available both for GIVEN and F-marked elements, the contrastive DP *a macskaajtó* can appear there.

The reason why there are altogether three available positions for APs in a Hungarian comparative subclause is due to the fact that the QP undergoes cyclic movement: first from within the VP to the edge of the FP, and subsequently from the FP to the lower [Spec,CP]. The AP can be stranded either in its base position or in the FP, in addition to being able to move up as high as the [Spec,CP].

I will not venture to examine the issue of positional differences here, since this is not my primary concern and would go far beyond the scope of the present investigation. What is important now is that though the information-structural properties of the lexical AP obviously play a crucial role in the formation of the comparative subclause, they do not have a bearing on whether Comparative Deletion happens or not. Comparative Deletion is a phenomenon linked to a specific syntactic position and is predictable from the formal properties of the comparative operator.

4 Attributive Comparative Deletion

4.1 Introduction

This chapter aims at providing an adequate explanation for the phenomenon of Attributive Comparative Deletion, as attested in English, by way of relating it to the regular mechanism of Comparative Deletion described in Chapter 3. I will show that Attributive Comparative Deletion can only be understood as a descriptive term referring to a phenomenon that is a result of the interaction of more general syntactic processes; in other words, there is no reason to postulate any special mechanism underlying Attributive Comparative Deletion in the grammar. Eliminating such a mechanism will allow one to achieve a unified analysis of all types of comparatives. On the other hand, Attributive Comparative Deletion is not a universal phenomenon: I will show that its appearance in English can be conditioned by independent, more general rules and that the absence of such restrictions may lead to the absence of Attributive Comparative Deletion in other languages. Again, I will first review some of the existing analyses, partly because in certain respects I will strongly rely on them and partly because the advantages of my proposal can best be understood when measured against these ones.

4.2 Earlier accounts

4.2.1 The problems to be discussed

Attributive Comparative Deletion is a peculiar phenomenon that involves the obligatory deletion of the quantified AP and the lexical verb from the comparative subclause if the quantified AP functions as an attribute within a nominal expression. Consider the examples in (1):

(1)   a.   Ralph bought a bigger cat than George did ~~buy~~ a ~~big~~ cat flap.
      b.   Ralph bought a bigger cat than George ~~bought~~ a ~~big~~ cat flap.
      c.   * Ralph bought a bigger cat than George bought a ~~big~~ cat flap.

    d. *Ralph bought a bigger cat than George bought a big cat flap.

    e. *Ralph bought a bigger cat than George ~~bought~~ a big cat flap.

    f. *Ralph bought a bigger cat than George did ~~buy~~ a big cat flap.

As can be seen, both the adjective (*big*) and the lexical verb (*buy*) have to be eliminated from the comparative subclause; this is possible either by eliminating the tensed lexical verb, as in (1b), or by deleting the lexical verb and leaving the auxiliary *do* bearing the tense morpheme intact, as in (1a). Note that both the verb and the adjective have to be deleted, as indicated by the ungrammaticality of (1c)–(1f).

Furthermore, the obligatory elimination of the adjective is not merely due to the fact that it is GIVEN; the overt presence of the attributive adjective is ungrammatical even if it is different from its matrix clausal counterpart, as shown by (2):

(2)   a. *Ralph bought a bigger cat than George ~~bought~~ a wide cat flap.

     b. *Ralph bought a bigger cat than George did ~~buy~~ a wide cat flap.

It seems that the elimination of the adjective from that particular position is obligatory.

On the other hand, note that the deletion of the lexical verb is required only if part of the DP is overt; in case the entire DP is eliminated, as in (3), the lexical verb can stay:

(3)   Ralph bought a bigger cat than George bought ~~a big cat~~.

A number of questions arise in connection with these phenomena. First, it has to be explained why the adjective has to be deleted and cannot appear overtly even if it is contrastive. Second, one has to account for the fact that the deletion of the adjective happens alongside the deletion of the lexical verb: apart from answering the question why this should be so, the issue of how this can be carried out also has to be addressed since in structures like (1a) and (1b) the adjective and the lexical verb do not seem to be adjacent. In other words, though the strong interrelatedness of the elimination of both these elements suggests that they are deleted by one and the same process, their apparently distinct positions also raise the possibility of there being two separate processes at hand – if so, one has to explain why and how these are interrelated.

In addition, the relation of Attributive Comparative Deletion to ordinary Comparative Deletion also has to be addressed; the fact that in structures such as (1a) and (1b) it is the lower copy that may remain overt suggests that CD takes place regularly in these structures too – if so, however, one has to account for the differences attested in the extent to which lower copies may remain overt.

Furthermore, the analysis of Attributive Comparative Deletion also has to take cross-linguistic differences into consideration. For instance, in languages like Hungarian the full structure may be visible in the subclause, as shown by (4):

(4) Rudolf   nagyobb macskát vett,   mint amilyen széles macskaajtót
     Rudolph bigger   cat.ACC bought.3SG than how   wide cat.flap.ACC
     Miklós vett.
     Mike   bought.3SG
     'Rudolph bought a bigger cat then Mike did a cat flap.'

On the other hand, languages such as German do not permit Attributive Comparative Deletion, as shown in (5):

(5) *Ralf hat eine   größere   Wohnung als Michael ein   Haus.
      Ralph has a.ACC.F bigger.ACC.F flat   than Michael a.ACC.N house
     'Ralph has a bigger flat than Michael a house.'

Therefore, a sound analysis for Attributive Comparative Deletion should account for cross-linguistic variation, besides providing an adequate explanation for the English data.

In what follows I will briefly review two analyses concerning Attributive Comparative Deletion. The first one is that of Kennedy & Merchant (2000), who provided the most detailed description of the phenomenon in English, also successfully explaining a number of related issues and making the occurrence of Attributive Comparative Deletion partially predictable in cross-linguistic terms. Second, I will also review the article by Reglero (2006), which makes use of the analysis by Kennedy & Merchant (2000) by extending it to Spanish, thus providing important insights into cross-linguistic variation in this respect.

4.2.2 Attributive modification – Kennedy & Merchant (2000)

Starting from the observation made by Pinkham (1982; 1985), Kennedy & Merchant (2000: 91–92) point out that Attributive Comparative Deletion proves to be a challenge to deletion analyses for Comparative Deletion since "in comparatives involving attributive adjectives, CD cannot target just the corresponding AP in the comparative clause." Consider the following example (Kennedy & Merchant 2000: 92, ex. 7a):

(6)   *Pico wrote a more interesting novel than Brio wrote a ___ play.

As Kennedy & Merchant (2000: 92) argue, any analysis treating Comparative Deletion as an unbounded deletion process targeting left-branch constituents (cf. Bresnan 1975) would face a serious problem here, in that attributive APs are canonical left-branch constituents and yet they cannot be deleted in constructions such as (6). In other words, such an analysis would predict (6) to be grammatical, which is clearly not the case.

One of the fundamental claims made by Kennedy & Merchant (2000: 103) is that the derivation of ill-formed attributive CD constructions contains left-branch extraction in the same way it happens in main clause *wh*-questions. The examples in (7) are essentially ruled out for the same reason (Kennedy & Merchant 2000: 103, exx. 25 and 26):

(7)   a.   * Erik drives a more expensive car than Polly drives **a motorcycle**.

   b.   * **How expensive** does Polly drive **a motorcycle**?

In both cases, a DegP is claimed to move out to a [Spec,CP] position from within the DP. This DegP is phonologically null in comparative subclauses such as in (7a), see Kennedy & Merchant (2000: 102–103).

The prediction is that languages that allow left-branch extraction in questions like (7b) should also allow constructions such as (7a), whereas languages that do not should have them. This prediction is borne out: Polish and Czech allow constructions like (7a) and (7b) alike, while Bulgarian and Greek do not (Kennedy & Merchant 2000: 104–109). Note that the unavailability of left-branch extraction in Greek (and Polish) is true for the constructions discussed here and does not necessarily have to hold for other structures. As far as Greek is concerned, it is known that Greek does allow certain left-branch extractions, cf. Uriagereka (2006: 281), based on Corver (1992) and Horrocks & Stavrou (1987). (On the relation between the article and the availability of extraction in Greek, see also Bošković 2005; 2012.)

Consider the examples in (8) from Polish (Kennedy & Merchant 2000: 104, exx. 29 and 31a):

(8)   a.   **Jak długą sztukę** napisał Paweł?
      how long play   wrote Pawel
      'How long a play did Pawel write?'

   b.   **Jak długą** napisał Paweł **sztukę**?
      how long   wrote Pawel play
      'How long a play did Pawel write?'

c. Jan napisał dłuższy list,　niż　Paweł napisał **sztukę**.

　　Jan wrote　longer　letter　than Pawel wrote　play

　　'Jan wrote a longer letter than Pawel wrote a play.'

As can be seen, Polish allows both the extraction of the entire nominal expression, as in (8a), or the extraction of the DegP attribute from within that nominal expression, as in (8b); the availability of (8b) predicts that (8c) should be grammatical, which is indeed the case (Kennedy & Merchant 2000: 104).

By contrast, consider the data in (9) from Greek (Kennedy & Merchant 2000: 106–107, exx. 35 and 37a):

(9)　a.　**Poso megalo aftokinito** agorase o　Petros?

　　　　how　big　　car　　　　bought the Petros

　　　　'How big a car did Petros buy?'

　　b.　* **Poso megalo** agorase o　Petros ena **aftokinito**?

　　　　how　big　　bought the Petros a　　car

　　　　'How big a car did Petros buy?'

　　c.　*O　Petros agorase ena megalitero aftokinito apoti　　o　Giannis

　　　　the Petros bought　a　bigger　　car　　　than.what the Giannis

　　　　agorase **ena dzip**.

　　　　bought a　jeep

　　　　'Petros bought a bigger car than Giannis did a jeep.'

Unlike in Polish, the extraction of the DegP out of a nominal expression is not allowed, as demonstrated by the ungrammaticality of (9b): only movement together with the rest of the DP is allowed, as in (9a). The fact that (9c) should be ungrammatical is predictable from the ungrammaticality of (9b).

Another prediction is that the elimination of the lexical verb or of the noun in constructions like (9c) should result in grammatical configurations, just as in the case of English. This is again fulfilled, as shown by the Greek data given in (10) below (Kennedy & Merchant 2000: 108, ex. 39):

(10)　a.　O　Petros agorase ena megalitero aftokinito apoti　　agorase o

　　　　the Petros bought　a　bigger　　car　　　than.what bought　the

　　　　Giannis.

　　　　Giannis

　　　　'Petros bought a bigger car than Giannis bought.'

> b. O   Petros agorase ena megalitero aftokinito apoti   o   Giannis.
>   the Petros bought a   bigger   car   than.what the Giannis
>
> 'Petros bought a bigger car than Giannis did.'
>
> c. O   Petros agorase ena megalitero aftokinito apoti   o   Giannis
>   the Petros bought a   bigger   car   than.what the Giannis
>   ___ ena dzip.
>   a   jeep
>
> 'Petros bought a bigger car than Giannis did a jeep.'

In (10a) the entire nominal expression containing the DegP is removed from the subclause, while in (10b) the finite verb is also eliminated; in turn, in (10c) only the finite verb is absent. Most importantly, all of these constructions are grammatical and the same observation holds for Bulgarian (Kennedy & Merchant 2000: 108–109).

What follows from all this is that constructions like (6) are ruled out because they violate the Left Branch Condition (Kennedy & Merchant 2000: 110). As pointed out by Kennedy & Merchant (2000: 109–116), the Left Branch Condition is essentially a PF constraint: the acceptability of the elliptical counterparts of constructions like (6) show that (6) cannot be ruled out by LF.

Essentially, Kennedy & Merchant (2000) claim that the operation responsible for ellipsis is VP-deletion. First of all, they adopt the view that pseudogapping is in fact an instance of VP-deletion, such that there is some additional mechanism that saves the remnant (Kennedy & Merchant 2000: 121, based on Kuno 1981). Consider the example in (11) for pseudogapping (Kennedy & Merchant 2000: 121, ex. 60a):

(11)   I eat pizza, but I don't seafood.

In this case, there is a DP remnant (*seafood*) in the second conjunct; Kennedy & Merchant (2000: 121–122) adopt the view formulated by Jayaseelan (1990) and Johnson (1997) that the DP moves out of its base position within the VP and is right-adjoined to the VP-node. Hence the structure of the string *but I don't seafood* should be as given in (12), based on Kennedy & Merchant (2000: 122, ex. 61):[1]

---

[1] Note that Kennedy & Merchant (2000) treat *don't* as a single inflection head and do not postulate a separate NegP; this may be a problem in itself, but since it has no bearing on the analysis, I will not attempt to provide an alternative to this later on either.

(12)

```
              IP
          ／      ＼
      DP_subj        I'
        |         ／    ＼
       I  I        VP
          |      ／    ＼
       don't  V̶P̶   DP_remnant
            ／   ＼    ／▔＼
        t_subj  V̶'̶  seafood
             ／   ＼
          V̶   t_remnant
            |
           eat
```

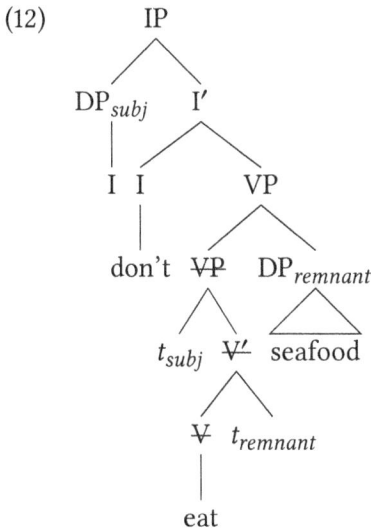

The same is claimed to take place in attributive comparatives; however, if the DP is moved to the right, the degree expression moves alongside with it, and therefore it could not be deleted (cf. Kennedy & Merchant 2000: 122–124).

In order to overcome this problem, Kennedy & Merchant (2000: 124–130) propose a revised analysis for the syntax of attributive modification. As argued by Kennedy & Merchant (2000: 124), certain DegPs[2] modifying nominal expressions end up in an inverted position. Consider the following examples (Kennedy & Merchant 2000: 124, exx. 65a, 66a, and 66c):

(13) a. **[How interesting a play]** did Brio write?

  b. I ate **[too big a piece]**.

  c. Bob didn't write **[as detailed a proposal]** as Sheila did.

As Kennedy & Merchant (2000: 129–130) note, based on Bresnan (1973), there is considerable variation as to which degree expressions must, can and cannot undergo inversion. The point is that if the DegP does move up to a position within the nominal expression, the uninterpretable [+wh] feature of the DegP – which is involved in Left Branch Condition effects – is transferred to some functional head in the nominal projection (Kennedy & Merchant 2000: 124).

The functional projection of this head is right above the DP, and is referred to as FP by Kennedy & Merchant (2000: 124–125). The structure of the string *how interesting a play* is as follows (Kennedy & Merchant 2000: 125, ex. 67):

---

[2]Kennedy & Merchant (2000) treat the bracketed constituents in (13) as DegPs throughout their paper. However, based on the analysis in Chapter 2, they should rather be treated as QPs.

(14)

```
                    FP
                  /    \
              DegP_i     F'
             /     \    /  \
     how interesting  F   DP
                          /  \
                         D    NP
                         |   / \
                         a  t_i play
```

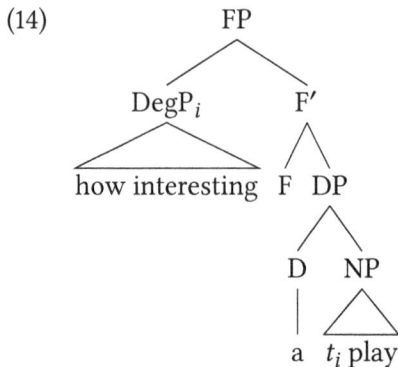

As can be seen, the DegP moves up to the [Spec,FP] position from within the NP, thus producing an inverted word order.

There are arguments in favour of such an analysis. First, in certain dialects the F position may be overtly filled by *of* (Kennedy & Merchant 2000: 125–126; cf. also Bolinger 1972; Abney 1987; Bowers 1987). Consider the examples in (15), taken from Kennedy & Merchant (2000: 125–126, exx. 68a, 69a and 69c):

(15) a. **[How long of a novel]** did Brio write?
      b. I ate **[too big of a piece]**.
      c. Bob didn't write **[as detailed of a proposal]** as Sheila did.

Second, there are certain ambiguities that can be explained only by accepting that the DegP may move to a [Spec,FP] position. This is demonstrated by the following set of examples (Kennedy & Merchant 2000: 127, ex. 70):

(16) a. I have written a successful play, but you have ___ a novel.
      b. I have written a successful play, but you have written a novel.
      c. I have written a successful play, but you have written a successful novel.

The sentence in (16a) is ambiguous between the two readings paraphrased in (16b) and (16c); cf. Kennedy & Merchant (2000: 127). As far as the one in (16b) is concerned, it is completely unsurprising: under the analysis proposed by Kennedy & Merchant (2000), what happens here is that "the remnant DP is removed from VP, and the VP is deleted" (Kennedy & Merchant 2000: 128). By contrast, the reading given in (16c) is unexpected inasmuch as deletion "appears to be 'reaching inside' the remnant DP to delete the attributive modifier along with VP" (Kennedy & Merchant 2000: 128). The way to overcome this apparent problem is to adopt the representation in (14) for structures like (16a): in that case, the VP and the attributive modifier are adjacent at PF – according to Kennedy & Merchant (2000: 129–130), the DP moves out of the FP, leaving the DegP in [Spec,FP] behind within the VP that counts as the extraction site.

Essentially, the same is claimed to happen in the case of attributive comparative structures (Kennedy & Merchant 2000: 130–134). The F head has to be eliminated because English lacks a [+wh] F head in the lexicon, as opposed to a [+wh] D head, which does exist (Kennedy & Merchant 2000: 130). The [+wh] feature is uninterpretable on the F head at PF; however, if deletion takes place, then it also eliminates this feature (Kennedy & Merchant 2000: 131). On the other hand, since the DP may scramble out of the FP, the DP itself is not affected by deletion (Kennedy & Merchant 2000: 131).

Consider the following example (Kennedy & Merchant 2000: 131, ex. 77):

(17) Pico wrote a more interesting novel than he did a play.

The processes taking place in (17) are summarised in (18); cf. Kennedy & Merchant (2000: 132, ex. 78):

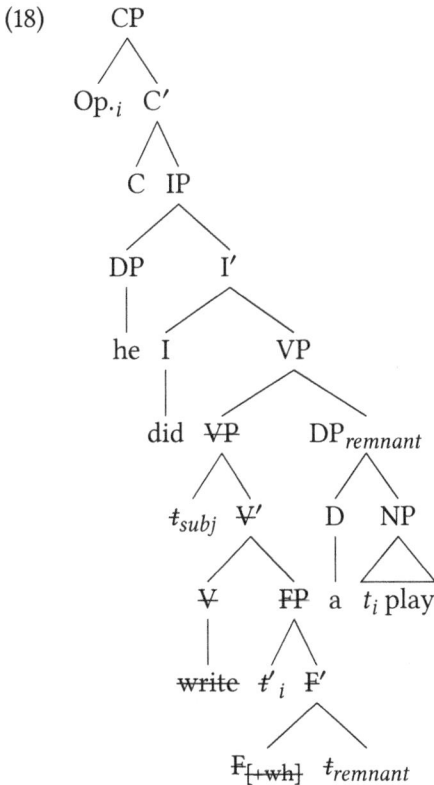

(18)

```
                CP
               /  \
          Op.ᵢ    C'
                 /  \
                C    IP
                    /  \
                  DP    I'
                  |    /  \
                 he   I    VP
                      |   /  \
                    did  V̶P̶   DP_remnant
                        /  \    /  \
                   t̶_subj  V̶'  D    NP
                         /  \   |   /\
                        V̶    FP a  tᵢ play
                        |   /  \
                    w̶r̶i̶t̶e̶  t'ᵢ  F'
                             /  \
                        F̶_[̶+̶w̶h̶]̶  t_remnant
```

As can be seen, the DP moves rightwards and is adjoined to the VP node; in turn, the lower VP node is deleted, alongside with the FP within it.

The analysis has its advantages, especially as far as the syntax of attributive modification is concerned, and also because verb gapping is treated as an instance of VP-deletion and not as a special process. In this respect, Kennedy & Merchant (2000) strongly rely on the results of Kuno (1981), Sag (1976), Levin (1986), Miller (1992), Jayaseelan (1990), Lasnik (1995) and Johnson (1997); but cf. also Coppock (2001) and Johnson (2004) for more recent analyses.

However, there are two main problems that arise in connection with the general mechanism of VP-ellipsis. First, the rightward movement of the DP is unmotivated; moreover, rightward movement – within a minimalist framework – is questionable in itself. Second, if VP-ellipsis targets a VP-constituent, it remains also unexplained what mechanism may select only the lower VP node.

In addition, there are two further problems concerning the application of this framework to attributive comparative structures. On the one hand, the DP moves from within the FP; however, there is no example in any analogous structure for the DP to move out – to the right – from its own functional extension generated this way: a sequence such as *how big did you see a cat is not grammatical either. On the other hand, the movement of the operator as indicated in (18) is not valid, chiefly because English has no other structures where the QP containing the operator moves out from within the FP – thus the sequence *how big did you see a cat is obviously not grammatical if we do not suppose the DP to be moving to the right either. At the same time, it would be rather ad hoc to assume that the QP containing the operator is phonologically empty in attributive structures: as was shown in Chapter 3, in predicative structures the QP contains a phonologically visible AP, and there is no reason for supposing that there would be a difference in the internal structure of the QP between predicative and attributive structures.

In sum, though the proposal of Kennedy & Merchant (2000) accounts for both why the AP must be deleted and how it can be adjacent to the lexical verb, the mechanism of VP-deletion has to be revised. Further, the analysis does not link Attributive Comparative Deletion to a more general theory on Comparative Deletion. This would be important especially because the higher copy seems to be deleted in attributive structures as well, thus the deletion taking place at the base-generation site has to be linked to the deletion of lower copies – in turn, the overt presence of a remnant DP also has to be linked to a more general theory on why and how lower copies may be phonologically realised.

Last but not least, though Kennedy & Merchant (2000) provide a cross-linguistic investigation as far as the extractability of the degree modifier from the DP

is concerned, they still do not address the issue of further cross-linguistic variation; that is, cases when the absence of Attributive Comparative Deletion effects
cannot be directly linked to the possibility of extracting attributive modifiers.

4.2.3 Gapping in Spanish – Reglero (2006)

Building on the findings of Kennedy & Merchant (2000), Reglero (2006) inves-
tigates the formation of Spanish subcomparative constructions, showing that
Spanish does not allow nominal subcomparatives in the way English does. The
importance of this study lies chiefly in that it provides further cross-linguistic
insights into the possible mechanisms behind Attributive Comparative Deletion
and in that it examines cases of nominal comparatives: this issue was neglected
by Kennedy & Merchant (2000), who considered only attributive structures.

As Reglero (2006: 67) points out, the term Comparative Subdeletion was used
by Bresnan (1972) to refer to constructions like (19), cf. Reglero (2006: 67, ex. 1):

(19)   Mary read more books than John read magazines.

For the derivation of (19), Reglero (2006: 68, ex. 4) adopts (20):

(20)   Mary read more books than Op_i John read [t_i many] magazines.

As opposed to English, Spanish does not allow constructions like (19); consider
the following example (Reglero 2006: 68, ex. 7):

(21)   * María leyó más libros que Juan leyó revistas.
       Mary read more books than John read magazines
       'Mary read more books than John read magazines.'

Relying on the observation of Price (1990), however, Reglero (2006: 68) notes
that constructions like (21) become fully grammatical if the verb is deleted from
the subclause. Consider the example in (22), taken from Reglero (2006: 68, ex. 8):

(22)   María leyó más libros que Juan revistas.
       Mary read more books than John magazines
       'Mary read more books than John read magazines.'

Reglero (2006: 68) refers to this as the "Obligatory Gapping" strategy; this
applies even if the verb in the subclause is different from the one in the matrix
clause, as shown by the ungrammaticality of (23), cf. Reglero (2006: 69, ex. 11):

(23) * María leyó más libros que Juan compró revistas.
      Mary read more books than John bought magazines
      'Mary read more books than John bought magazines.'

This shows that the verb must be deleted regardless of whether it is redundant or not, hence there is some other requirement at work here (Reglero 2006: 69).

As Reglero (2006: 69) notes, the chief difference from ordinary gapping is that verb deletion in constructions like (22) is obligatory. Based on the analyses of Lasnik (1995) and Kennedy & Merchant (2000) for English, Reglero (2006: 69–70) proposes that the object *revistas* contains a strong feature "that needs to be checked either by movement, or by PF deletion of the strong feature in PF." The derivation of the subclause in (22) is given in (24), see Reglero (2006: 70, ex. 14):

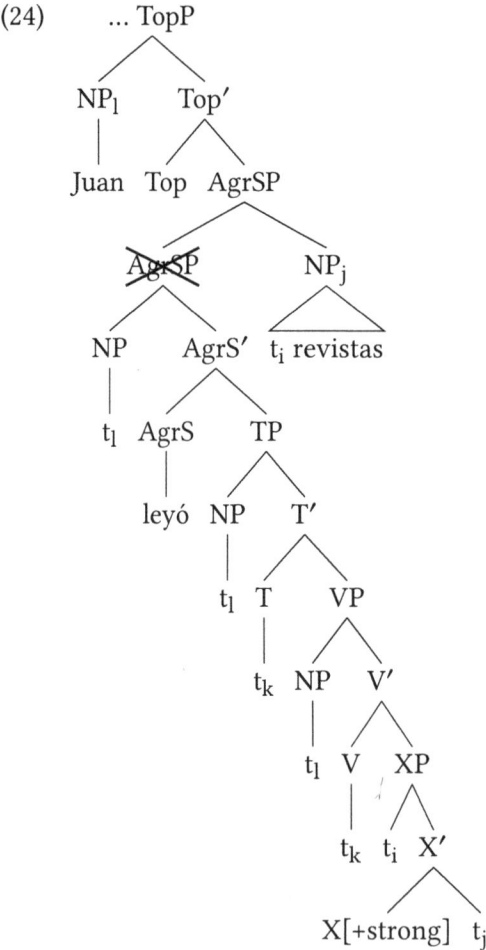

(24)   ... TopP

NP_1 Top'

Juan   Top AgrSP

~~AgrSP~~ NP_j

NP   AgrS' t_i revistas

t_1 AgrS   TP

leyó NP   T'

t_1 T   VP

t_k NP   V'

t_1 V   XP

t_k t_i X'

X[+strong] t_j

There is reason to believe that subjects move up as high as the topic projection in Spanish comparative subclauses (see Reglero 2006: 70–72). If so, it is possible to delete the AgrSP without affecting the subject.

Essentially, the proposal made by Reglero (2006) is similar to what Kennedy & Merchant (2000) claimed in connection with English; however, there is also an important difference in that in Spanish an AgrSP is deleted, whereas in English there is VP-ellipsis. As for English, it was shown that though the lexical verb must be eliminated, an auxiliary or modal that is located higher (e.g. *do*) may remain overt. This is not the case in Spanish (Reglero 2006: 73, ex. 25):

(25) * María puede leer más libros que Juan puede revistas.
       Mary can   read more books than John can   magazines

      'Mary can read more books than John can magazines.'

The ungrammaticality of (25) shows that the projection affected by deletion is indeed larger than the VP. Just as was proposed by Kennedy & Merchant (2000), deletion takes place because an uninterpretable feature must be eliminated, which is present on the XP in (24) because the degree expression moves up to its specifier in the same way it does to the FP in Kennedy & Merchant (2000); see Reglero (2006: 73–74).

As for the rightward movement of the object NP *revistas* in (24), Reglero (2006: 75–77) claims that it undergoes Heavy NP Shift (HNPS) and is adjoined relatively high in the structure because in Spanish objects moving out of quantified phrases (e.g. in the case of floating quantifiers) land high. This ensures that when the lower AgrSP node is deleted, not only the subject in [Spec,TP] but also the object adjoined to the AgrSP escapes deletion.

Again, there are a number of problems that arise with this proposal, most of which have already been mentioned in connection with Kennedy & Merchant (2000). In particular, the rightward movement of the nominal expression is not motivated enough and it is not plausible that this movement would be an instance of HNPS since the nominal expression in question is not (necessarily) heavy at all. Besides this, the deletion mechanism is again problematic since it is not clear how the lower but not the higher AgrSP node is selected.

Moreover, it is not quite clear why this particular deletion has to take place in Spanish but not in English; in addition, the difference between attributive and nominal structures in English in this respect is not addressed either, though this would be fairly important in understanding the reasons behind Attributive Comparative Deletion.

4.3 Verb deletion – an alternative approach

In the following, based on Bacskai-Atkari (2012b), I will present an analysis for Attributive Comparative Deletion, as found in English, by adopting the structure given by Kennedy & Merchant (2000) for the syntax of attributive modification and by proposing a different approach to VP-ellipsis from the one found in Kennedy & Merchant (2000) and in Reglero (2006).

The starting point of the argumentation is the assumption, presented in detail in Chapter 3, that if deletion takes place at PF, it cannot affect F-marked material. This is highlighted by Reich (2007: 472–473) as a rule constraining verb deletion and, with respect to VP-ellipsis, he basically implies that if the object is F-marked, then the F-markedness of this object in itself may withstand deletion. Consider the examples in (26):

(26) a. Ralph likes cats and Mike [$_{VP}$ likes [$_{DP}$ dogs]$_F$].
  b. Ralph likes cats and Mike [$_{VP}$ ~~likes~~ [$_{DP}$ dogs]$_F$].
  c. * Ralph likes cats and Mike [$_{VP}$ ~~likes~~ [$_{DP}$ ~~dogs~~]$_F$].

The full structure is shown in (26a). In case deletion takes place, as in (26b), the following happens: the V head (*likes*) is deleted but the F-marked DP (*dogs*) remains overt. Should the DP be eliminated too, which would no longer be gapping but stripping, then the sentence would not be grammatical since the F-marked DP could not be recovered from the context, as shown in (26c).

Following this, it can still be maintained that verb gapping is an instance of VP-ellipsis: deletion targets the GIVEN VP, within which there is an F-marked DP. Since deletion operations proceed in a left-to-right fashion at PF (which is why it is the copies on the left edge that remain from a movement chain, cf. Bošković & Nunes 2007), when the PF mechanism working this way arrives at the DP, it stops.

This is further reinforced by the fact that when there is no F-marked DP, as in (27), then there is nothing to prevent the elimination of the DP:

(27) a. Ralph likes cats and Mike [$_{VP}$ likes [$_{DP}$ cats]].
  b. * Ralph likes cats and Mike [$_{VP}$ ~~likes~~ [$_{DP}$ cats]].
  c. Ralph likes cats and Mike [$_{VP}$ ~~likes~~ [$_{DP}$ ~~eats~~]] too.

Taking the sentence in (27a), where the DP (*cats*) is not F-marked, it can be seen that in case VP-ellipsis happens, only the entire VP can be deleted, as in (27c); the elimination of the single V head, as in (27b), is not sufficient. If verb gapping existed as a separate mechanism targeting the V head as such, then (27b) should be grammatical. On the other hand, the phenomenon can be explained well with the mechanism of VP-ellipsis described above: as there is no F-marked DP within the VP, deletion will naturally affect the DP, too. Note that the reason why (27c) contains *too* is precisely because it is a stripping construction: without the presence of *too*, coordination would be interpreted as holding between the two DPs *cats* and *Mike* and thus not containing ellipsis. I will not try to explain here why this should be so as it would go far beyond the scope of the present investigation; for a more elaborate discussion, see Vicente (2010).

Similarly, it is also VP-deletion that takes place in attributive comparatives: here the F-marked constituent is the DP, not the FP. Consider the examples given in (28):

(28) a. * Ralph bought a bigger cat than Mike [$_{VP}$ bought [$_{FP}$ x-big [$_{DP}$ a cat flap]$_F$]].

  b. * Ralph bought a bigger cat than Mike [$_{VP}$ ~~bought~~ [$_{FP}$ x-big [$_{DP}$ a cat flap]$_F$]].

  c. Ralph bought a bigger cat than Mike [$_{VP}$ ~~bought~~ [$_{FP}$ ~~x-big~~ [$_{DP}$ a cat flap]$_F$]].

  d. * Ralph bought a bigger cat than Mike [$_{VP}$ ~~bought~~ [$_{FP}$ ~~x-big~~ [$_{DP}$ ~~a cat flap~~]$_F$]].

The sentence containing the full structure overtly in (28a) is ungrammatical because the QP (*x-big*) in the subclause should be deleted. The reason why (28b) is not grammatical either is that VP-ellipsis affects only the V head though the FP, which is GIVEN, cannot stop deletion at this point. The only grammatical sentence is (28c), in which VP-ellipsis is stopped by the first F-marked projection, that is, the DP (*a cat flap*). The sentence in (28d) is again ungrammatical since the F-marked DP is also deleted.

VP-ellipsis is thus an optional process that may save the construction from ungrammaticality; in this respect it is similar to sluicing (see the relevant discussion presented in Chapter 3), hence the phenomenon is not unique.

4.4 The lack of Attributive Comparative Deletion

One of the most important questions concerning the analysis above is whether it can be maintained when tested against cross-linguistic data. The chief claim is that Attributive Comparative Deletion is not a separate mechanism in itself but the surface realisation of two more general processes: Comparative Deletion and VP-ellipsis. Therefore, the prediction is that in languages where either of the two processes is missing, Attributive Comparative Deletion will not be attested. In what follows, I will briefly examine two languages in this respect, Hungarian and German, which were both claimed in the introduction of the present chapter to lack Attributive Comparative Deletion constructions.

The fundamental difference between English and Hungarian lies in the fact that the former but not the latter exhibits Comparative Deletion. Recall that in English both copies of the degree expression are eliminated from the subclause by default, as shown in (29):

(29)   a.   Mary is taller than [x-tall] George was [x-tall].
       b.   Mary bought bigger cats than [x-big-cats] George saw [x-big-cats].

As was argued for in Chapter 3, the reason behind this is that there is an Overtness Requirement on the operator in the [Spec,CP] position, such that an overt AP (or NP) is not licensed if the operator is phonologically zero. Since, however, the syntactic features are checked off for the movement chain, the lower copy of the QP (or the nominal expression containing that QP) can be regularly deleted and may remain overt only in case it is contrastive.

However, this is clearly not the case in Hungarian, which has overt operators and the higher copy can remain overt, as demonstrated by (30):

(30)   a.   Mari magasabb, mint amilyen magas Gyuri   volt.
            Mary taller   than how   tall   George was.3SG
            'Mary is taller than George was.'

       b.   Mari nagyobb macskákat vett,   mint amilyen nagy macskákat
            Mary bigger   cats.ACC   bought.3SG than how   big   cats.ACC
            Gyuri   látott.
            George saw.3SG
            'Mary bought bigger cats than George saw.'

As was discussed in Chapter 3, the QP (*amilyen magas* 'how tall') and the quantified DP (*amilyen nagy macskákat* 'how big cats') may remain overt in the subclause even if they are logically identical with their counterparts in the matrix clause. Moreover, these elements are overt in the [Spec,CP] position and not in their base position, as in Hungarian there is clearly no Comparative Deletion eliminating these constituents.

The higher copy of the QP or the quantified DP in the subclause is not obligatorily deleted and so the lower copy can be regularly deleted. Thus the expectation is that Attributive Comparative Deletion will not be attested in Hungarian. This prediction is borne out by the data, exemplified in (4), repeated here as (31):

(31) Rudolf   nagyobb macskát vett,   mint amilyen széles macskaajtót
      Rudolph bigger   cat.ACC bought.3SG than how   wide cat.flap.ACC
      Miklós vett.
      Mike   bought.3SG
      'Rudolph bought a bigger cat then Mike did a cat flap.'

The full DP *amilyen széles macskaajtót* 'how big a cat flap' is overtly located in [Spec,CP], as CD does not eliminate it; therefore, the lower copy can regularly be deleted without any part of it remaining. It can thus be concluded that Hungarian does not have Attributive Comparative Deletion because it does not have Comparative Deletion at all.

As was seen in Chapter 3, Comparative Deletion is not attested in German in the way it is in English. Consider:

(32) a. ? Maria ist größer als   Johann **groß** ist.
         Mary is taller than John   tall   is
         'Mary is taller than John.'

      b. Der   Tisch ist länger als   das   Büro **breit** ist.
          the.M table is longer than the.N office wide is
          'The table is longer than the office is wide.' ⸱

As shown by the acceptability of (32b), German is similar to English in that it allows subcomparatives in predicative structures. However, German is also different from Hungarian in that the movement of the entire degree expression to the [Spec,CP] position would result in Comparative Deletion in the same way as it applies in English, since the comparative operator is zero in both cases, resulting in a violation of the Overtness Requirement. On the other hand, the possibility of moving the operator on its own in predicative structures is an option not available in English, hence the acceptability of structures like (32a). In other words, if there is a copy to be realised overtly in German, then it is the lower one, just as in English.

However, the operator cannot be extracted on its own if the QP is a modifier within a DP, and since the quantified DP cannot occur overtly in the [Spec,CP] position, this may suggest that German actually has Attributive Comparative

Deletion in the same way as it is attested in English. This is not the case, as shown by (33):

(33)   a.   * Ralf   hat eine   größere   Wohnung als   Michael ein
           Ralph has a.ACC.F bigger.ACC.F flat   than Michael a.ACC.N
           Haus.
           house
           'Ralph has a bigger flat than Michael a house.'

       b.   * Ralf   kauft schnellere Hunde als   Michael Katzen.
           Ralph buys faster.PL   dogs   than Michael cats
           'The dogs Ralph buys are faster than the cats that Michael buys.'

The sentences in (33) are not grammatical though the QP is eliminated from the subclause. Since this deletion is VP-ellipsis in English, the root of the problem with (33) may be related to VP-ellipsis in German: German is known to lack VP-deletion in the way English has it (Winkler 2005: 120–124; Merchant 2004: 671). Moreover, the German comparative subclause is verb-final, just as any other subclause in German: this is also attested by (32); therefore, a prenominal modifier and a verb could not be deleted together, even though the QP is located at the left edge of the plural nominal expression in (33b).

However, the chief problem is that German does not require the deletion of the QP in the lower copy in the way English does. The following construction is fully grammatical for several speakers:

(34)   Ralf   hat eine   größere   Katze als   Michael eine   breite
       Ralph has a.ACC.F bigger.ACC.F cat   than Michael a.ACC.F wide.ACC.F
       Katzenklappe hat.
       cat.flap   has.
       'Ralph's cat is bigger than Michael's cat flap is wide.'

While the acceptability of (34) shows inter-speaker variation (with no identifiable regional differences), the point here is that speakers who accept (34) still do not accept (33). In (34), the QP *breit(e)* 'wide' can remain overt as part of the DP in the lower copy of that DP; note also that this QP is not inverted, that is, it is not moved to a [Spec,FP] position: this should be clear from the fact that it appears between the indefinite article *eine* 'a' and the noun head *Katzenklappe* 'cat flap'. I will return to the question of inverted and non-inverted QP modifiers in §4.6; for the time being, suffice it to say that the lower copy of the entire DP can remain in a German comparative subclause just as the entire copy of a QP can in predicative structures. That is, in structures like (34) the entire DP moves up to the [Spec,CP] position, since the QP cannot be extracted on its own. The higher copy is eliminated by Comparative Deletion just as in English because the Overtness Requirement on the operator is not met. However, the entire lower copy may remain overt in German, unlike in English, and this is presumably related to the fact that German does not display the kind of inversion English does.

4.5 The Overtness Requirement revisited

The analysis so far captures important cross-linguistic differences and is fully able to relate the phenomenon of Attributive Comparative Deletion to whether and how Comparative Deletion is attested in the language. In other words, Attributive Comparative Deletion is a phenomenon that results from Comparative Deletion and VP-ellipsis. The way VP-ellipsis is available in a given language is naturally subject to more general rules and, as was shown in Chapter 3, so is Comparative Deletion, in that it is reducible to an Overtness Requirement that holds on elements moving to a [Spec,CP] position.

Therefore, Attributive Comparative Deletion is not attested in cases when the higher copy of the quantified expression can be overtly realised in the [Spec,CP] position, that is, when there is a phonologically visible operator. Problems seem to arise when it is the lower copy that should be pronounced. This is true for languages such as English, where the operator is a Deg head and cannot be extracted in predicative structures either, and it also holds for languages like German, where the QP modifier operator could be extracted from a single QP but not from within a DP, as that would be a case of violating the Left Branch Condition. However, as was pointed out by Kennedy & Merchant (2000), in languages where the QP can be extracted from the nominal expression, such as Polish or Czech, Attributive Comparative Deletion does not arise.

In other words, Attributive Comparative Deletion arises when there is an inverted QP that moves to the [Spec,FP] position in the extended nominal expression. As was shown by Kennedy & Merchant (2000), precisely this QP is ungrammatical; however, they do not address the question why this should be so. In what follows I will argue that this is due to an Overtness Requirement on the operator element and that this Overtness Requirement is essentially the same as the one that underlies Comparative Deletion, thus extending the Overtness Requirement in the CP-domain to the nominal domain.

As was shown by Kennedy & Merchant (2000: 124–130), certain quantified expressions undergo upward movement within the nominal expression, landing in the specifier position of a functional projection (FP) above the DP layer. For the time being, I adopt the analysis given by Kennedy & Merchant (2000) in that the nominal expression *a novel* in examples like (35) is indeed a DP; I will return to this issue in §4.6, showing that the different layers in the nominal expression show different behaviour with respect to projecting an FP layer (and hence attributive modification), and I will treat *a novel* rather as a NumP.

Recall the following contrast:

(35) a. [FP [QP How interesting]i [DP a [NP ti novel]]] did Ralph read?

  b. * [DP A [NP [QP how interesting] novel]] did Ralph read?

As can be seen, the construction is grammatical only if the QP moves up to the FP level, as in (35a): if it stays in its base position, as in (35b), the result is ungrammatical. The quantified expression in this case contains a *wh*-operator (*how*), which has to move upwards because of its [EDGE] feature; in addition, in the analysis given by Kennedy & Merchant (2000), this is how the entire nominal expression acquires a [+wh] feature, which can be checked off in the [Spec,CP] position. Otherwise, the [+wh] feature is claimed to be uninterpretable on the F head for PF. Essentially, the same kind of movement is assumed to take place in Attributive Comparative Deletion structures as well: however, since in these cases the higher copy is not pronounced either (due to Comparative Deletion, see Chapter 3), the lower copy cannot be automatically eliminated. This is why, as has been seen, VP-ellipsis applies, which can delete the lexical verb and the AP together since these are indeed adjacent at PF, as illustrated in (36):

(36) Ralph bought a bigger cat than George did [VP buy [FP [QP x-big]i [DP a [NP ti cat flap]]]].

The issue here is why the particular position of the QP is ungrammatical. According to Kennedy & Merchant (2000), the reason should be the presence of an unchecked [+wh] – or, in comparative subclauses, rather a [+rel] – feature on an F head. This is problematic for a number of reasons: first, the feature under discussion is checked off in the higher copy and therefore should no longer cause a problem for any copy in the movement chain. Second, the F head is not visible in these cases and it is thus not straightforward why a given feature on an invisible head should in itself be a PF-violation.

More importantly, as was also discussed by Kennedy & Merchant (2000), there are constructions that clearly do not involve the movement of the entire nominal expression to an operator position and yet inversion is attested. For instance, the degree element *too* also requires inversion, as illustrated in (37):

(37)　a.　Ralph bought [FP [QP too big]i [DP a [NP *t*i cat]]].
　　　b.　* Ralph bought [DP a [NP [QP too big] cat]].

In the case of (37a), it does not seem valid that the F head is equipped with a [+wh] feature that happens to be uninterpretable at PF: the QP itself is not [+wh] in nature and the whole FP does not move up to a [+wh] position. Moreover, the construction is grammatical so there seems to be no PF-violation at hand.

As was mentioned, while movement to [Spec,FP] is obligatory for *too*, as is for *so*, QP degree modifiers (e.g. *more, enough, quite*) generally involve this movement optionally, see Kennedy & Merchant (2000: 129–130), based on Bresnan (1973: 287–288). Yet, as noted by the same authors, there is one construction which does not allow this movement and this is the case of bare adjectives (which are nevertheless analysed as QPs containing a null degree element marking the positive degree). As was shown in Chapter 2 in detail, gradable adjectives are in the specifier of a DegP irrespectively of whether the degree is absolute, comparative or superlative, since the degree itself is expressed by the Deg head and not the AP itself. Moreover, modifiers are located in the [Spec,QP] position and these show agreement with the Q head with respect to its degree, whereby the absolute degree also has its modifiers as well, e.g. *very*.

Consider now the examples in (38):

(38)　a.　* Ralph bought [FP [QP big]i [DP a [NP *t*i cat]]].
　　　b.　Ralph bought [DP a [NP [QP big] cat]].

One may think that this is so because bare adjectives cannot move to the [Spec,FP] position at all; indeed, if they lacked a degree element, this would be a plausible consequence. However, it appears that even positive adjectives can undergo this movement, as shown in (16). Observe the following sentence of the same type:

(39)　Ralph saw a lilac cat and Mike did a tiger.

Recall that sentences like (39) are ambiguous between two readings (see Kennedy & Merchant 2000: 127–131): under one reading Mike saw a tiger, which was not necessarily lilac, while under the other reading Mike saw a lilac tiger. Therefore, in the first case the adjective *lilac* is not even underlyingly present in the second clause, whereas in the second case it has to be deleted, given that the information it carries is also present. The two structures are shown in (40a) and (40b), respectively:

(40) a. Ralph saw a lilac cat and Mike did [~~VP~~ ~~see~~ [DP a [NP tiger]]].

  b. Ralph saw a lilac cat and Mike did [~~VP~~ ~~see~~ [~~FP~~ [~~QP~~ ~~lilac~~]ᵢ [DP a [NP t_i tiger]]]].

The deletion of the adjective together with the verb in (40b) is possible only if the adjective moves up to the specifier of the FP. Note that in this case deletion saves the construction from ungrammaticality as the overt presence of *lilac* in (40b) would not be grammatical, just as in (38a) above.

It has to be mentioned that the acceptability of pseudogapping constructions seems to show interesting dialectal and/or idiolectal differences. Some speakers do not find structures like (40) natural and prefer a construction like (41) below:

(41) Ralph saw a lilac cat as Mike did a tiger.

On the other hand, there is a difference in the availability of the two readings: a reading like (40a) is generally more available than one like (40b), and speakers who get an interpretation like (40b) also get (40a) but not vice versa. This should not be surprising, as the derivation in (40a) is more economical than the one in (40b): apart from the fact that there is more material elided in (40b), there is also an extra movement operation. The same applies to structures like (41) above and also to cases like (42) where the degree expression is more complex:

(42) Ralph saw a most interesting play as did Peter a movie.

In this case, the ambiguity of the sentence depends on the presence/absence of the QP *most interesting* in the subordinate clause in the underlying structure.

At any rate, it seems that inverted degree expressions are ungrammatical precisely when there is no overt degree element. These QPs move to a left-peripheral position within the extended nominal expression and just as the [Spec,CP] position is reserved for elements with an overt operator (see Chapter 3), the [Spec,FP] position must have an overt degree element to avoid PF-uninterpretability.

This implies that the Overtness Requirement is not specific to comparative structures. This is further reinforced by the fact that it can be observed in the [Spec,CP] position in structures other than comparatives. That is, in relative clauses that may contain the sequence of a relative operator and some lexical projection. Though this construction is generally not widespread, there are still some examples such as the one from Hungarian given in (43):

(43) a. Mari Judith Hermann könyvét   olvasta,   **amely könyvet**
          Mary Judith Hermann book.POSS.ACC read.PST.3SG which book.ACC
          egyébként   még én küldtem neki   Berlinből.
          incidentally still I   sent.1SG she.DAT Berlin.ELA

          'Mary was reading Judith Hermann's book, which actually I had sent
          her from Berlin.'

      b. Leégett   a gyár,   **amely esemény** megmozgatta a
          down.burned.3SG the factory which event   PRT.moved.3SG the
          várost.
          city.ACC

          'The factory burned down, which moved the city.'

Such constructions are relatively rare, presumably because they either involve
the repetition of the matrix clausal nominal expression, as in (43a), or the noun
in the subclause must be general enough to be an anaphor for the entire matrix
clause, as in (43b). The configuration is also grammatical in the absence of an
overt NP, as in (44):

(44) a. Mari Judith Hermann könyvét   olvasta,   **amelyet**
          Mary Judith Hermann book.POSS.ACC read.PST.3SG which.ACC
          egyébként   még én küldtem neki   Berlinből.
          incidentally still I   sent.1SG she.DAT Berlin.ELA

          'Mary was reading Judith Hermann's book, which actually I had sent
          her from Berlin.'

      b. Leégett   a gyár,   **ami** megmozgatta a   várost.
          down.burned.3SG the factory what PRT.moved.3SG the city.ACC

          'The factory burned down, which moved the city.'

In (44a) the operator takes the accusative case suffix and, just like in (43a),
marks the relative nature of the clause; in (44b) the relative pronoun *ami* 'what'
refers back to the entire matrix clause just as the nominal expression in (43b).
However, an overt NP is not grammatical in the [Spec,CP] position without an
overt operator:

(45) a. * Mari Judith Hermann könyvét   olvasta,   **könyvet**
            Mary Judith Hermann book.POSS.ACC read.PST.3SG book.ACC
            egyébként   még én küldtem neki   Berlinből.
            incidentally still I   sent.1SG she.DAT Berlin.ELA

            'Mary was reading Judith Hermann's book, which actually I had
            sent her from Berlin.'

    b. *Leégett   a   gyár,   **esemény** megmozgatta a   várost.
        down.burned.3SG the factory event   PRT.moved.3SG the city.ACC
        'The factory burned down, which moved the city.'

The reason behind the ungrammaticality of (45) is that Hungarian lacks zero relative operators. Moreover, even if there were a zero operator, it would not be interpretable for PF to have overt material in a [+rel] position without an overt element representing [+rel].[3] Note that this does not exclude the possibility of having null operators in [Spec,CP] on their own if they are available, such as the zero relative operator in English, because in that case there would be no visible lexical material to cause uninterpretability either.

It seems justifiable that the Overtness Requirement holds in a similar way in [Spec,CP] positions as in [Spec,FP] positions at left edges of nominal expressions.[4] Considering this, the following generalisation arises: certain phrase-sized constituents moving leftwards to an operator position must have an overt marker

---

[3]It has to be mentioned that some strings that look like the ones in (43) may in fact be grammatical. Consider the examples in (i):

   (i)   a. Mari Judith Hermann könyvét   olvasta,   **a könyvet** egyébként még
          Mary Judith Hermann book.POSS.ACC read.PST.3SG the book.ACC incidentally still
          én küldtem neki   Berlinből.
          I   sent.1SG she.DAT Berlin.ELA

          'Mary was reading Judith Hermann's book; actually, I had sent it to her from Berlin.'

      b. Leégett   a   gyár,   **ez az esemény** megmozgatta a   várost.
         down.burned.3SG the factory this the event   PRT.moved.3SG the city.ACC
         'The factory burned down; this event moved the city.'

    However, these are instances of coordination, and therefore the DPs *a könyvet* and *ez az esemény*, respectively, are not in a [Spec,CP] position.

[4]The scope of the present investigation does not enable a broader investigation of the issue in the sense that there might be other overtness issues related to left-peripheral positions. For instance, topicalised subordinate clauses in English seem to constitute such a case:

   (i) I know [CP **(that)** he arrived late].

  (ii) [CP ***(That)** he arrived late] is surprising.

    As indicated, the complementiser *that* can be omitted in (i), where it appears at the right edge, but not when it does so at the left edge, that is, when it is topicalised, as in (ii). The phenomenon is not restricted to English; for instance, Poletto (1995) observes a similar issue in Italian. The investigation of this problem would go far beyond the scope of the present book, and I will therefore leave this question open here.

on their left edge so that the configuration converges. The overt marker may be the head but may also be a specifier element. In either case, the topmost projection of the given phrase is equipped with certain features either because the head itself inherently has that feature or because it acquires that feature via specifier–head agreement. These features are interpretable at LF but the same is not necessarily true for PF: a feature that is interpretable at LF is not necessarily so at PF, and vice versa (cf. Tsimpli & Dimitrakopoulou 2007: 223).

In the case of Comparative Deletion and the obligatory overtness of relative operators, there is a zero element bearing the [+rel] feature followed by overt material. Consider the grammatical,[5] non-deleting examples in (46) from Dutch:

(46)   a. Maria is groter dan **hoe groot** Jan is.
          Mary is taller than how tall   John is

          'Mary is taller than John is.'

       b. De tafel is langer dan **hoe breed** het   kantoor is.
          the table is longer than how wide the.N office   is

          'The table is longer than the office is wide.'

The PF string for *hoe groot* 'how tall' is as follows:

(47)   hoe$_{[+rel]}$ groot

The [+rel] feature on *hoe* instructs PF to align the left edge of the phrase with the left edge of a phonological unit. However, in cases where the operator is phonologically zero, the PF string is the following:

(48) $_{[+rel]}$ tall

This causes a problem for PF because the [+rel] feature on its own, that is, without any visible element carrying it, is not alignable.

The problem is fundamentally similar in the case of Attributive Comparative Deletion and the movement of quantified expressions to the left edge of a functional FP. In a string such as *how big a cat*, PF sees the following string:

(49)   how$_{[+wh]}$ big

By contrast, the zero comparative operator in English attributive comparative structures produces a string similar to the one in (48):

---

[5] As pointed out in Chapter 3, there is variation in the acceptability of *hoe* 'how' in these cases; the present discussion applies to dialects where *hoe* is available as a comparative operator.

(50) [+rel] big

The [+rel] feature is not interpretable for PF without a visible element: the string should be aligned to the left edge of the extended nominal expression (FP).

Given the similarity between (47) and (49) on the one hand and between (48) and (50) on the other hand, it seems reasonable to assume the existence of some generalised pattern. Instead of the separate operator features [+wh] and [+rel], there is a general operator feature: an operator feature is essentially responsible for elements moving to the left edge (cf. Müller 2003) and thus the generalised feature may be called simply [EDGE]. This predicts that a zero *wh*-element or a relative pronoun is not ungrammatical in itself but they become PF-uninterpretable if they move to the edge, that is, if they are equipped with an [EDGE] feature.

The generalised PF-interpretable configuration of strings containing [EDGE] features is given in (51):

(51) $X_{[EDGE]}$ Y

The syntactic status of X and Y, as well as their exact structural relation, is not of importance in terms of PF-interpretability: X itself is naturally a head, such that it may be a head taking Y as its complement, or it may be the head of a phrase that is located in the specifier of the phrase headed by Y. In either case, the [EDGE] feature itself is located on a phonologically visible head and the structure converges.

By contrast, the PF-uninterpretable configuration should be assigned the representation in (52):

(52) [EDGE] Y

The syntactic status of Y is not important here as PF-uninterpretability arises because the [EDGE] feature is not attached to any phonologically visible material.

4.6 More on attributive modification

Since the reason behind Attributive Comparative Deletion in English is that an inverted AP is not allowed in an edge position without an overt operator element there, it is worth examining how languages and structures differ in this respect. The expectation is that if the QP does not invert, then PF-uninterpretability does not arise since the QP is not in an edge position.

It has been seen that in English certain QPs require movement to the [Spec,FP] whereas others do not. Based on the analysis given by Kennedy & Merchant (2000), the examples in (53) all involve this kind of movement:

(53)   a. [How big a cat] did Ralph see?

     b. Ralph bought [too big a cat].

     c. Ralph bought a bigger house than Michael did [a flat].

Underlyingly, in accordance with what has been claimed in the previous sections, the structures of the bracketed constituents are shown in (54), respectively:

(54)   a. [$_{FP}$ [$_{QP}$ how big]$_i$ [$_{DP}$ a [$_{NP}$ t_i cat]]]

     b. [$_{FP}$ [$_{QP}$ too big]$_i$ [$_{DP}$ a [$_{NP}$ t_i cat]]]

     c. [$_{FP}$ [$_{QP}$ x-big]$_i$ [$_{DP}$ a [$_{NP}$ i flat]]]

Inversion is dependent on two factors: whether the nominal expression enables the projection of an FP, and whether the QP can undergo such movement. Regarding latter condition, it has already been shown that not all QPs require this kind of inversion: still, it is expected that the properties of the QP can be projected to the entire nominal expression via feature percolation. Consider the following examples involving the optional movement of the QP *more intelligent*:

(55)   a.   I have never seen [a more intelligent dog].

     b. ? I have never seen [more intelligent a dog].

In line with Kennedy & Merchant (2000: 130) and Bresnan (1973: 287–288), the structure involving inversion, as shown in (55b), is slightly less acceptable than the non-inverted one in (55a). The possibility of (55b) shows that *more*, composed of the Deg head *-er* and the Q head *much*, can move to [Spec,FP] if that position is generated, but it is also grammatical in its base position. By contrast, the Q heads in (54) require movement obligatorily. Since the structures in (55) are otherwise equivalent, it is reasonable to claim that feature percolation is possible without movement and movement is triggered rather by the properties of the individual quantifiers. As the QP appears in a [Spec,NP] position it can enter into an agreement relationship with the N head, which in turn can project its features upwards in the structure. Thus, inversion does not stem from the inability of a nominal expression to be marked for quantification otherwise; rather, an [EDGE] feature of a quantifier needs to be satisfied by movement to an edge position.

On the other hand, the availability of a [Spec,FP] position seems to be dependent on the internal structure of the nominal expression as well. Consider:

(56)   a.   [How big a dog] did Peter see?

     b. * [How big dogs] did Peter see?

As has been established, structures like (56a) involve the obligatory movement of the QP to the [Spec,FP] position, which suggests that *how* requires inversion. It follows that in (56b) inversion should happen in order to derive a grammatical configuration; however, (56b) is not grammatical. The difference between (56a) and (56b) is that the latter involves a plural, while the former involved the indefinite article *a*. If one were to claim that in both cases there is a single DP above the NP (disregarding now the FP), then the difference between (56a) and (56b) would be unaccounted for.

Instead, I propose that the reason why (56a) allows inversion is that the DP layer is not present in the structure, and hence extraction is possible; furthermore, the indefinite article is the head of a NumP. As Zamparelli (2008: 11) describes, the NumP must always be present in English, partly because it is responsible for agreement as well, contrary to Romance languages that have a separate AgrP for this. The NumP may be headed by numerals (e.g. *one*, *two*) or by indefinite articles. The DP layer appears above the NumP, which is also shown by the fact that Num heads may co-occur with the definite article:

(57) a. [**The two** dogs] are sleeping.

  b. [**Two** dogs] are sleeping.

In (57a), the nominal expression is definite as it contains the D head *the*; by contrast, the nominal expression in (57b) is indefinite. As should be obvious, *two* in itself does not determine [±def] as it may occur in both constructions; in this way, the [−def] nature of the nominal expression does not come from the Num head itself but rather from an indefinite zero D head, in the same way as [+def] is marked by *the* in (57). The structure of the DPs in (57) is shown in (58):

(58)

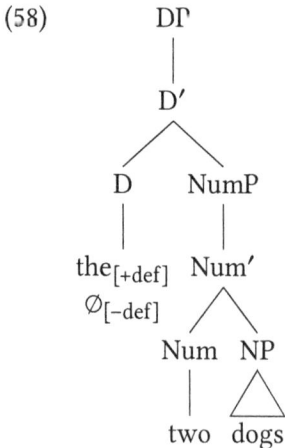

As can be seen, definiteness is encoded in the DP layer and not in the NumP for Num heads like *two*. However, if the Num head is an indefinite article, the situation is quite different because the indefinite article is unambiguously associated with [−def], and thus there is no reason for introducing a DP layer for marking definiteness separately. Hence, a nominal expression such as *a dog* should be assigned the following structure:

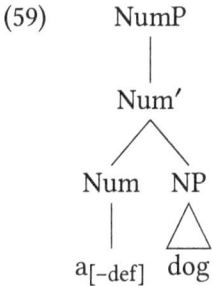

(59)   NumP
            |
        Num′
       ╱‾‾‾╲
    Num NP
     | △
  a$_{[-def]}$ dog

The structural difference between (58) and (59) has a bearing on the availability of inversion, as demonstrated by the contrast in (56). In cases like (56a), that is, with the string *how big a dog*, an FP layer is projected on top of the NumP, as shown in (60):

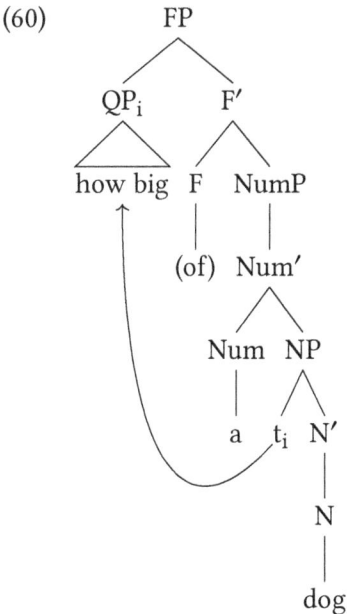

(60)   FP
        ╱‾‾‾‾╲
     QP$_i$ F′
    △   ╱‾╲
  how big F NumP
        | |
      (of) Num′
           ╱‾╲
        Num NP
         | ╱╲
         a t$_i$ N′
               |
               N
               |
            dog

As can be seen, the QP can be extracted from within the NP and move to the [Spec,FP] position. Depending on the dialect, the F head can be filled by *of*, and precisely due to this option, I do not want to claim that the FP is in fact a DP, since *of* is clearly not a D head and, unlike D heads in structures like (58), *of* clearly plays no role in marking definiteness.

By contrast, a structure like (56b) involves the plural, that is, *how big dogs*, and the maximal projection, disregarding the FP, is a DP, not a NumP, as given in (58), since definiteness is not inherently determined by the Num head. Note that by assuming that in structures like (60) there is a NumP layer generated instead of a DP, I propose an analysis that is fundamentally different from the one presented by Kennedy & Merchant (2000), who do not distinguish between these functional layers in the nominal expression and do not discuss the NumP.

It would be highly problematic to claim that DPs project an FP layer just as NumPs do: the DP is a phase boundary in itself, and therefore the left edge of the nominal expression is already created. Thus there is no [Spec,FP] position for the QP to move to. The key difference between the FP and the DP is precisely this: once the FP is projected, it requires material to move to its specifier and, as far as PF is concerned, this material has to be associated with a phonologically visible marker equipped with designated properties. The DP specifier is not an edge position in this sense, since there is no requirement that would rule out [Spec,DP] positions that remain unfilled. Consider the following representation:

(61)

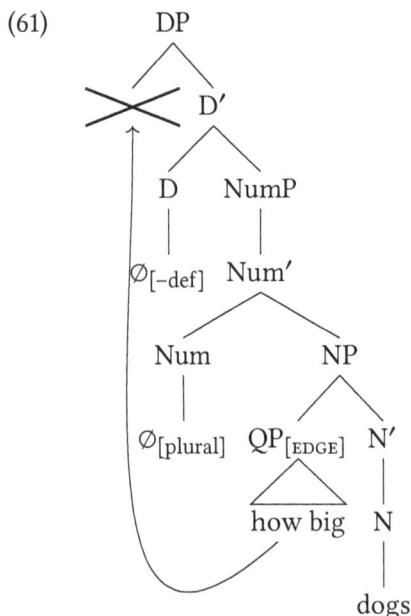

Movement is not available in the way it is in (60). Therefore, the problem with strings like *how big dogs* is that though the [EDGE] feature of the QP should be checked, there is no element that would attract it to a relevant specifier position, and thus the structure is ungrammatical.

This accounts well for differences between (56a) and (56b). There is one more difference to be explained, shown in (62):

(62)   a.   * [How big cats] did Ralph see?
       b.   [How many cats] did Ralph see?

Interestingly, it seems that while a QP like *how big* cannot modify a plural nominal expression, a QP like *how many* can.[6] The same difference holds in comparative subclauses:

(63)   a.   * Ralph bought a bigger house than Michael bought [a flat].
       b.   Ralph bought more houses than Michael bought [flats].

The difference lies in the fact that English requires VP-ellipsis in attributive comparatives like (63a), as shown by Kennedy & Merchant (2000), but does not do so in nominal comparatives like (63b), as also pointed out by Reglero (2006).

Observing the difference between (62a) and (62b), it should be clear that the nominal expressions themselves have the same layers, that is, a DP and a NumP above the NP (the DP being responsible for definiteness and the NumP for marking the plural), and therefore the difference in the acceptability of the two structures stems from differences that hold within the QPs. In other words, QPs such as *how many, more* and *x-many* are different from ones like *how big*, and this difference is encoded in the quantifiers.

Recall from Chapter 2 that the Deg head and the Q head are distinct projections but the upward movement of the Deg head to the Q head may result in composite forms. For instance, the movement of *-er* to *much* results in *more* in strings like *more intelligent*, and the movement of *-er* to *many* results in *more* in strings like *more cats*. Note that while both cases result in the surface form *more*, the Q heads themselves (*much* or *many*) are different.

In (62), the Deg head itself is *how*, and the Q head is a zero in (62a) and *many* in (62b); as was argued for in Chapter 2, the upward movement of the Deg head to the Q head results in a reverse order, that is, the original Deg head is adjoined

---

[6]As will be shown later in connection with German, there are interesting cross-linguistic differences in this respect; at this point, what is important for us is that English does not allow constructions like (63a).

from the right, in line with the Linear Correspondence Axiom (see Kayne 1994) and the Mirror Principle (see Baker 1985; 1988). The zero Q head requires movement to a [Spec,FP] position, as in constructions such as *how big a cat*; however, the DP in (62a) has the structure given in (61), and there is no [Spec,FP] position available; consequently, (62a) is ungrammatical. By contrast, *many* in (62b) does not require movement, and thus the QP may remain in situ, that is, within the NP. It should be obvious that only the Q head can be held responsible for obligatory movement as the Deg head is *how* in both cases.

Turning now to the structures given in (63), it seems plausible that the Q heads (though zero in both cases) differ in a similar way, that is, the one in (63a) requires movement to the [Spec,FP] position, which results in obligatory Attributive Comparative Deletion. This condition of which is not met in (63a), hence its ungrammaticality. By contrast, the Q head in the subclause in (63b) does not require movement to a [Spec,FP] position and as the (phonologically not visible) QP is not inverted, the Overtness Requirement on left-peripheral elements is not violated, since the FP layer is not generated at all.

It is the idiosyncratic property of a given Q head whether it is equipped with the [EDGE] feature triggering movement or not, and it is not directly linked to other features. Therefore, while certain quantifiers in English require inversion, this may not be true for their counterparts in other languages; this was seen in connection with Reglero (2006) in terms of differences between English and Spanish nominal comparatives. As was discussed in §4.3, German does not show Attributive Comparative Deletion because no inversion is required. In (53a) and (53b), it was shown that QPs such as *how big* and *too big* are inverted in English. Consider now the examples in (64) from German:

(64) a. [Eine   wie große   Katze] hat Ralf   gekauft?
          a.ACC.F how big.ACC.F cat   has Ralph bought.PTCP
          'How big a cat did Ralph buy?'

      b. *[Wie große   eine   Katze] hat Ralf   gekauft?
          how big.ACC.F a.ACC.F cat   has Ralph bought.PTCP
          'How big a cat did Ralph buy?'

      c. Ralf hat [eine   zu große   Katze] gekauft.
          Ralph has a.ACC.F too big.ACC.F cat   bought.PTCP
          'Ralph bought too big a cat.'

      d. *Ralf hat [zu große   eine   Katze] gekauft.
          Ralph has too big.ACC.F a.ACC.F cat   bought.PTCP
          'Ralph bought too big a cat.'

As can be seen, German not only allows the non-inverted orders given in (64a) and (64c), but actually requires them: (64b) and (64d) – which are structurally parallel with the English examples in (53a) and (53b) – are ungrammatical. This shows that even in cases involving an indefinite nominal expression, the FP layer is not generated. I do not wish to investigate the internal structure of German nominal expressions here; the point is rather that since German obviously lacks the FP in structures involving overt operators, there is nothing unexpected in the claim that the FP is not generated in comparative subclauses such as the one in (34), repeated here as (65), which is acceptable (depending on the speaker):

(65) Ralf hat eine   größere   Katze als Michael eine   breite
      Ralph has a.ACC.F bigger.ACC.F cat   than Michael a.ACC.F wide.ACC.F
      Katzenklappe hat.
      cat.flap   has.
      'Ralph's cat is bigger than Michael's cat flap is wide.'

Since the QP in the subclause in (65) is obviously within the NP and the result is grammatical, it is expected that the German QP, contrary to the English one, does not have to be deleted.

On the other hand, it is likewise expected that, unlike English in (62a), German allows plurals to appear together with QPs such as *how big*. Consider:

(66) [Wie große   Katzen] hat Ralf   gesehen?
       how big.ACC.PL cats   has Ralph seen
      'How big were the cats that Ralph saw?'

Since there is no requirement on the QP in German to move to [Spec,FP], structures like (66) are grammatical, whereas they are not derivable in English.

All this shows that Attributive Comparative Deletion is not a separate mechanism as such but is the surface result of various other factors that interact with each other, namely: whether there is Comparative Deletion in the [Spec,CP] position (due to the Overtness Requirement), whether the QP has to move to a [Spec,FP] position within the extended nominal projection, and whether the language has VP-ellipsis.

5 Lower copies and movement chains

5.1 Introduction

In Chapter 3, I argued that Comparative Deletion is an epiphenomenon that is primarily related to the Overtness Requirement on left-peripheral elements, which states that overt lexical material is licensed in an operator position only if the operator itself is overt. As was shown, there are four logical possibilities, depending on whether the operator moves on its own, and whether the operator is overt or not. If the operator is able to strand a lexical AP or NP (or there is no lexical XP base-generated together with the operator at all), the lexical XP is spelt out in its base position, and the overtness of the operator is immaterial, as is the information structural status of the lexical XP. If an overt operator takes the lexical XP along to the [Spec,CP] position, the lexical XP is licensed irrespective of its information-structural status. However, if a phonologically zero operator takes the lexical XP to the clausal left periphery, the entire phrase in [Spec,CP] has to be deleted in order to avoid a violation of the Overtness Requirement. In this case, the lower copy of the movement chain (in the base position) is realised overtly if it is contrastive. This leads to an asymmetry between contrastive and non-contrastive XPs: in the case of the latter, the absence of any overt copy results in the surface phenomenon traditionally referred to as Comparative Deletion. The realisation of contrastive XPs, on the other hand, appears to be straightforward. Using data mainly from Slavic, this chapter will demonstrate that the availability of the lower copy for overt realisation is not universal. Further, I will argue that the difference between English and Slavic in this respect lies chiefly in the availability of multiple *wh*-fronting in Slavic. In order to gain a better understanding of multiple operator movement and movement chains, I will start by reviewing the analysis of Bošković (2002).

5.2 Multiple operator movement – Bošković (2002)

When there are multiple *wh*-elements in a single clause, different languages show different behaviour with respect to where the individual *wh*-elements appear. As

Bošković (2002: 352–353) shows, traditionally four types are assumed: languages where only one *wh*-element is fronted, while the others remain in situ (e.g. English); languages where none of the *wh*-elements is fronted, hence *wh*-in-situ languages (e.g. Chinese); languages that show both of these options (e.g. French); and languages where the fronting of multiple (and in fact all) *wh*-elements occurs (e.g. Bulgarian, based on Rudin 1988). The last option is illustrated by example in (1) from Bulgarian (Bošković 2002: 352, ex. 5):

(1) **Na kogo kakvo** dade Ivan?
     to who what gave Ivan
     'What did Ivan give to who?'

As can be seen, both *na kogo* 'to whom' and *kakvo* 'what' are fronted. While the traditional assumption is that multiple fronting languages constitute a separate type, Bošković (2002) claims that multiple *wh*-fronting languages fall into the three other types, and they exhibit a special type of *wh*-in-situ elements.

One key argument comes from superiority effects in multiple *wh*-fronting languages, which show a parallel distribution to *wh*-fronting in non-multiple-*wh*-fronting languages (Bošković 2002: 353–357). That is, there are languages that always exhibit superiority effects (e.g. Bulgarian, hence parallel to English), there are languages that exhibit superiority in contexts where French-type languages require fronting, but not in others (e.g. Serbo-Croatian, hence parallel to French); and there are languages that exhibit no superiority effects at all (e.g. Russian, thus parallel to Chinese); see Bošković (2002: 355). Consider the examples in (2) from Serbo-Croatian (Bošković 2002: 353, exx. 6 and 7):

(2) a. Ko   koga voli?
         who whom loves
         'Who loves whom?'

     b. Koga ko   voli?
         whom who loves
         'Who loves whom?'

     c. [Ko   koga voli], taj   o   njemu i   govori.
         who whom loves that-one about him   even talks
         'Everyone talks about the person they love.'

d. ?* [Koga ko   voli], taj   o   njemu / o   njemu taj
      whom who loves that-one about him   about him   that-one

   i   govori.
   even talks

'Everyone talks about the person they love.'

As can be seen in (2a) and (2b), there is no superiority effect in short-distance matrix questions with a null C: the order of the fronted subject and object is free. By contrast, in the embedded context demonstrated in (2c)–(2d), only the configuration where the subject precedes the object is grammatical, as in (2c): the reverse order, given in (2d), is ungrammatical. The same applies to pattern involving long-distance movement or an overt question particle *li* in C (Bošković 2002: 354). Bulgarian shows superiority effects in all of these contexts (Bošković 2002: 354), while Russian demonstrates no superiority effects in any of these contexts (Bošković 2002: 354–355, following Stepanov 1998).

According to Bošković (2002: 355), superiority effects are attested in the languages under scrutiny whenever *wh*-movement is obligatory, that is, whenever there is a strong [+wh] feature on C. Serbo-Croatian is similar to French in that it does not require *wh*-movement in all contexts, and thus superiority effects cannot be observed in short-distance matrix questions with a null C. At the same time, all *wh*-phrases undergo fronting in Serbo-Croatian, as well as in Bulgarian and Russian, hence no *wh*-phrase is licensed in situ: Bošković (2002: 355) argues that this is independent from a [+wh] feature on C, since that can be checked off only once. Obligatory fronting is illustrated in (3) below for Serbo-Croatian:

(3) a. Ko šta   kupuje?
         who what buys

         'Who buys what?'

    b. ?* Ko   kupuje šta?
           who buys   what

          'Who buys what?'

The fronting requirement applies to echo questions as well (Bošković 2012: 356): this applies not only to Serbo-Croatian, Bulgarian and Russian but also to Polish (see Wachowicz 1974) and Hungarian (see É. Kiss 1987). Consider the example in (4) from Serbo-Croatian (Bošković 2012: 356, ex. 16a):

(4) ?* Ivan kupuje šta?
     Ivan buys   what
     'Ivan buys what?

Following Stjepanović (1999) and the original idea of Horvath (1986), Bošković (2012: 356–357) argues that the driving force underlying this kind of fronting is focus, which can be observed in the case of non-*wh* elements as well. This is illustrated by the examples in (5) from Serbo-Croatian (Bošković 2012: 357, ex. 17):

(5) a. JOVANA savjetuje.
        Jovan.ACC advises

        'She/He advises Jovan.'

   b. ?* Savjetuje JOVANA.
        advises   Jovan.ACC

        'She/He advises Jovan.'

Crucially, multiple *wh*-fronting languages demonstrate predictable behaviour with respect to the interpretation of multiple questions (Bošković 2012: 357–359). In languages like English and German, multiple *wh*-questions are compatible with a pair-list answer only (and not with single-pair answers), and the same holds for Bulgarian and Romanian. Serbo-Croatian, Russian and Polish, however, just like French, allow single-pair answers as well.

As noted by Bošković (2012: 359–379), there are certain exceptions to the obligatoriness of fronting all *wh*-phrases in multiple *wh*-fronting languages. There are three types of exceptions: semantic, phonological, and syntactic.

Regarding semantic exceptions, D-linked *wh*-phrases and particular echo *wh*-phrases are allowed to remain in situ (Bošković 2012: 359–364). The exception with a D-linked *wh*-phrase is illustrated in (6) below for Serbo-Croatian (Bošković 2012: 360, ex. 26a):

(6) Ko je kupio koju knjigu?
    who is bought which book
    'Who bought which book?'

As noted by Bošković (2012: 359), the phenomenon has been observed in the literature for various languages, such as by Wachowicz (1974) for Polish, and by Pesetsky (1987; 1989) for Polish, Czech, Russian and Romanian. Bošković (2012: 360) argues that this is so because the "range of reference of D-linked *wh*-phrases is [...] discourse-given", and they are therefore expected not to undergo focus fronting. The same applies to *wh*-phrases in echo questions, especially with a surprise reading (rather than a clarification reading) because the *wh*-phrase in these cases is known to the speaker as well, hence it represents GIVEN information (Bošković 2012: 362–364).

Regarding phonological exceptions, Bošković (2012: 364–376) shows that two homophonous *wh*-phrases are not allowed to be fronted at the same time if they are adjacent to each other. Consider the example in (7) from Serbo-Croatian (Bošković 2012: 364, ex. 37):

(7) Šta   uslovljava šta?
    what conditions what
    'What conditions what?'

As can be seen, in this case the second *wh*-element is licensed to appear in situ. The configuration involving adjacent, phonologically identical *wh*-phrases is ruled out only if the two *wh*-words are adjacent: if an adverb appears between the two, the structure is licensed (Bošković 2012: 364), which indicates that the rule applies at PF rather than in syntax. In addition, it cannot be a result of violating a superiority constraint, since the rule applies to any two *wh*-elements, not just the highest one and the one immediately below it, while superiority effects are relevant only for the highest *wh*-element (Bošković 2012: 365–367). The ban on identical *wh*-phrases is strictly phonological in nature: for instance, the sequence *kogo na kogo* 'whom to whom' is licensed in Bulgarian, while **na kogo kogo* 'to whom whom' is not (Bošković 2002: 365–367, following Billings & Rudin 1996). At the same time, a *wh*-phrase is licensed in situ only in the second case, indicating that the in-situ option is only a last resort (Bošković 2002: 367).

To account for the phenomenon, Bošković (2002: 367–376) argues that while PF normally spells out the highest copy of a movement chain, in these cases a lower copy is spelt out. As pointed out by Bošković (2002: 367–368), the availability of spelling out lower copies at PF has been proposed by a number of authors in the literature (for instance by Bobaljik 1995, Runner 1998, Pesetsky 1997; 1998, Richards 1997, Roberts 1997, and Nunes 1999), and the idea is essentially similar to spelling out non-trivial copies at LF, as argued by Chomsky (1995). In this sense, spelling out the lower copy of a *wh*-element in Slavic is a last resort option to avoid PF-violation, which would result from the spelling out of two consecutive, phonologically identical *wh*-elements.

Regarding syntactic exceptions, Bošković (2002: 376–379) shows that it is possible for *wh*-phrases to stay in situ when they are extracted out of non-*wh*-islands, as noted by Comorovski (1996) for Romanian. Consider the examples in (8) from Romanian (Bošković 2002: 377, ex. 65):

(8) a. Ion a   auzit zvonul   că Petru a cumpărat CE?
           Ion has heard the.rumour that Petru has bought   what

           'Ion heard the rumour that Petru has bought what?'

    b. *Ce   a   auzit Ion zvonul   că Petru a   cumpărat?
           what has heard Ion the.rumour that Petru has bought

           'Ion heard the rumour that Petru has bought what?'

As can be seen, in this case the *wh*-element *ce* 'what' has to remain in situ. While islands are generally assumed to be syntactic in nature, Bošković (2002: 377–379) argues that islandhood is a PF property to some extent, and that realising a copy within the island may save the construction from island violation which would arise when spelling out the higher copy of the same movement chain.

Bošković (2002) argues convincingly that multiple *wh*-fronting languages do not behave in a uniform fashion, but he also shows that exceptions to the movement of *wh*-phrases are restricted and can either be explained by the focussed nature of fronted *wh*-elements or by the copy theory of movement. These exceptions are therefore essentially predictable.

5.3 Predicative comparatives in Czech and Polish

As was discussed in Chapter 3 in detail, English allows the realisation of contrastive lower copies in subcomparative structures, while non-contrastive lower copies must be eliminated. This is demonstrated in (9):

(9)   a. *Ralph is taller than Peter is **tall**.
     b. The table is longer than the office is **wide**.

I argued that the higher copy of the quantified expression, landing in the lower [Spec,CP] via operator movement, is deleted in Standard English due to the Overtness Requirement, while the lower copy is regularly eliminated, unless it is contrastive. Consider the examples in (10):

(10)   a. Ralph is taller than ~~x-tall~~ Peter is ~~x-tall~~.
      b. The table is longer than ~~x-wide~~ the office is **wide**.

As should be obvious, the contrast between (9a) and (9b) is dependent on certain factors. First, the operator has to be covert: the higher copy would be fully realised with an overt operator (since it would obey the Overtness Requirement), irrespectively of whether the AP is contrastive or not (as is the case for non-standard English *how*). Second, the operator has to be a Deg head and thus not extractable from the QP: non-contrastive lower copies are not ruled out in languages where the zero operator can be extracted (as was shown for German). Third, the realisation of the contrastive lower copy must be allowed.

When considering cross-linguistic data, it is obvious that the English pattern cannot be universal and that even the third condition is not always met. The following examples show that the lower copy cannot be realised in Czech (cf. Bacskai-Atkari 2015):

(11)   a.   * Marie je vyšší, než je **vysoký** Karel.
            Mary is taller than is tall   Charles
            'Mary is taller than Charles.'

      b.   * Ten stůl je delší, než je ta   kancelář **široká**.
            that desk is longer than is that office   wide
            'The desk is longer than the office is wide.'

The question arises why Czech does not allow the realisation of the contrastive lower copy in (11b). In principle, one may think this is because Czech has no zero operator at all, and indeed, we saw in Chapter 3 that Czech does in fact have an overt operator, *jak* 'how'. If this is indeed the reason, then Czech is essentially similar to Hungarian (see Chapter 3). The relevant examples are repeated in (12):

(12)   a.   ?? Marie je vyšší, než **jak vysoký** je Karel.
            Mary is taller than how tall   is Charles
            'Marie is taller than Charles.'

      b.   ? Marie je vyšší, než **jak** je **vysoký** Karel.
            Mary is taller than how is tall   Charles
            'Marie is taller than Charles.'

      c.   ?? Ten stůl je delší, než **jak široká** je ta   kancelář.
            that desk is longer than how wide   is that office
            'The desk is longer than the office is wide.'

      d.   Ten stůl je delší, než **jak** je ta   kancelář **široká**.
            that desk is longer than how is that office   wide
            'The desk is longer than the office is wide.'

As can be seen, the operator *jak* may either appear together with the AP in [Spec,CP] or the AP may be stranded; in either case, it does not make any significant difference whether the AP is contrastive or not. This behaviour is expected on the basis of cross-linguistic data for comparatives with overt operators.

However, the fact that Czech has an overt comparative operator does not actually explain the ungrammaticality of (11). Namely, the same ungrammaticality can be observed in Polish:

(13) a. * Maria jest wyższa niż Karol   jest **wysoki**.
          Mary is   taller   than Charles is   tall

          'Mary is taller than Charles.'

    b. */?? Stół jest dłuższy niż   biuro jest **szerokie**.
          desk is   longer   than office is   wide

          'The desk is longer than the office is wide.'

In contrast to Czech, Polish has no overt comparative operators either. A possible candidate would be the degree operator *jak* 'how', which is available in interrogatives (cf. the data of Borsley & Jaworska 1981: 81), as demonstrated in (14):

(14) a. **Jak wysoki** jest Karol?
          how tall   is   Charles

          'How tall is Charles?'

    b. */?? **Jak** jest Karol   **wysoki**?
          how is   Charles tall

          'How tall is Charles?'

However, *jak* is not available in comparative subclauses (cf. Bacskai-Atkari 2015):

(15) a. * Maria jest wyższa niż **jak wysoki** jest Karol.
          Mary is   taller   than how tall   is   Charles

          'Mary is taller than Charles.'

    b. */?? Stół jest dłuższy niż **jak szerokie** jest biuro .
          desk is   longer   than how wide   is   office

          'The desk is longer than the office is wide.'

The data in (15) clearly show that the reason why both sentences in (13) are ungrammatical cannot be the availability of an overt operator because Polish does not allow the operator to be overt at all. This also implies that the operator (required by degree semantics) has to be zero.

In other words, the problem with Polish is essentially the following. First, the ungrammaticality of (13) cannot be attributed to the availability of an overt operator, hence Polish is different from languages like Hungarian in this respect. Second, while Polish has a zero operator, it cannot be extracted on its own and moved to the [Spec,CP], as was shown to be the case in German and Dutch in Chapter 3, since in that case both sentences in (13) should be grammatical. Third, the zero operator in Polish should then be similar to the English one, which is a non-extractable Deg head (see Chapter 3); however, in that case one would expect the realisation of a contrastive lower copy to be possible, which is again not met, since (13b) is ungrammatical. It seems, then, that the sentences in (13) are ungrammatical because even contrastive lower copies of a movement chain are not licensed to be realised in comparatives in Polish.

Before turning to the issue of why this should be so, let me first review some properties of attributive comparatives in Czech and Polish. In particular, I will argue that there is a zero operator in Czech as well, and that the ungrammaticality of (11) goes back to the same reasons as that of its Polish counterpart, and can be explained in a principled way. In this way, Czech will be shown to be similar to Polish rather than to Hungarian.

5.4 Attributive comparatives in Czech and Polish

As was shown in Chapter 4, based on the analysis given by Kennedy & Merchant (2000), the QP is extractable from the nominal expression in Czech and Polish, and this property is not restricted to the comparative subclause but it can be observed in interrogatives as well, where the QP is visible. Observe the examples in (16) from Czech (Kennedy & Merchant 2000: 104, ex. 30):

(16) a. **Jak velké auto** Václav koupil?
          how big   car   Václav bought
          'How big a car did Václav buy?'

      b. **Jak velké** Václav koupil **auto**?
          how big   Václav bought car
          'How big a car did Václav buy?'

As can be seen, it is possible to move the entire nominal expression containing the QP, as in (16a), but it is also possible that the QP *jak velké* 'how big' moves out on its own, and the noun is stranded. The same can be observed in Polish, as shown by the example in (17), taken from Kennedy & Merchant (2000: 104, ex. 29):

(17)   a. **Jak długą sztukę** napisał Paweł?
            how long play   wrote Pawel
            'How long a play did Pawel write?'

       b. **Jak długą** napisał Paweł **sztukę**?
            how long   wrote   Pawel play
            'How long a play did Pawel write?'

In comparative subclauses, it is possible to have an overt lexical verb and a remnant NP, showing that the QP has moved out on its own. This is illustrated in (18) for Czech (Kennedy & Merchant 2000: 105, ex. 32b):

(18)   Václav koupil větší   auto než Tomáš ztratil loď.
        Václav bought bigger car   than Tomáš lost   boat
        'Václav bought a bigger car than the boat that Tomáš lost.'

The same is true for Polish, as shown by (19) below (Kennedy & Merchant 2000: 104, ex. 31a):

(19)   Jan napisał dłuższy list,   niż   Paweł napisał sztukę.
        Jan wrote   longer letter than Pawel wrote   play
        'Jan wrote a longer letter than Pawel wrote a play.'

In these cases, the higher copy of the QP is deleted in a [Spec,CP] position due to the Overtness Requirement. The remnant NP is not affected because it is not a lower copy itself, and hence its overt realisation does not require enforcing the pronunciation of a lower copy. The point is that there is a zero operator in Czech and Polish that can combine with lexical APs. If so, it is expected that the same zero operator can combine with APs if the AP is in a predicative position, too.

5.5 Movement chains

Based on what was said above, it seems that in Czech and Polish, the zero operator taking lexical APs is non-extractable, just as in English. This predicts that lower copies of non-contrastive APs are unacceptable just as they are in English; the relevant examples are repeated in (20), where (20a) is from Czech and (20b) is from Polish:

(20) a. * Marie je vyšší, než   je **vysoký** Karel.
          Mary is taller than is tall   Charles

      'Mary is taller than Charles.'

   b. * Maria jest wyższa niż   Karol   jest **wysoki**.
          Mary is   taller than Charles is   tall

      'Mary is taller than Charles.'

The higher copy of the QP is deleted in [Spec,CP] due to the Overtness Requirement, and the lower copy should be eliminated regularly as a lower copy; in (20), the lower copy is not F-marked either and there is thus no reason for it to stay overt, just like in the English counterpart of the sentences.

However, as was seen earlier, the lower copy is not licensed with F-marked APs either in Czech and Polish, as shown by (21a) for Czech and by (21b) for Polish:

(21) a. * Ten stůl je delší, než   je ta   kancelář **široká**.
          that desk is longer than is that office   wide

      'The desk is longer than the office is wide.'

   b. */?? Stół jest dłuższy niż   biuro jest **szerokie**.
            desk is   longer than office is   wide

      'The desk is longer than the office is wide.'

I assume that this is because Czech and Polish generally do not license the realisation of lower copies of a movement chain, in line with the analysis given by Bošković (2002). In order to capture the cross-linguistic differences, consider the abstract representations in (22), using *tall* as the adjective, THAN for the comparative complementiser and HOW for an overt comparative operator (not to be taken as the English operator), as well as $\emptyset$ for a zero operator:

(22) a. THAN HOW tall ... ~~HOW tall~~

   b. THAN HOW ... ~~HOW~~ tall

   c. * THAN $\emptyset$ tall ... ~~$\emptyset$ tall~~

   d. THAN ~~$\emptyset$ tall~~ ... ~~$\emptyset$ tall~~

   e. * THAN ~~$\emptyset$ tall~~ ... $\emptyset$ tall

   f. THAN $\emptyset$ ... ~~$\emptyset$~~ tall

   g. THAN HOW $tall_F$ ... ~~HOW tall_F~~

   h. THAN HOW ... ~~HOW~~ $tall_F$

    i.   * THAN ∅ tall$_F$ ... ~~⊘ tall$_F$~~

    j.   THAN ~~⊘ tall$_F$~~ ... ∅ tall$_F$

    k.   * THAN ~~⊘ tall$_F$~~ ... ~~⊘ tall$_F$~~

    l.   THAN ∅ ... ~~⊘~~ tall$_F$

In examples (22a)–(22f), the adjective is not contrastive, while in examples (22g)–(22l) it is. In (22a) and (22g), the operator is overt and it takes the adjective to the [Spec,CP] position, and both elements remain overt: it does not matter whether the adjective is contrastive or not, since the higher copy can be regularly spelt out. This can be observed in the case of English (substandard) *how* and Czech *jak* 'how'; note that this option is available for all overt comparative operators taking an AP. In (22b) and (22h), the operator is overt and it does not take the adjective to the [Spec,CP]; this option (stranding) is not available for all overt operators, but this can be observed in the case of Czech *jak*. Again, it does not matter whether the AP is contrastive or not, since it does not take part in movement at all.

In (22c) and (22i), the operator is zero and it takes the lexical AP to [Spec,CP]: the configuration is illicit because the higher copy is not eliminated, even though it violates the Overtness Requirement, according to which overt lexical material is licensed in an operator position only if the operator itself is overt. The information structural status of the AP is irrelevant in this respect. If the operator can be extracted on its own, as in (22f) and (22l), the Overtness Requirement is satisfied since no AP moves to the [Spec,CP] at all, and the AP can be realised in its base position, irrespective of whether it is contrastive or not: this can be observed in German and Dutch with the zero comparative operators.

Nevertheless, an AP moving to [Spec,CP] with a zero operator does not mean that the structure is ruled out: the grammatical possibilities are dependent on certain properties of movement chains. In (22d), the lower copy of the AP is realised: the configuration is ruled out because a lower copy of a movement chain is licensed only under special circumstances, and since the AP is not contrastive, there is no reason to enforce the realisation of its lower copy. Hence, regular deletion should take place, as in (22e), which is a grammatical configuration, as is known from Standard English. The ungrammaticality of (22d) and the grammaticality of (22e) are not language-specific, though: they follow from universal principles of grammar. Similarly, the configuration in (22k) is ruled out universally as in this case both copies of a contrastive element are deleted, and the AP is not recoverable. However, the configuration in (22j) is subject to cross-linguistic variation: in this case, the higher copy is regularly eliminated by the Overtness

Requirement, and the lower copy is realised because the AP is F-marked. For this, it is necessary for the language to allow the realisation of lower copies of a movement chain, in case the pronunciation of the higher copy would cause a violation at PF. This is possible in English, but not in Czech and Polish.

Recall from §5.2 that the realisation of lower copies is very restricted in Slavic, as shown by Bošković (2002). There are three major kinds of exceptions. First, D-linked *wh*-phrases may be realised in situ because the range of reference is actually discourse-given, and the phrase is not expected to undergo focus fronting. This obviously does not apply to (21), where the APs are not discourse-given, as opposed to D-linked nominal expressions (such as *which book*), where the NP is taken to be discourse-given. Moreover, as far as D-linked *wh*-phrases are concerned, Bošković (2002) argues that they do not undergo movement: this is possible because the [wh] feature on C has already been checked by the first *wh*-constituent moving there, and all other *wh*-phrases are subject to some kind of focus fronting. In the comparative subclause, however, the [rel] feature on the C head can be checked off only if the only relative operator of the clause moves there, which is the comparative operator itself, and as this cannot be separated from the AP, the AP takes part in movement as well. Apart from D-linked *wh*-phrases, certain echo *wh*-elements may also remain in situ: again, this is not applicable to the case of comparatives, and comparative operator movement is not compatible with the assumption of the operator element remaining in situ.

Second, the lower copy of certain *wh*-phrases may be realised if the *wh*-element is phonologically adjacent to another fronted *wh*-element that is immediately adjacent to it. This clearly cannot be the reason for the ungrammaticality of (21), as there is no second operator element in the clause and the operator is not even overt in the first place.

Third, the realisation of the lower copy is possible if the pronunciation of the higher copy would be an instance of island violation (non-*wh*-islands). This is again not the case in (21), where the operator + AP combination moves regularly to [Spec,CP] from a predicative position, and there is no island at all, hence no island violation can occur either.

In sum, the ungrammaticality of (21) lies in the unavailability of the lower copy of the QP in Czech and Polish, as the conditions under which lower copies can be realised are not satisfied here. Note also that the contrastive AP in (21) in its base position is ungrammatical as a lower copy but there is nothing ruling out the realisation of contrastive phrases here: on the contrary, as was shown in Chapter 3 in connection with Czech, this is precisely the position where contrastive elements are preferably located in the clause in these languages (see also Šimík & Wierzba 2012).

5.6 More on cross-linguistic differences

So far, we have seen that there is evidently an important connection between multiple *wh*-fronting languages and the availability of predicative subcomparatives. Namely, if a multiple *wh*-fronting language has a zero Deg operator, then the lower copy of the entire degree expression cannot be realised even if the AP is contrastive, and predicative subcomparatives are thus not derivable with the operators in question. However, this does not imply that all multiple *wh*-fronting languages lack predicative subcomparatives: it is predicted that these structures will be absent if the operator is a Deg head and it is zero, but in all other cases the AP either appears in [Spec,CP] or does not move at all, and thus the question of realising a lower copy does not arise in the first place.

We have already seen that Czech allows the overt operator *jak* 'how', which is extractable. But even Slavic languages may allow an extractable operator (as in German and Dutch); consider the examples in (23) from Serbo-Croatian:[1]

(23) a. Pavao je viši nego (što) je **visok** Petar.
          Paul is taller than what is tall   Peter

      'Paul is taller than Peter.'

      b. Pavao je viši nego (što) je Petar **visok**.
          Paul is taller than what is Peter tall

      'Paul is taller than Peter.'

      c. Sto je duži   nego (što) je **visok** ured.
          table is longer than what is wide office

      'The table is longer than the office is wide.'

      d. Sto je duži   nego (što) je ured **visok**.
          table is longer than what is office wide

      'The table is longer than the office is wide.'

Note that individual speakers may differ regarding their judgements and preferences concerning the presence/absence of *što* 'what'; since this kind of variation is not immediately relevant to our present discussion, I will not investigate the issue here. Suffice it to say that *što* is a lower C head, similarly to English *what*, as discussed in Chapter 3 (see Bacskai-Atkari 2016 on the role of lower complementisers and the status of *što*).

The point is that Serbo-Croatian allows the realisation of the AP in the subclause, not only when it is contrastive, as in (23c) and (23d), but also when it is not,

---

[1]I owe many thanks to Boban Arsenijević for his help with the Serbo-Croatian data.

as in (23a) and (23b). The AP can appear either clause-finally or clause-internally in both constellations, there being no information-structural constraints on its preferred position. The possibility of (23c) and (23d) contrasts with the data from Czech and Polish, while all the three languages are multiple *wh*-fronting languages. However, the grammaticality of (23a) and (23b) indicates that the Serbo-Croatian zero comparative operator differs from the ones in Czech and Polish: it is a QP modifier, which can be extracted on its own, just like in German and Dutch, whereas the zero operator in Czech and Polish is a Deg head, just like in English. Hence, the AP in (23c) and (23d) is not the realisation of a contrastive lower copy but a stranded AP, just like (23a) and (23b) contain a stranded AP, too. It can thus be concluded that the ban on realising lower copies of a movement chain is relevant in the derivation of comparatives only if the operator is a zero Deg head but not otherwise.

It seems that the Standard English pattern is highly unusual: while Czech and Polish also have a zero, non-extractable comparative operator, they do not allow the realisation of contrastive lower copies either, and thus they do not show the asymmetric pattern attested in English. However, English is not completely unique: Norwegian shows the same asymmetry. Consider the examples in (24):[2]

(24) a. * Mary er eldre enn Peter er **gamal**.
          Mary is older than Peter is old

          'Mary is older than Peter.'

    b. ? Katten er feitere enn kattedøra er **vid**.
          the.cat is fatter than the.cat.flap is wide

          'The cat is fatter than the cat flap is wide.'

The same applies to Icelandic, as shown by (25):[3]

(25) a. * María er eldri en það sem Pétur er **gamall**.
          Mary is older than what that Peter is old

          'Mary is older than Peter.'

---

[2]The Norwegian data stem from the cross-Germanic survey I conducted as part of my project "The syntax of functional left peripheries and its relation to information structure" in 2016/2017. Both informants marked (24a) as ungrammatical; (24b) was marked with two question marks by my informant from Rogaland county, while my informant from Vest-Agder county marked it as perfectly grammatical. The markedness of (24b) can be attributed to the fact that subcomparatives are generally far more difficult to parse than ordinary comparatives, since they involve more than a single dimension of comparison, rather than to true dialectal differences.

[3]The Icelandic data stem from the cross-Germanic survey mentioned above. My two informants, one from Reykjavík and the other from Austurland (Eastern Region), had the same judgements.

b. Kötturinn er feita en kattahurðin er **breið**.
the.cat is fatter than cat.flap is wide

'The cat is fatter than the cat flap is wide.'

Let me sum up the cross-linguistic differences in predicative comparatives, based on the findings presented in Chapter 3 and Chapter 5. There are three major factors determining the overt realisation of the quantified expression: whether the operator is overt, whether it is extractable, and whether lower copies of a movement chain can be realised if the pronunciation of the higher copy would cause the derivation to crash at PF. The possibilities are summarised in (26):

(26)

operator overt?
- YES
  - operator extractable?
    - YES
      - Czech (*jak*) Hungarian (*amennyire*)
    - NO
      - English (*how*) Dutch (*hoe*) Hungarian (*amilyen*)
- NO
  - operator extractable?
    - YES
      - German (Ø) Dutch (Ø) Estonian (Ø) Serbo-Croatian (Ø)
    - NO
      - lower copies available?
        - YES
          - English (Ø) Norwegian (Ø) Icelandic (Ø)
        - NO
          - Czech (Ø) Polish (Ø)

As can be seen, the first question is whether the operator is overt or not. This determines whether the information-structural properties of the AP taken by the operator matter inasmuch as, with overt operators, the pattern is essentially symmetric and both types of APs are available, while there is variation if the operator is covert. With overt operators, the AP can (and sometimes must) be realised in [Spec,CP] together with the operator, while this option is excluded with covert operators, which may only allow the realisation of the AP in its base position.

If the operator is overt, the next question is whether it is extractable. This decides on the possible positions of the AP in the subclause, that is, whether it is restricted to appear in the [Spec,CP] with the given operator or whether it may be stranded in a lower position, while the operator still has to move to [Spec,CP]. If the operator is extractable, the AP can move up together with the operator or it may be stranded. If it moves up to [Spec,CP], its information-structural properties are not relevant, and both contrastive and non-contrastive APs are licensed here equally. If the AP is stranded, its preferred position in the clause largely depends on the information-structural requirements of the given language, and contrastive and non-contrastive APs may differ in terms of their preferred positions. This can be observed in Czech and Hungarian (see Chapter 3).

If the operator is overt and not extractable, the AP always moves up with the operator to [Spec,CP], and the information structural status of the AP is not relevant. This was observed in English, Dutch and Hungarian (see Chapter 3).

If the operator is not overt, then the next question is again whether it is extractable or not. Contrary to what we saw in the case of overt operators, this question here not only decides on the possible positions of the AP in the subclause but it crucially decides whether non-contrastive APs can be realised or not: namely, if the AP moves up to [Spec,CP] together with the covert operator, it must be eliminated because it violates the Overtness Requirement. If the covert operator is extractable, the AP may be stranded, irrespective of its information-structural status, and so even non-contrastive APs can be realised overtly. This can be observed in German, Dutch and Estonian (see Chapter 3).

If the operator is not overt and is not extractable either, then the next question is whether the language allows the realisation of lower copies of a movement chain in cases where the pronunciation of the higher copy would cause the derivation to crash at PF. This decides whether contrastive APs can be realised (and hence whether subcomparatives are possible): the higher copy is deleted in any case due to the Overtness Requirement and non-contrastive lower copies are regularly eliminated as lower copies of a movement chain, thus the only question is whether contrastive lower copies can overwrite the general rule of deleting lower copies. This is possible in English, resulting in the classical "Comparative Deletion" pattern with non-contrastive APs, as opposed to subcomparatives with contrastive APs. However, the realisation of lower copies is not possible in languages like Czech and Polish, and subcomparatives are thus not derivable: a contrastive lower copy cannot be realised, yet the complete elimination of non-given elements is universally prohibited.

The importance of this is that the English pattern, where Comparative Deletion refers to the obligatory elimination of a non-contrastive AP from the comparative subclause, is not universal: in fact, it is highly language-specific, and it can only be regarded as a result of several factors. Thus, Comparative Deletion cannot be regarded as a universal phenomenon or a parameter either, and the analysis of the particular English pattern cannot be solely based on Standard English data but must take other languages and non-standard varieties into consideration.

6 Ellipsis without Comparative Deletion

6.1 Introduction

The last chapter of this book is devoted to the examination of ellipsis phenomena which, alongside the phenomenon of Comparative Deletion, are also responsible for the derivation of comparative subclauses. So far, I have been dealing with the elimination of the degree expression itself, that is, a QP or a DP containing a QP in the subclause (though Chapter 4 also examined the case of VP-ellipsis in English to a limited extent). The importance of taking other deletion phenomena into consideration is that comparative subclauses tend to be highly elliptical, resulting in there being only one overt constituent following the complementiser. In languages like English, this means that in addition to Comparative Deletion, ellipsis also takes place. In other languages, such as Hungarian, where Comparative Deletion is not attested since comparative operators are overt, the question arises how the degree expression is covered by ellipsis. As I will show, there is no movement to the lower [Spec,CP] position in such cases, and hence the well-formedness of the construction can be repaired only via ellipsis, which in turn eliminates larger units than the quantified expression itself.

6.2 Ellipsis in English

6.2.1 VP-ellipsis revisited

First of all, let us consider ellipsis phenomena in English comparatives, which operate in addition to the Overtness Requirement, and which are responsible for the formation of typical comparative constructions that tend to overtly involve only contrastive elements in the comparative subclause. Though these processes are typically instances of VP-ellipsis, I will show that the ellipsis domain can also be larger, even though the mechanism of ellipsis is essentially the same. As was already seen in Chapter 4, comparative subclauses may involve VP-ellipsis, which is an optional deletion operation. To gain a fuller picture of its role in the formation of comparatives, let us first have a look at the data from various subtypes of comparatives.

As far as predicative structures are concerned, the following pattern arises:

(1)   a. The table is longer than the office is wide.
      b. Ralph is more enthusiastic than Jason is.
      c. Ralph is more enthusiastic than Jason.

The full string is represented in (1a), where the lower copy of the QP (*wide*) remains overt, since it is contrastive. As there is no contrastive QP in the subclause in (1b), the lower copy is regularly eliminated but there is no VP-ellipsis; finally, in (1c) the verb is eliminated since it is recoverable.

The picture is slightly more complicated in nominal comparatives:

(2)   a. Ralph bought more houses than Michael bought flats.
      b. Ralph bought more houses than Michael did flats.
      c. Ralph bought more houses than Michael did.
      d. Ralph bought more houses than Michael.

As was shown in Chapter 4, nominal comparatives allow a full structure to appear in the subclause, as in (2a); the lexical verb may be eliminated, as in (2b), resulting in a gapping construction. By contrast, in (2c) not only the lexical verb but also the nominal expression is eliminated, under identity with its matrix clausal antecedent; the same is true for (2d), where the auxiliary is also absent and there is only one overt DP (*Michael*).

Finally, attributive comparatives show the following distribution:

(3)   a. Ralph bought a bigger house than Michael did a flat.
      b. Ralph bought a bigger house than Michael did.
      c. Ralph bought a bigger house than Michael.

The structure parallel to the one in (2a) is not allowed, as shown in Chapter 4, and hence the lexical verb must be eliminated, as in (3a). If the NP is GIVEN, as in (3b) and (3c), then it is also deleted: this may result in an overt auxiliary, as in (3b) or just a single overt DP (*Michael*), as in (3c).

Note that I consider all the cases containing a single DP following *than* (see (1c), (2d) and (3c) above) to be instances of reduced clausal comparatives and not of phrasal comparatives. The term "phrasal comparative" is often used in the literature on comparatives either to mean reduced clauses or genuine phrases (see Merchant 2009, Bhatt & Takahashi 2011) but to avoid confusion, I will refrain from treating reduced clausal comparatives as phrasal comparatives. Originally,

Hankamer (1973) proposed that there are two distinct *than* elements in English: a complementiser taking clauses and a preposition taking nominal expressions as its complement. There are a number of counterarguments to this (see also the discussion below): for instance, as Bhatt & Takahashi (2011) argue, it is expected that there are semantic differences between clausal arguments and individual (DP-sized) arguments, but this is not attested for English.[1] In particular, the "Reduction Analysis" (see, for instance, Lechner 1999, Lechner 2001, Lechner 2004; Merchant 2009) correctly predicts the behaviour of binding patterns, while the "Direct Analysis" (see, for instance, Heim 1985) does not (Bhatt & Takahashi 2011: 586–590). Of course, this does not mean that there are no languages with true phrasal comparatives: as Bhatt & Takahashi (2011: 590–613) show, Hindi-Urdu and Japanese have cases exactly like that, and therefore the category of the comparative complement and the properties of the degree head are subject to cross-linguistic variation.[2]

I claim that, in all of the elliptical cases in (1)–(3) above, the mechanism responsible for eliding the verb is ordinary ellipsis (either VP-ellipsis or TP-ellipsis). In other words, there is no specific ellipsis mechanism applying in comparative subclauses, that is, there is no need for a separate process such as Comparative Ellipsis (see also the analyses of Kennedy 2002, Lechner 2004, Merchant 2009). Based on Merchant (2001), I assume that ellipsis is carried out via an [E] feature that is present on a functional head, which instructs PF to eliminate its complement, that is, the head itself remains intact. Moreover, based on the discussion given in Chapter 4, I also assume that the presence of an F-marked constituent may stop the linear deletion process; note that this is prosodically licensed if the

---

[1]Neither are differences attested in island sensitivity, see Merchant (2009: 160–161).

[2]It is very likely that cross-linguistic variation is fined-grained and that even comparatives that are invariably phrasal on the surface may have a more complex structure. As shown convincingly by Merchant (2009), one such instance is that of Greek comparatives with the preposition *apo* 'from', which is always followed by an accusative-marked DP. However, these constructions show island sensitivity, which is unexpected if there is no movement in the structure, that is, if one would take a surfacist approach and assume that there is merely a DP complement. Merchant (2009: 151–160) argues that there is either overt or covert movement; if one adopts the analysis that the DP moves overtly, it lands higher than the CP it is base-generated in and ends in the complement of the prepositions *apo*, and is assigned accusative case (see Merchant 2009: 151–156 for details). In Bacskai Atkari (2017), I adopted this view for Greek comparatives with *apo* and showed that this approach correctly predicts that *apo*-comparatives pattern with clausal comparatives and not with ordinary phrasal comparatives in certain ambiguous constructions. I cannot discuss the issue of clausal and phrasal comparatives here in more detail, but it should be obvious that a clausal analysis for reduced comparative clauses is altogether favourable for English and also for similar constructions from other languages to be dealt with in this chapter.

constituent is also aligned to the right edge of an Intonational Phrase (cf. Szendrői 2001, based on Selkirk 1984; 1986, Nespor & Vogel 1986, Chen 1987, Inkelas 1989, McCarthy & Prince 1993, Neeleman & Weerman 1999, Truckenbrodt 1999 among others).

In the case of VP-ellipsis, the [E] feature can be located in a v node above the VP (or any thematic vP). This is schematically represented in (4):

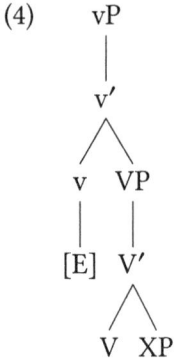

(4) vP
      |
      v′
     / \
    v   VP
    | |
   [E]   V′
        / \
       V   XP

As can be seen, the [E] feature is located in the v head above the VP, and deletion at PF affects the complement of v, that is, the VP (the domain of ellipsis), as shown in (5):

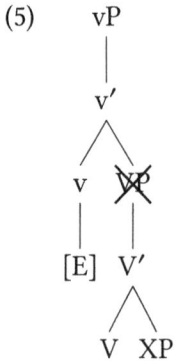

(5) vP
      |
      v′
     / \
    v   V̶P̶
    | |
   [E]   V′
        / \
       V   XP

This leaves the v head itself intact and deletes the following VP, including the V head and the XP in the complement position of the V head. However, if the XP (or a constituent thereof) is contrastive, then it can withstand deletion, as demonstrated in (6):

(6) a. $v_{[E]}$ [~~$_{VP}$ V [XP]~~]
     b. $v_{[E]}$ [~~$_{VP}$ V~~ [XP]$_F$]

Note that the presence of the [E] feature is optional in itself; on the other hand, if the XP is a non-contrastive lower copy, it is regularly deleted as a lower copy, independently of the [E] feature and hence VP-ellipsis.

Let us turn to the cases outlined at the beginning of this section. In predicative structures like (1), the v node is headed by the copula (*is*) and the XP is a QP:

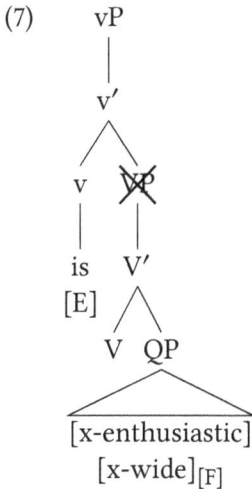

(7)

```
        vP
        |
        v′
       ╱╲
      v   X̶P̶
      |    |
      is   V′
     [E]  ╱╲
         V  QP
        ╱──────╲
   [x-enthusiastic]
      [x-wide][F]
```

Obviously, if the [E] feature is not present on the v node, then the QP *x-enthusiastic* is deleted regularly as a lower copy, resulting in the structure in (1b), while the QP *x-wide* is realised overtly since it is F-marked, as in (1a). The representation in (7) shows the case when the [E] feature is present on the v head: the ellipsis domain is the VP and the v head itself (*is*) remains intact. This means that a non-contrastive QP such as *x-enthusiastic* is deleted, resulting in a configuration like (1b), but note that the same configuration emerges even without the presence of the [E] feature. On the other hand, a contrastive QP such as *x-wide* is not deleted, resulting in a configuration like (1a), which is again the same output that emerges without the presence of the [E] feature.

At this point, it may seem that the presence of the [E] feature does not make any difference as far as the final structure is concerned; furthermore, it does not seem to matter either whether the verb itself is GIVEN or not, since the [E] feature does not delete the verb. The importance of the [E] feature will become clearer when considering attributive and nominative structures; before turning to them, however, let me briefly discuss one issue related to predicative structures that is crucial in understanding the importance of where the [E] feature is located.

Let us suppose that the [E] feature can be located on a node immediately dominating the vP headed by *is*, that is, the I/T head. This would mean that the I/T head is not affected by deletion but its complement is, and the ellipsis domain would be the entire vP and not just the VP, as in (7). Following the analysis given above, this would mean that if the QP is GIVEN, the entire vP is deleted, while a contrastive QP is overt (but the v head is not). In other words, this would predict that both examples in (8) should be grammatical, which is not the case:

(8) a. Ralph is more enthusiastic than Jason ~~is enthusiastic~~.
     b. * The table is longer than the office ~~is~~ wide.

The ungrammaticality of (8b) shows that the [E] feature cannot be located above the vP node containing *is*. On the other hand, the grammaticality of (8a) raises the question how the auxiliary can still be eliminated.

One possibility has to do with phase theory. Note that the vP in question is a phase boundary and hence in structures like (8a) the entire vP-phase is eliminated at PF. This is perfectly possible because it affects only recoverable material, while this option would render an invalid construction in the case of (8b). I adopt the view that phases can be split: that is, material is transferred only to PF or LF (Marušič 2005: 129–130, based on Felser 2004, Bobaljik & Wurmbrand 2005; cf. also Marušič & Žaucer 2006). In the particular case, this means that the vP headed by *is* in (8a) is not transferred to PF but only to LF; therefore its absence is actually due to the lack of PF-transfer and not to PF-deletion.

The other possibility has to do with the FP Merchant (2001) assumes for ellipsis structures: the head of this functional projection hosts the feature [E] and the remnant is moved to the specifier of the FP and thus escapes deletion. One advantage of assuming the availability of the FP is that this projection is not tied to the notion of tense and can appear in tenseless clauses as well. Consider the examples in (9) showing pronominal remnants:

(9) a. ? Ralph is taller than I.
     b. Ralph is taller than **me**.

The remnant is preferably in the accusative case, possibly also to phonological reasons; note also that in English, the default case is the accusative (see Schütze 2001). At the same time, as was also pointed out by Bhatt & Takahashi (2011: 618), the nominative remnant is not excluded either, indicating that *than* is not a preposition assigning accusative case to the pronoun (contrary to Hankamer 1973). The appearance of the accusative case on the remnant is rather due to the absence of the TP projection in the subclause, yet the gradable argument cannot be realised even if it is contrastive. Thus, some kind of ellipsis still applies, even though it is not TP-ellipsis (see Bacskai-Atkari 2014b for an analysis).

On the other hand, the FP analysis cannot handle Attributive Comparative Deletion without assuming rightward movement of the remnant, since gapping and pseudogapping constructions are different from sluicing in that the second remnant cannot be located at the left periphery. Since this chapter is primarily devoted to gapping constructions, I will continue to use an FP-less analysis. However, note that I do not wish to theoretically exclude the availability of the FP. On the contrary, I would like to stress that in cases where there is only a single remnant, the FP-style sluicing analysis is possible and English very probably has several ways of deriving the same surface structure.

Related to this, it is worth mentioning that the present chapter will deal with the derivation of elliptical tensed clauses, that is, the type given in (9a) but not that in (9b). The availability of (9a) shows that full, tensed comparative clauses can be reduced to a single remnant in English (apart from examples where the remnant XP is not even a DP but an AP or a PP), and I would like to show that these structures can be derived without either requiring a designated "Comparative Ellipsis" process or by assuming that comparative subclauses are coordinated at some point in the derivation, as is done by Lechner (1999; 2004). If the DP remnant is not pronominal in English, it is case ambiguous, and could potentially be derived on a par with (9b), see the details given in Bacskai-Atkari (2014b). For reasons of space, I cannot discuss these constructions here; the point here is to show how clausal ellipsis in comparatives works.

Let us now turn to nominal comparatives, as given in (2). In these structures, the v node either is zero or is headed by the auxiliary *do*; the XP is a DP functioning as the object. The case with no overt auxiliary is illustrated in (10):

(10)

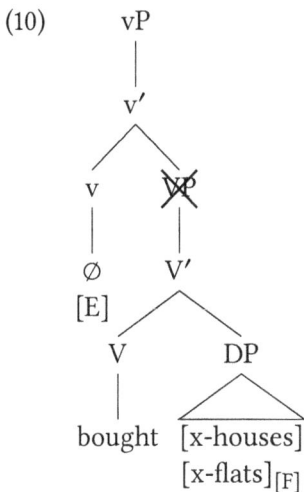

If there is an [E] feature, then it is on the v head. If there is no [E] feature, the VP is not elided; however, since the DP is actually a lower copy, it is deleted regularly as a lower copy (and hence *houses* is not overt), while it remains overt if it is contrastive (as in the case of *flats*). The picture is slightly different if the [E] feature is present, since in that case the VP is the ellipsis domain: if the DP is not contrastive, this eliminates the entire VP but if the DP is contrastive, it stays overt.

Naturally, it is also possible that the v head is filled by the auxiliary *do*:

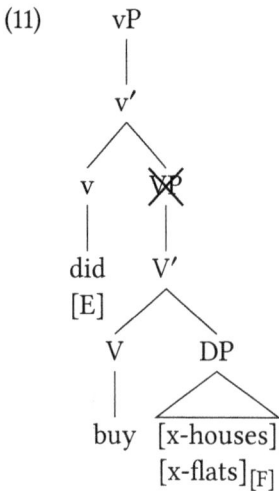

(11)
```
        vP
        |
        v′
       / \
      v   V̶P̶
      |    |
     did   V′
     [E]  / \
         V   DP
         |   /\
       buy  [x-houses]
            [x-flats][F]
```

The insertion of the auxiliary is motivated because in the absence of the lexical verb the tense morpheme could not be spelt out: in other words, the dummy auxiliary appears when there is an [E] feature on the v head but not otherwise, since the overt co-occurrence of *did* and *buy* in structures like (11) would violate general rules of economy. The ellipsis domain is the VP, and only contrastive elements, such as the DP *flats*, can withstand linear deletion, as in (2b); otherwise the entire VP is eliminated at PF, as in (2c).

Finally, let us consider what happens in attributive comparatives. The crucial difference from nominal comparatives lies in the presence of a functional FP layer above the NumP (see Chapter 4), the specifier of which hosts the QP. Again, the v head may or may not be filled by the dummy auxiliary. In (12) below, there is no overt v head:

(12)

```
            vP
            |
            v′
           /  \
          v    XP
          |    |
          Ø    V′
         [E]  /  \
             V    FP
             |   /  \
         bought QP   F′
               /\   /  \
           x-big  F   NumP
                  |   /\
                  Ø [a house]
                    [a flat][F]
```

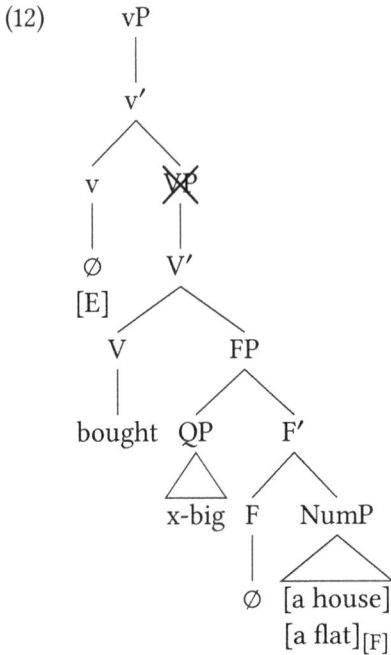

If the entire FP is GIVEN, then it can be deleted regularly as a lower copy. In these cases, if there is no [E] feature on the v head, the lexical V may remain overt in the structure. Otherwise, as was argued for in Chapter 4 in detail, the presence of the [E] feature on the v head is necessary, since the QP must be eliminated. Recall also that this requirement is not sensitive to whether the lexical AP is contrastive or not but stems from an Overtness Requirement on operators moving to a left-peripheral position, and therefore a contrastive AP would render an ungrammatical configuration.

It follows that the presence of the [E] feature on the v head causes the elimination of the lexical V and also of the QP, and only a contrastive NumP (such as *a flat*) may remain overt. If the NumP is not contrastive, the entire FP can be eliminated as a lower copy.

The situation is essentially the same if the v node contains the dummy auxiliary, as in (13):

(13) vP
```
            vP
            |
            v'
           /  \
          v    XP̶
          |     |
         did    V'
         [E]   /  \
              V    FP
              |   /  \
            buy  QP   F'
                /\   / \
            x-big  F  NumP
                   |  /  \
                   Ø [a house]
                     [a flat][F]
```

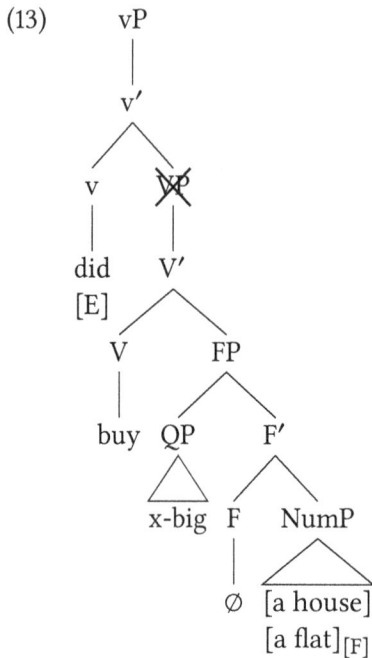

Again, the lexical verb and the QP are deleted, and the dummy auxiliary *did* remains overt; the NumP is elided if it is not contrastive, as in (3b), and withstands linear deletion if it is contrastive, as in (3a).

6.2.2 Different domains of ellipsis and syntactic ambiguity

The analysis presented so far provides a unified account for ellipsis phenomena in English comparatives. Elliptical clauses tend to overtly contain only a single contrasted constituent. In the examples considered so far this constituent was invariably the subject, but this is not necessarily the case, as shown by (14) below:

(14)   More girls ate sandwiches than hamburgers.

In this case, the remaining DP constituent in the subclause is *hamburgers*, which is an object. The derivation of the subclause is outlined in (15):

(15)   [CP than [CP [DP x-many girls] [IP [DP x-many girls] [VP ate [DP hamburgers]F]]]]

As can be seen, the highest copy of the quantified DP (*x-many girls*) in the [Spec,CP] position is eliminated due to the Overtness Requirement. In addition, the rest of the clause is elided except for the object DP (*hamburgers*), which is possible because the lower copies of the quantified DP and the lexical verb are not contrastive.

Since the lower copy of the subject DP is regularly eliminated, and VP-ellipsis can take place independently, there is no reason to suppose that the two processes are connected. However, this is not necessarily so in cases when the subject and the quantified expression are independent. Consider:

(16)　Mary drank ale more often than sherry.

The derivation is shown in (17):

(17)　[$_{CP}$ than [$_{CP}$ ~~[$_{QP}$ x-often]~~ ~~[$_{IP}$ [$_{DP}$ Mary]~~ ~~[$_{VP}$ drank~~ [$_{DP}$ sherry]$_F$] ~~[$_{QP}$ x-often]]]]~~

In this case, the lower copy of the quantified adverb (*x-often*) is elided in its base position; the subject DP *Mary* and the lexical verb are deleted together. This is possible if the [E] feature is located on the C head and ellipsis in this case naturally affects both the subject and the verb, neither of which are F-marked.

As shown by Merchant (2001), ellipsis is carried out via an [E] feature that is present on a functional head: in sluicing, for instance, this functional head is a C in English. In cases like (15), then, if the [E] feature is located on the lower C head, ellipsis affects the non-contrastive lexical verb. This option is preferable to locating the [E] feature on the v head because it is preferable to elide the maximal unit (cf. Merchant 2008). Similarly to the case of VP-ellipsis, an F-marked constituent blocks the linear deletion process and hence the DP *hamburgers* remains overt.

The availability of [E] on both C and v is responsible for certain structural ambiguities. Consider the examples in (18):

(18)　a. I love you more than Peter.

　　　b. I'm a linguist. I like ambiguity more than most people.

In both cases, the DP following *than* can be interpreted either as the subject or the object, as there is no overt case distinction. Taking the example in (18a), the ellipsis domain for a structure containing *Peter* as the subject is shown below:

(19)

```
                CP
                |
                C′
              /    \
            C        CP
            |       /   \
          than   Op.ᵢ    C′
                        /  \
                       C    IP
                           /   \
                        DPⱼ     I′
                        /\     /\
                     Peter  I   vP
                                |
                                v′
                              /    \
                            v        vP
                            |      /    \
                            Ø   tⱼ loves you tᵢ
                           [E]
```

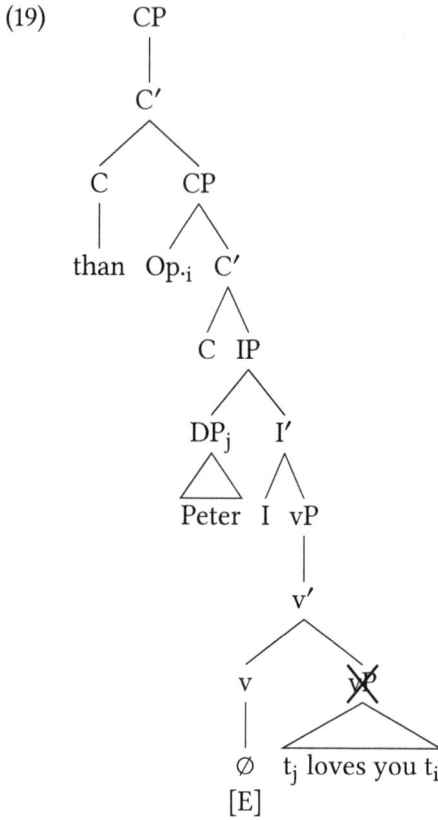

As can be seen, in this case the contrastive element is the subject, and the [E] feature can only be located on a v head and not on C; since there is no contrastive element in the ellipsis domain, the entire vP is eliminated.

By contrast, if *Peter* in (18a) is an object, the the ellipsis domain is the complement of a C head equipped with the [E] feature, as illustrated in (20):

(20)

```
        CP
        |
        C'
       /  \
      C    CP
      |   /  \
    than Op-i C'
            /  \
           C    IP̶
           |   /  \
           Ø  DP_j I'
          [E]      / \
               I  I  vP
                      |
                      v'
                     / \
                    v   vP
                  t_j love [Peter]_F t_i
```

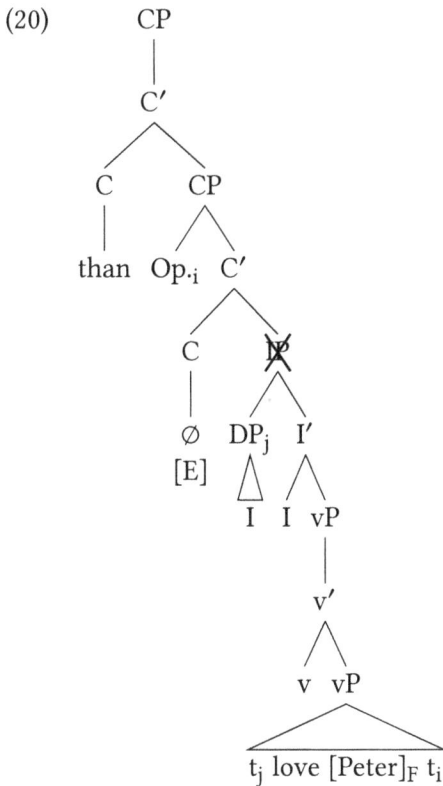

Ellipsis hence affects the entire IP and stops only at the F-marked DP *Peter*. If the [E] feature were located on a v head (as in (19)), then the subject would also remain overt and (21) should be grammatical, which is not the case:

(21) *I love you more than I Peter.

The fact that the feature [E] is located as high as possible in the structure is essentially in line with economy requirements. The elimination of a larger unit is thus the result of a single process but the possibility of [E] appearing on a lower functional head is not excluded either.

Thus, ambiguity may result from there being two possible underlying structures, with respect to the position of a remnant DP in the subclause. On the other hand, ambiguity may also be the result of which projection is responsible for withstanding deletion. Consider the following example:[3]

(22) More people die each year from falling coconuts than sharks.

---

[3]I am indebted to Jenneke van der Wal for calling my attention to this particular example.

The sentence in (22) is ambiguous and the three possible readings are para-phrased with fuller structures in (23) below:

(23)   a.   More people die each year from falling coconuts than sharks do.

b.   More people die each year from falling coconuts than from sharks.

c.   More people die each year from falling coconuts than from falling sharks.

The most plausible meaning is the one given in (23b) but the other two mean-ings are also available and congruent. To derive the sentence in (22) with the meaning of (23a), the [E] feature has to be present on the v head and the entire VP is elided; the subject DP *sharks* is left intact because it falls outside of the ellipsis domain. Note that the DP *x-many sharks* is the quantified expression in the subclause and hence it is moved from the VP first into the [Spec,IP] position as the subject and then further to the [Spec,CP] position as the quantified ex-pression. The copy in the [Spec,CP] position is eliminated due to the Overtness Requirement and the lowest copy would have to be regularly deleted anyway. For the sake of convenience, I do not include these copies in the representation in (24), which shows exclusively the effect of VP-ellipsis:

(24)   [$_{CP}$ than [$_{IP}$ [$_{DP}$ x-many sharks]$_F$ [$_{vP}$ ~~[$_{VP}$ die [$_{PP}$ from falling coconuts]]]]]

Naturally, the [E] feature cannot be located on the C head since then the con-trastive DP (*sharks*) would stop the deletion process from applying further.

By contrast, in order to derive the readings in (23b) and (23c), the [E] feature is present on the C head and it stops only at the clause-final contrastive element, which is either a full DP or a part thereof. In the case of the reading given in (23b), ellipsis is as illustrated in (25):

(25)   [$_{CP}$ than ~~[$_{IP}$ [$_{DP}$ x-many people]~~ ~~[$_{vP}$ [$_{VP}$ die [$_{PP}$ from~~ [$_{DP}$ sharks]$_F$]]]]]

By contrast, for a reading such as the one in (23c), there has to be an AP present within the DP as well, which is also elided, as shown in (26):

(26)   [$_{CP}$ than ~~[$_{IP}$ [$_{DP}$ x-many people]~~ ~~[$_{vP}$ [$_{VP}$ die [$_{PP}$ from~~ [$_{DP}$ ~~[$_{AP}$ falling]~~ [$_{NP}$ sharks]$_F$]]]]]

Note also that the PP may be able to withstand deletion too, as in (23b), which is then derived as given in (27):

(27)   [$_{CP}$ than ~~[$_{IP}$ [$_{DP}$ x-many people]~~ ~~[$_{vP}$ [$_{VP}$ die~~ [$_{PP}$ from [$_{DP}$ sharks]]$_F$]]]]

This is possible because F-marking may affect either the entire PP or the DP: just as an F-marked lexical element (the noun *sharks*) can project this property up to the DP level, the same may be projected up to the PP.

Naturally, the ellipsis processes described above could be examined in other constructions as well; however, since the aim of the present investigation is not to provide a unified account for ellipsis but to investigate the structure of comparative constructions, I will leave such questions open here. The advantage of the analysis presented in this section lies in the fact that it provides a unified framework for the various outputs, which are hence the results of otherwise optional processes and general requirements on GIVEN/contrastive lower copies. While the presence of an [E] feature on a functional head is in itself optional, once this option is taken, the way ellipsis applies is predictable. In other words, all deletion rules applying in English comparatives can be reduced to general principles. Again, note that the analysis presented here applies only to tensed clauses; see Bacskai-Atkari (2014b) on tenseless clauses in English.

6.3 Ellipsis in Hungarian

6.3.1 Sluicing and VP-ellipsis

The question arises whether and to what extent the analysis given in §6.2 can be applied to other languages, such as Hungarian; in English, the higher copy of the quantified expression is regularly eliminated in the [Spec,CP] position due to the Overtness Requirement but this is not so in languages that have overt comparative operators. Yet, the final linear structure of comparative subclauses in Hungarian tends to be strikingly similar to their English counterparts: that is, only contrastive elements are preserved and the quantified expression is not visible either.

First of all, let us consider examples containing a GIVEN verb: in all of these cases there is a synonymous pair of sentences where one contains a full subclause and the other shows the result of ellipsis. I will argue that in these elliptical examples the [E] feature is located on a functional head right above the TP/IP and lower than the CP, and the effects are essentially similar to sluicing and VP-ellipsis in English.

Consider the following examples for predicative structures:

(28) a. Mari magasabb volt,   mint **amilyen magas** Péter **volt.**
          Mary taller   was.3SG than how   tall   Peter was.3SG
          'Mary was taller than Peter.'

      b. Mari magasabb volt,   mint Péter.
          Mary taller   was.3SG than Peter
          'Mary was taller than Peter.'

The sentence in (28a) represents the full structure of a predicative comparative subclause, that is, the subclause where no ellipsis has taken place. By contrast, the one in (28b) is the result of ellipsis, since only a contrastive DP (*Péter*) remains overt and both the finite verb (*volt*) and the quantified expression (*amilyen magas*) are elided. As far as their semantics is concerned, the two sentences are equivalent. The question that arises is how the quantified expression is deleted since Comparative Deletion is not applicable (the operator being visible); furthermore, (28a) suggests that the quantified expression and the finite verb are not even adjacent.

Before attempting to provide an answer to this, let us see some examples for nominal comparatives:

(29) a. Mari több macskát vett,   mint **ahány**   **macskát** Péter
          Mary more cat.ACC bought.3SG than how.many cat.ACC   Peter
          vett.
          bought.3SG
          'Mary bought more cats than Peter did.'

      b. Mari több macskát vett,   mint Péter.
          Mary more cat.ACC bought.3SG than Peter
          'Mary bought more cats than Peter did.'

The (more) complete string is given in (29a) and the one in (29b) is the result of ellipsis affecting the quantified DP (*ahány macskát*) and the lexical verb (*vett*). The picture is similar in the case of attributive structures:

(30) a. Mari nagyobb macskát vett,   mint **amilyen nagy macskát**
          Mary bigger   cat.ACC bought.3SG than how   big   cat.ACC
          Péter **vett.**
          Peter bought.3SG
          'Mary bought a bigger cat than Peter did.'

b. Mari nagyobb macskát vett,   mint Péter.
  Mary bigger   cat.ACC bought.3SG than Peter
  'Mary bought a bigger cat than Peter did.'

Again, (30a) shows the complete string containing the finite verb and the quantified DP (*amilyen nagy macskát*), while in (30b) these elements have been elided from the subordinate clause. Both in (29) and in (30), it seems that the quantified expression and the finite verb are not adjacent. Therefore, the question posed in connection with (28) remains: that is, how both of these elements can be elided if the elements are not adjacent. There are two basic possibilities. First, there might be two different processes involved (even though the elimination of the highest copy of the quantified expression cannot be the result of Comparative Deletion). Second, there may be a single process that is able to affect both elements that are adjacent at some point. In what follows, I will argue for the latter.

That there is indeed a correlation between the deletion of the quantified expression and the finite verb is shown by the phenomenon descriptively termed Comparative Verb Gapping by Bacskai-Atkari & Kántor (2012). This is the observation "that if the operator is deleted, the finite verb must also be deleted" (Bacskai-Atkari & Kántor 2012: 49). In other words, while examples (28)–(30) clearly show that structures containing both the quantified expression and the finite verb are grammatical and so are ones where both of these elements are elided, the absence of an overt quantified expression seems to require the deletion of the finite verb. This is demonstrated by the ungrammaticality of the following sentences (see also the examples given in Bacskai-Atkari & Kántor 2012: 54–56):

(31) a. * Mari magasabb volt,   mint Péter **volt**.
        Mary taller   was.3SG than Peter was.3SG
        'Mary was taller than Peter.'

  b. * Mari több macskát vett,   mint Péter **vett**.
        Mary more cat.ACC   bought.3SG than Peter bought.3SG
        'Mary bought more cats than Peter did.'

  c. * Mari nagyobb macskát vett,   mint Péter **vett**.
        Mary bigger   cat.ACC bought.3SG than Peter bought.3SG
        'Mary bought a bigger cat than Peter did.'

The ungrammaticality of the examples in (31) shows that the deletion of the quantified expression should affect the GIVEN finite verb as well.

The core argument of Bacskai-Atkari & Kántor (2012: 56–59) is that when there is no overt quantified expression in a Hungarian comparative subclause, it is so because the operator failed to undergo movement to the [Spec,CP] position before spell-out to PF. However, it is ungrammatical to have a phrase containing a relative operator in its base position; more precisely, there is an unchecked [+rel] feature on the operator, and the construction can be saved only by deletion (Bacskai-Atkari & Kántor 2012: 58).

Interestingly, the phenomenon is not restricted to comparative subclauses but can be found in certain relative clauses as well; consider the following set of examples (based on Bacskai-Atkari & Kántor 2012: 59, ex. 32):

(32)   a.   Ugyanazt   a   könyvet olvasom, mint **amit**   Péter **olvas**.
           that.same.ACC the book.ACC read.1SG as   what.ACC Peter reads
           'I am reading the same book that Peter is reading.'

       b.   Ugyanazt   a   könyvet olvasom, mint **amit**   Péter.
           that.same.ACC the book.ACC read.1SG as   what.ACC Peter
           'I am reading the same book that Peter is reading.'

       c. *Ugyanazt   a   könyvet olvasom, mint Péter **olvas**.
           that.same.ACC the book.ACC read.1SG as   Peter reads
           'I am reading the same book that Peter is reading.'

       d.   Ugyanazt   a   könyvet olvasom, mint Péter.
           that.same.ACC the book.ACC read.1SG as   Peter
           'I am reading the same book that Peter is reading.'

The relative clauses in (32) differ from ordinary relative clauses in that they also contain the complementiser *mint* 'as'. However, the structure is not comparative: only non-degree equation is involved in the sense that a given entity is identified with another one, but note that there are no degree expressions either in the matrix clause or in the subordinate clause. The point is that since there is an overt complementiser at the left periphery, the relative operator *amit* 'what' may be deleted, which would not be possible otherwise. Since Hungarian lacks zero relative operators, the absence of an overt relative operator from a relative clause can only be the result of deletion.

The full version is given in (32a), containing both the operator and the finite verb (*olvas*); note that the verb can be elided even if the operator is overt, as shown by (32b) and the same would be true for comparatives as well (cf. Bacskai-Atkari & Kántor 2012: 59). The ungrammatical configuration in (32c) lacks an overt operator but the finite verb is present; finally, the construction in which both the operator and the finite verb are deleted is again grammatical, as in (32d). This reinforces the hypothesis that the absence of the operator (or of the phrase containing the operator) is due to some ellipsis process that takes place in the verbal domain: that is, when the operator fails to move up to the [Spec,CP] position.

It has to be highlighted that ordinary relative clauses in Hungarian do not contain the complementiser *mint* 'as': they are introduced by a zero complementiser and contain overt relative operators, there being no zero relative operators in Hungarian. If, however, there is an overt *mint* in the subclause, the relative operator is licensed to be absent (under the conditions discussed in connection with (32) above) since there is an overt marker introducing the subordinate clause. In other words, the sentences in (32a) and (32b) would be grammatical without *mint* as well. It is also worth mentioning that the pronoun in the matrix clause is a composite of the prefix *ugyan-* 'same' and the pronoun *azt* 'that.ACC' but it could appear in the simple form of *azt* as well; however, for most of my informants, the constructions sound more natural with the emphatic version given in (32). Since the pronoun is also marked for case, the DP containing the lexical noun (*a könyvet* 'the book') can also be left out. The variations concerning relative clause constructions containing the matrix pronominal element *ugyanazt* and the overt relative pronoun *amit* are summarised in (33) below:

(33) Ugyanazt   (a   könyvet) olvasom, (mint) amit   Péter (olvas).
      that.same.ACC the book.ACC read.1SG as   what.ACC Peter reads

      'I am reading the same (book) that Peter is reading.'

Interestingly, the same options are available for comparatives expressing equality; these contain the matrix clausal pronoun *olyan* 'so' or *ugyanolyan* 'self-same' and if there is an overt comparative operator in the subclause, the complementiser *mint* can be left out, as in (34):

(34) Ugyanolyan könyvet   olvasok, (mint) amilyet   Péter (olvas).
      self.same   book.ACC read.1SG as   how.ACC Peter reads

      'The book I am reading is like the one Peter is reading.'

Again, the noun can be left out of the matrix clause, provided that the pronoun *ugyanolyan* takes the relevant case endings (this of course results in a change in the meaning), as given in (35):

(35) Ugyanolyat   olvasok, (mint) amilyet Péter (olvas).
       self.same.ACC read.1SG as   how.ACC Peter reads
       'What I am reading is like what Peter is reading.'

The same option is available in ordinary comparative subclause expressing equality, as illustrated in (36):

(36) Mari olyan magas, (mint) amilyen az anyja.
       Mary as   tall   as   how   the mother.POSS
       'Mary is as tall as her mother.'

However, this is not possible in comparatives expressing inequality, as demonstrated by (37):

(37) Mari magasabb, *(mint) amilyen az anyja.
       Mary taller   than how   the mother.POSS
       'Mary is taller than her mother.'

This shows that there is a difference in the selectional restrictions between the two types: while the degree element *olyan* may select for a comparative subclause introduced by *mint* or by zero, the degree element *-bb* '-er' selects exclusively for *mint* as a C head. The requirement to have an overt relative operator in the subordinate clause in the absence of *mint* is a requirement that holds in the subclause and is essentially one that makes the presence of some overt clause-type marker necessary: in this respect, a relative operator is sufficient because it is also equipped with the [+rel] feature and in comparatives also with a [+compr] feature. I will not venture to investigate the difference between *olyan* and *-bb* in this respect, especially as the phenomenon is attested cross-linguistically and the requirement to have overt complementisers in comparative subclauses expressing inequality seems to be universally applicable (see Bacskai-Atkari 2016 for a detailed analysis).

Let us now return to the clauses in (28b), (29b) and (30b), repeated here for the sake of convenience in (38):

(38) a. Mari magasabb volt,   mint Péter.
          Mary taller   was.3SG than Peter
          'Mary was taller than Peter.'

       b. Mari több macskát vett,   mint Péter.
          Mary more cat.ACC bought.3SG than Peter
          'Mary bought more cats than Peter did.'

    c. Mari nagyobb macskát vett,   mint Péter.

        Mary bigger   cat.ACC bought.3SG than Peter

     'Mary bought a bigger cat than Peter did.'

Bacskai-Atkari & Kántor (2012: 57–59) argue in these constructions containing ellipsis sluicing takes place: therefore, they all contain an [E] feature on the F (focus) head and thus the complement of the F head is elided, as given in (39):[4]

(39)

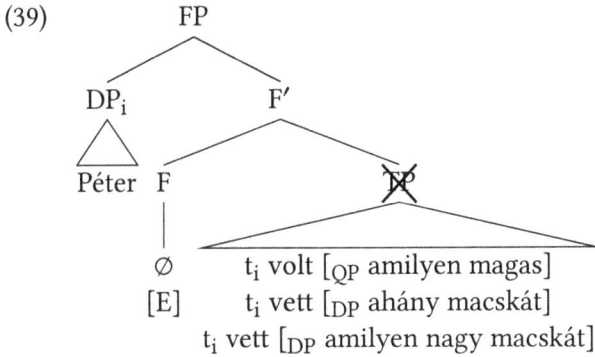

FP

DP$_i$ F′

Péter   F

       ∅   t$_i$ volt [$_{QP}$ amilyen magas]
     [E]   t$_i$ vett [$_{DP}$ ahány macskát]
           t$_i$ vett [$_{DP}$ amilyen nagy macskát]

The analysis follows van Craenenbroeck & Lipták (2006), who claim that sluicing in Hungarian is carried out by an [E] feature on the F head; on the other hand, it is also a fairly standard assumption that PF may save a construction via deletion, which eliminates some uninterpretable feature (see the discussion in Chapter 4 and also Kennedy & Merchant 2000: 131 and Merchant 2009: 145–151).

As Chapter 3 argued in connection with extractable degree operators, the quantified expression moves up first to the edge of the verbal domain and subsequently to [Spec,CP], and a contrastive lexical AP is preferably stranded in [Spec,FP]. In the elliptical examples, however, there is obviously no movement to the edge of the verbal domain since then the lexical element in the quantified expression should precede the focussed DP *Péter*, which is not the case. Alternatively, the ellipsis domain could be larger by way of placing the [E] feature on a C head, but then the entire subclause would have to be elided. Since the FP is a functional projection above the TP, the ellipsis process is indeed similar to English sluicing. On the other hand, since the FP is the highest projection to which the verb may move and the constituent located in [Spec,TP] regularly moves up

---

[4]Bacskai-Atkari & Kántor (2012) identify the FP as a FocP, and no TP below it, just a functional vP, in line with more traditional analyses of the Hungarian clause. I follow É. Kiss (2008a) in assuming the presence of a TP below the FP, but I differ from her analysis in that I do not treat the FP as a designated Focus projection. This has the advantage that the ability of the F head to host an [E] feature follows naturally from its status as a left-peripheral functional head.

to the [Spec,FP] position (cf. É. Kiss 2008a), locating the [E] feature on F is also similar to VP-ellipsis in English. The point is that if there is an [E] feaure on the F head, the verb does not move up to F, unlike in non-elliptical constructions.

On the other hand, note that the informational structural status of the quantified expression does not affect the ellipsis processes as in English. The reason behind this is that they are not the lower copies of a moved constituent that may be realised overtly under special conditions, but are the only copies since movement has not taken place. Furthermore, due to the presence of an overt operator with unchecked features, they are ungrammatical in their base position irrespectively of whether they are contrastive or not. Consequently, elliptical comparatives of the type in (39) are only possible if the quantified expression is GIVEN since the elimination of an F-marked phrase would violate recoverability.

6.3.2 Contrastive verbs in predicative structures

The question arises what happens if the verb is not GIVEN. Consider the following example of a predicative structure (see also Bacskai-Atkari & Kántor 2012: 55):

(40) Mari magasabb, mint Péter **volt**.
      Mary taller   than Peter was.3SG

      'Mary is taller than Peter was.'

As can be seen, the finite verb (*volt*) is overt in the subclause but no overt quantified expression is present. However, unlike the sentences in (31), it is still grammatical. The difference is that *volt* in (40) is not GIVEN since the zero copula in the matrix clause is in the present tense, and hence the past tense of *volt* expresses new information that would not be recoverable if the verb were elided.

This is possible if the [E] feature is located on a functional head lower than the F head; this was proposed by Bacskai-Atkari & Kántor (2011) and the relevant functional projection was identified as the AspP (aspectual phrase). I would like to take a slightly different approach here, as far as the projection is concerned, which I identify as a functional vP below the TP, identical to the PredP proposed by É. Kiss (2008a). Essentially, the projection is reminiscent of the functional vP hosting the copula in English predicative structures. The [E] feature cannot be located on this v head in (31a) because the [E] feature has to be located as high as possible. In (31a), the copula does not carry new information, and should therefore be deleted. This is enabled if the [E] is on the F head, as in (28b).

Note that even though the copula remains overt and carries new information in (40), the main stress still falls on the focussed DP *Péter*, just as in (28b). This is not surprising since the copula is a function word: as stated by the Lexical Category Condition (Truckenbrodt 1999: 226) and the Principle of Categorial Invisibility of Function Words (Selkirk 1984: 226), function words are to be treated as invisible with respect to constraints holding at the syntax-phonology mapping, and they do not receive main stress but are rather phonologically dependent on another element. In (40), it is the preceding DP *Péter* (cf. É. Kiss 2002: 74). On the other hand, main stress is assigned to the DP because Intonational Phrases are left-headed in Hungarian: main stress falls on the focussed constituent in a focus construction and not on the main (lexical) verb (cf. Szendrői 2001: 50–53).[5]

The derivation of (40) is schematically given in (41):

(41)

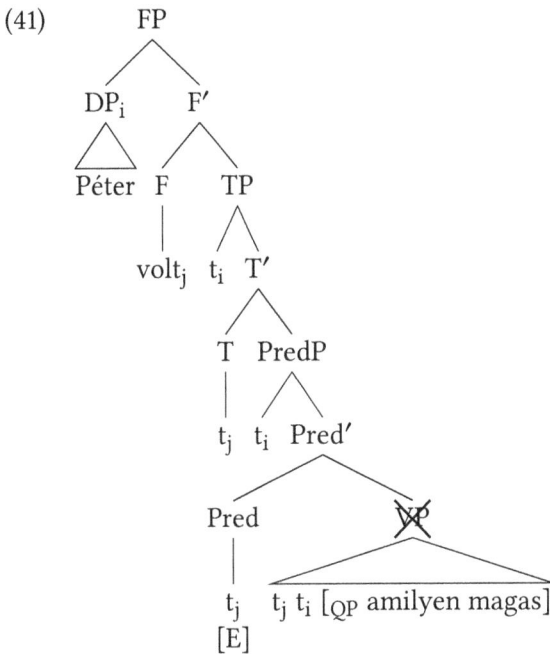

---

[5]In other words, nuclear stress falls on the leftmost element that may bear nuclear stress. This excludes topics from being assigned main stress as topics are treated as extrametrical (cf. Szendrői 2001: 49, based on Truckenbrodt 1999). On the other hand, the complementiser is not to be stressed either, as shown by Kenesei & Vogel (1989; 1995). Complementisers belong to the same Intonational Phrase as the entire subclause. However, based on the Lexical Category Condition (Truckenbrodt 1999: 226) and the Principle of Categorial Invisibility of Function Words (Selkirk 1984: 226), function words are to be treated as invisible with respect to constraints holding at the syntax–phonology mapping: consequently, the complementiser *mint* 'than' may not receive strong stress. Sato & Dobashi (2012) show for English that complementisers are phonologically dependent on the word that immediately follows them. Since the present investigation is not centred on prosody and the mapping rules between syntax and prosodic structure, I will not elaborate on these issues any further here; for a recent discussion on the syntax-prosody mapping in Hungarian comparatives, see Bacskai-Atkari (2013a).

As described by É. Kiss (2008a), the constituent landing in the specifier of FP (her FocP) first moves to the specifier of a Predicative Phrase (PredP) and to the specifier of the TP; the lexical verb moves along. In (41), the verb is a copula and is base-generated in Pred, just as the English copula is base-generated in a functional v head instead of V. The difference from (39) lies in the fact that here the [E] feature is located on the Pred head, not the F head. This is possible because the Pred is a functional head (essentially, a functional v head). If the [E] feature were located on F, then verb movement again would not take place, just as in (39). However, it is possible to base-generate the copula on a head containing [E]; in this case, the copula can again move higher to the F head. As the copula is contrastive, locating the [E] feature on Pred is in line with the requirement to delete the maximal GIVEN constituent. The point is that the copula can be inserted into Pred irrespectively of whether there is an [E] feature or not. The same does not hold for the F head, which does not trigger verb movement if the [E] feature is present, and verb movement is not obligatory either if the clause is not finite (see É. Kiss 2008a).

6.3.3 Contrastive verbs in attributive and nominal structures

The importance of all this becomes obvious when considering nominal and attributive comparative examples such as (42), where the verb that carries new information is a lexical one and as such is actually F-marked:

(42)   a. ? Mari több macskát vett,   mint Péter **látott**.
                Mary more cat.ACC bought.3SG than Peter saw.3SG
                'Mary bought more cats than Peter saw.'

        b. ? Mari nagyobb macskát vett,   mint Péter **látott**.
                Mary bigger   cat.ACC bought.3SG than Peter saw.3SG
                'Mary bought a bigger cat than Peter saw.'

As can be seen, the lexical verb in the subclause (*látott*) is different from the one in the matrix clause (*vett*); the sentences are acceptable but marked (the individual ratings of my informants differed as far as the degree of markedness is concerned).

Since the present investigation is not particularly concerned with the theory of focus in general, I do not attempt to address the issue of verbs and focus in detail. As shown by Kenesei (2006), instances where the verb seems to be focussed do not involve the focussing of the V head as such but either the VP or the entire proposition is focussed. This is actually in line with my analysis here and the examples in this section clearly demonstrate that it is not merely a verb in the subclause that is contrasted with the one in the matrix clause but rather an entire proposition: there are other elements that are contrastive, such as the subject DP in the examples in (42). However, since in the construction under scrutiny, contrastive elements are located above the VP (all thematic vP layers) and elements that are left in the thematic verbal domain are non-contrastive, what really matters to us here is indeed the status of the lexical verbal head. This behaves differently with respect to the ellipsis domain depending on whether there is propositional contrast or not.

In (39), the lexical verb (*vett*) moves up from a functional v head (assuming a layered analysis of the Hungarian verb phrase, see É. Kiss 2008b, É. Kiss 2009) to T but not beyond, since the F head contains an [E] feature. This means that, in order to derive the constructions in (42), the lexical verb has to move up to F despite the presence of the [E] feature, which regularly does not require verb movement to F. Since the quantified DPs are not present overtly, ellipsis must have taken place, as should be obvious from the discussion in the previous subsection. Since the lexical verb has to undergo a movement operation that it would not take otherwise, the construction is marked.

Moreover, in (42) the main stress has to fall on the verb in the subordinate clause; this follows from the fact that there are two propositions compared in (42), and the contrast is expressed by the main verb. However, this would not be possible if the DP *Péter* were located in [Spec,FP] because then the main stress would be assigned to that constituent. Therefore, the DP *Péter* in (42) has to move to a topic position in order to escape both ellipsis and main stress (see Szendrői 2001 on the extrametricality of topics).

As was mentioned before, contrastive verbs involve the contrast between entire propositions and not merely verbal heads; in (42), for instance, the subject DPs in the two clauses are also different. Though contrastive elements tend to appear preverbally, it is also possible to have contrastive elements that follow the verb. Consider the following example:

(43) Nagyobb macskát vettem   **ma,**   mint amekkorát láttam **tegnap.**
      bigger   cat.ACC bought.1SG today than how.big.ACC saw.1SG yesterday
      'I bought a bigger cat today than the one I saw yesterday.'

In this case, the adjuncts *ma* 'today' and *tegnap* 'yesterday' are also contrasted and they are phonologically prominent. In this position, as pointed out by Szendrői (2001: 53–55), elements receive extra stress by an additional prosodic rule and not by the nuclear stress rule. By default, it is more economical to move a phrase to the FP for stress assignment than to leave it in the VP but the verb in (43) above is also contrastive and would not receive main stress by default if there were an element in the [Spec,FP] position. This is in line with the analysis given by Kenesei (2006), in that in the case of VP-focus or propositional focus the contrastive elements following the verb are assigned focal stress. Note that this construction is not possible if the verb is not contrastive, that is, when there is no propositional contrast, as shown by (44):

(44)   * Nagyobb macskát vettem   **ma**,   mint amekkorát   vettem
           bigger   cat.ACC   bought.1SG today   than how.big.ACC bought.1SG
           tegnap.
           yesterday
           'I bought a bigger cat today than yesterday.'

In this case the adverb *tegnap* should move up to the [Spec,FP] position in order to give a felicitous construction.

Turning back to (42), there are a number of arguments in favour of the analysis, regarding both of the movement of the lexical verb and the non-focussed nature of the subject DP. Evidence comes from constructions involving a verbal particle; consider first the following examples that do not involve ellipsis:

(45)   a.   Mari   több   macskát vett,   mint **ahány**   macskát Péter
             Mary more cat.ACC   bought.3SG than how.many cat.ACC   Peter
             meglátott.
             PRT.saw.3SG
             'Mary bought more cats than Peter noticed.'

       b.   Mari   nagyobb macskát vett,   mint **amekkora macskát** Péter
             Mary more   cat.ACC   bought.3SG than how.big   cat.ACC   Peter
             meglátott.
             PRT.saw.3SG
             'Mary bought a bigger cat than Peter noticed.'

In (45), the comparative subclause contains the verbal particle *meg*, which precedes the lexical verb: adopting the analysis given by É. Kiss (2008b), this is because the particle moves to the specifier of PredP. In other words, a verbal particle preceding the lexical verb is in complementary distribution with a focussed constituent that would also move to this position (before moving further up to the specifier of the TP and of the FP) and the verbal particle + verb order is indicative of the fact that there is no focussed constituent in the [Spec,FP] position and the DP *Péter* in (45) is a topic (though contrastive). The main sentential stress in

(45) hence falls on the leftmost element of the Intonational Phrase, which is the verbal particle *meg* (cf. Szendrői 2001).

The structure of the subclauses in (45) is represented in (46):[6]

(46)

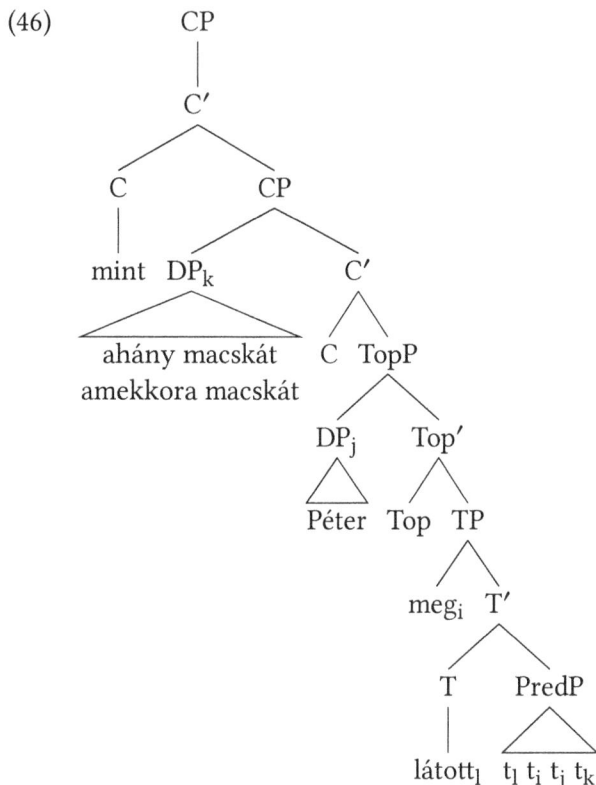

Since the quantified DP moves up to the [Spec,CP] position, there is no ellipsis taking place. As there is no FP (there being no focussed constituent) and [Spec,TP] is filled by the verbal particle *meg*, main sentential stress falls on this element, which renders a felicitous sentence since the main contrast involved in the comparison is expressed by the verb.

---

[6]I follow generally accepted views regarding the structure of a Hungarian finite (subordinate) clause, see for instance in É. Kiss (2002), in that a focussed constituent may be preceded by topics and topics are immediately below the CP-layer. Of course, there are other possible functional projections that can otherwise occur but since my examples contain none of them, I am not particularly concerned with whether they are underlyingly present even when they are not overtly filled. Note also that, since I am using a non-cartographic approach, the distinction between various functional projections in the syntax is less important here than usually assumed in the literature.

When the verb is not contrastive, the situation is different:

(47) a. Mari több macskát látott,   mint **ahány**   macskát Péter **látott**
          Mary more cat.ACC saw.3SG than how.many cat.ACC Peter saw.3SG

          meg.
          PRT

          'Mary saw more cats than Peter noticed.'

      b. Mari nagyobb macskát látott,   mint **amekkora macskát** Péter
          Mary bigger   cat.ACC saw.3SG than how.big   cat.ACC Peter

          látott   meg.
          saw.3SG PRT

          'Mary saw a bigger cat than Peter noticed.'

The subclauses in (47) contain the DP *Péter* as the focussed constituent; following É. Kiss (2008a), this DP is located in the specifier of the FP, and the verbal
particle does not move up, resulting in the non-neutral verb + verbal particle
order. Since the leftmost constituent in this case is the focussed DP, main stress
will fall on this constituent; this again renders a felicitous structure as the main
contrast in (47) is expressed by the DP. The structure of the subclause is shown
in (48):

(48)

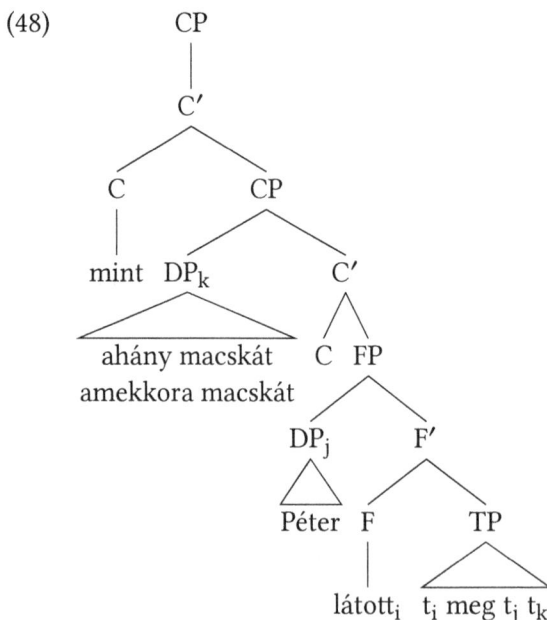

One of the chief differences between (46) and (48) is that there is no topicalised
constituent in (48) since the DP *Péter* moves to the FP; on the other hand, as has

been said, the presence of the DP in the [Spec,FP] position excludes the possibility of the verbal particle (*meg*) also moving out of the VP, since both constituents cannot land in [Spec,PredP]. The structures in (46) and (48) are not interchangeable: that is, whether the lexical verb is contrastive or not determines what constituent may move to [Spec,PredP] to result in a felicitous structure. On the other hand, the position of the verbal particle (its relative position to the verb) is indicative of which constituent has moved out.

Naturally, it is also possible to have full comparative subclauses without verbal particles:

(49)   a.   Mari több macskát vett,   mint **ahány**   macskát Péter
            Mary more cat.ACC bought.3SG than how.many cat.ACC Peter
            látott.
            saw.3SG
            'Mary bought more cats than Peter saw.'

       b.   Mari nagyobb macskát vett,   mint **amekkora macskát** Péter
            Mary bigger   cat.ACC bought.3SG than how.big   cat.ACC Peter
            látott.
            saw.3SG
            'Mary bought a bigger cat than Peter saw.'

       c.   Mari több macskát látott,   mint **ahány**   macskát Péter **látott.**
            Mary more cat.ACC saw.3SG than how.many cat.ACC   Peter saw.3SG
            'Mary saw more cats than Peter did.'

       d.   Mari nagyobb macskát látott,   mint **amekkora macskát** Péter
            Mary bigger   cat.ACC saw.3SG than how.big   cat.ACC Peter
            látott.
            saw.3SG
            'Mary saw a bigger cat than Peter did.'

In these cases, the surface word order in itself is not indicative of the underlying syntactic differences; however, the main stress falls on the lexical verb (*látott*) in (49a) and (49b), while it falls on the DP *Péter* in (49c) and (49d).

The structure of the subclauses in (49a) and (49b) is given in (50) below:

(50)

```
              CP
              |
              C′
           ╱      ╲
          C        CP
          |      ╱    ╲
        mint  DP_k     C′
             ╱    ╲   ╱  ╲
      ahány macskát  C  TopP
      amekkora macskát   ╱  ╲
                      DP_j    Top′
                     ╱  ╲    ╱  ╲
                  Péter  Top   TP
                                |
                                T′
                              ╱    ╲
                             T      PredP
                             |     ╱  ╲
                          látott_i  t_i t_j t_k
```

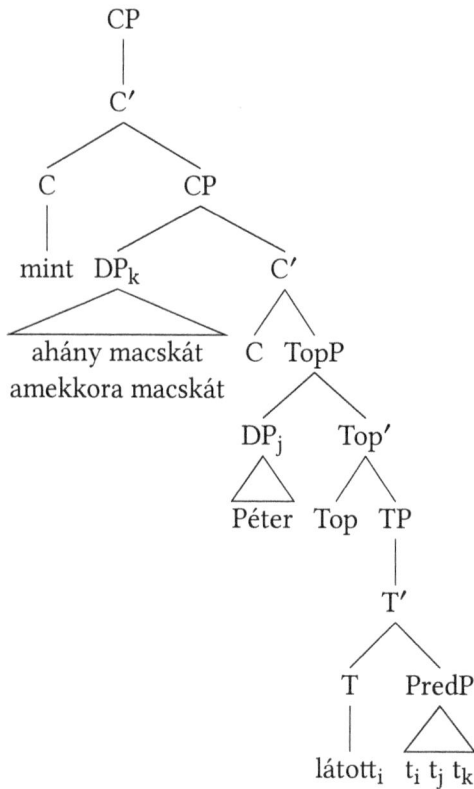

In line with É. Kiss (2008b), there is no FP in these cases: the main stress falls on the lexical verb anyway and the DP moves to a topic position,[7] and thus there is nothing that could potentially be located in the [Spec,FP] position.

By contrast, the structure of (49c) and (49d) is as given in (51):

---

[7] Note that topics may also be contrastive, and therefore the DP *Péter* can be located in a topic position even though it is contrasted with the DP *Mari* in the matrix clause. As described for instance by É. Kiss (2007: 72–78), in case a clause contains multiple contrastive elements, contrastive topics always precede the focus, which is essentially in line with the assumption that the focus is at the left edge of the FP and hence receives main stress, while elements located above it cannot be interpreted as foci. Note also that contrastive elements may occasionally also appear in a postverbal position, in which case they receive extra stress by an additional prosodic rule, as was described before (and see Szendrői 2001).

(51)

```
              CP
              |
              C′
            /    \
          C       CP
          |      /   \
      mint  DPₖ       C′
          /‾‾‾‾\     /  \
    ahány macskát   C  FP
    amekkora macskát    /  \
                     DPⱼ    F′
                    /\     /  \
                Péter   F    TP
                        |    |
                    látottᵢ  T′
                            /  \
                          T   PredP
                          |    /\
                         tᵢ  tᵢ tⱼ tₖ
```

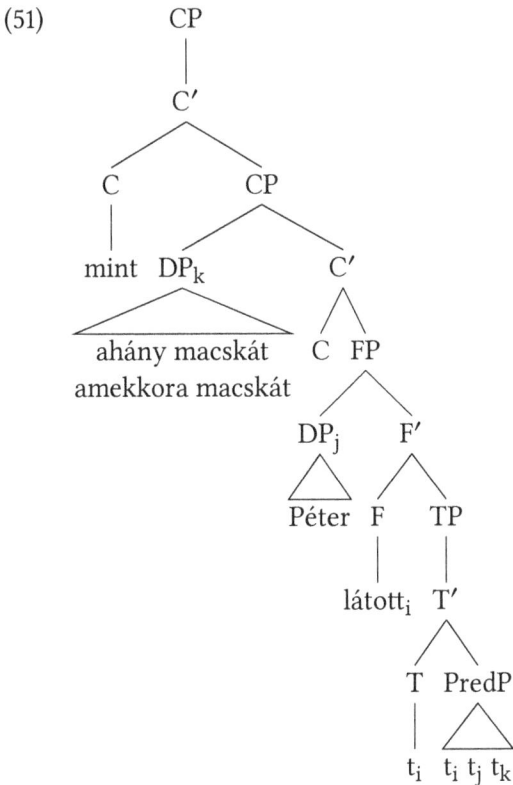

The only difference from (48) is that there is no verbal particle but, since the verbal particle is located within the thematic PredP in (48) as well, this makes no difference as far as the FP is concerned.

To conclude, it should be obvious that if the verb is contrastive, then the FP is not generated, since anything in [Spec,FP] would have to bear main stress. Main stress is thus assigned to the verb in T, and if there is a verbal particle, which phonologically attaches itself to the verb, main stress falls on the particle (which thus constitutes the first syllable of a phonological word). Otherwise, main stress would fall on a constituent distinct from the verb and the sentence would not be felicitous. In these cases, a contrastive DP is topicalised, while it appears in the [Spec,FP] position if the verb is GIVEN.

Based on all this, the structure of the subclauses in (42) is the following:

(52)

CP
|
C'

C   TopP

mint   DP$_j$ Top'

Péter   Top   TP
|
T'

T   PredP

látott$_i$ Pred'

Pred   ⊗VP

t$_i$ t$_i$ t$_j$ [$_{DP}$ ahány/amekkora macskát]
[E]

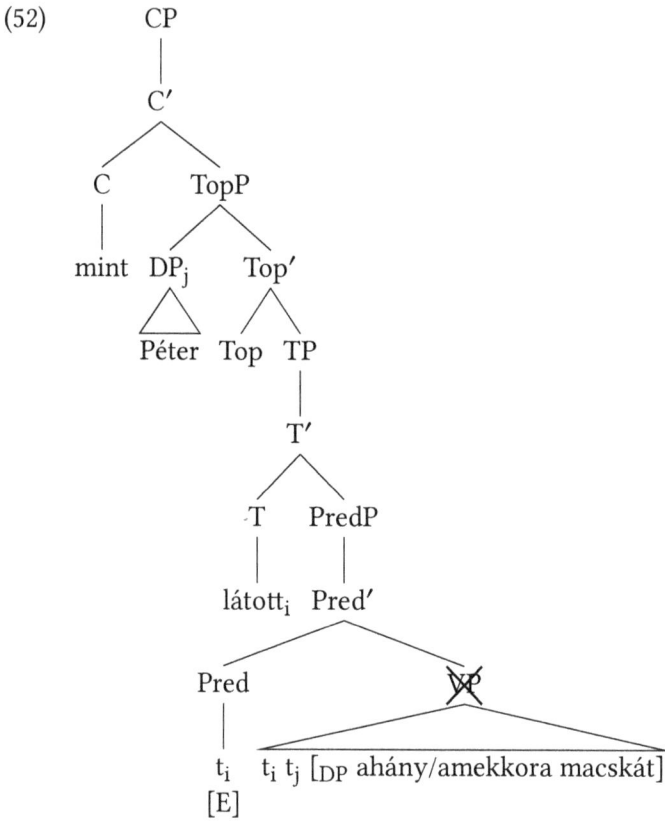

In (42), the verb must move out of the VP in order to escape deletion. This is similar to what was observed in connection with (40), yet there is a crucial difference as well. In (40), the copula is base-generated in Pred, and the [E] feature is added to Pred that happens to contain lexical material already. In (42), however, the lexical verb is generated in the VP and must move to the Pred head, which already contains an [E] feature, and, as was argued previously, the movement of the verb is normally not triggered by a head that contains the [E] feature. While the violation of this constraint does not result in ungrammaticality, the structure is marked due to an extra movement step, hence the markedness of the sentences in (42). As there is no focussed constituent, the FP is not generated and the verb moves only as far as T. The lexical verb can thus be assigned main sentential stress in the prosody: the DP *Péter* is topicalised and falls outside the domain of nuclear stress.

One might wonder whether the DP *Péter* is a focus, hence a constituent located in a [Spec,FP] position. However, taking such a stance would be problematic for various reasons; first, it would contradict the data shown by comparatives with a full subclause, as in (45), (47) and (49). Second, it would wrongly predict that if there is a verbal particle, then it should follow the verb, which is not the case:

(53)   a. * Mari több macskát vett,   mint Péter **látott   meg**.
             Mary more cat.ACC bought.3SG than Peter saw.3SG PRT
             'Mary bought more cats than Peter noticed.'

       b. * Mari nagyobb macskát vett,   mint Péter **látott   meg**.
             Mary bigger   cat.ACC bought.3SG than Peter saw.3SG PRT
             'Mary bought a bigger cat than Peter noticed.'

The reason why the focus status of the DP *Péter* would trigger the verb + verbal particle order is that the [Spec,FP] would then be occupied by this DP and the verb would move up to F, leaving the particle behind, and thus the particle would necessarily follow the verb. However, the sentences in (53) are not acceptable, which indicates that the DP *Péter* cannot be in [Spec,FP]. If both a preverbal DP and the verb are contrastive (that is, there is VP-focus or propositional focus), then it is the verb that should bear the pitch accent and not the DP. Similarly, as was also mentioned before, if there are two contrastive DPs, then the first one is a contrastive topic and the second one a focus, the latter bearing nuclear stress. In order to ensure that the DP does not get nuclear stress, it has to move to a topic position and since topics can also be contrastive, this does not result in semantic incongruence either. The correct intonation pattern can be assigned to the overt elements in the subclause in (42) but not in (53), where the postverbal position of the verbal particle clearly indicates that the [Spec,FP] is filled by another element (the DP *Péter*).

Moreover, if there is a verbal particle, it moves to the [Spec,PredP] and subsequently to the [Spec,TP] position and the verb moves to Pred and subsequently to T, resulting in the verbal particle + verb order, as indicated by the acceptability of the following examples:

(54)   a. ? Mari több macskát vett,   mint Péter **meglátott**.
             Mary more cat.ACC bought.3SG than Peter PRT.saw.3SG
             'Mary bought more cats than Peter noticed.'

       b. ? Mari nagyobb macskát vett,   mint Péter **meglátott**.
             Mary bigger   cat.ACC bought.3SG than Peter PRT.saw.3SG
             'Mary bought a bigger cat than Peter noticed.'

The acceptability of the sentences in (54) is similar to that of the ones in (42); again, individual ratings may differ with respect to the degree of markedness. This is not surprising since the structure should be essentially the same as the one given in (52), except that there is a verbal particle in the [Spec,PredP] position:

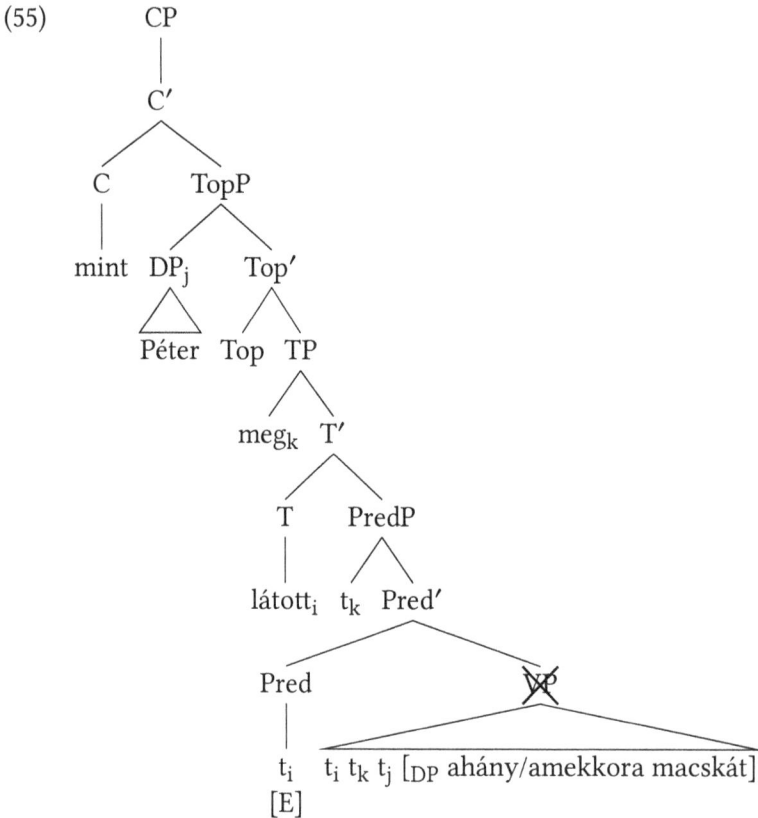

(55)
```
                        CP
                        |
                        C'
                  _____|_____
                 C           TopP
                 |         ____|____
               mint     DP_j       Top'
                        /\        ___|___
                     Péter      Top     TP
                               _____|_____
                            meg_k           T'
                                       _____|_____
                                      T           PredP
                                      |         ____|____
                                  látott_i    t_k    Pred'
                                          _____|_____
                                        Pred            VP (crossed out)
                                         |          _____
                                         t_i   t_i t_k t_j [_DP ahány/amekkora macskát]
                                        [E]
```

Just as in (52), the [E] feature is located on the Pred head and hence the domain of ellipsis is the VP; again, the lexical verb moves up to the Pred head and subsequently to T to escape deletion, which involves an extra step in the derivation since the Pred head contains an [E] feature; consequently, the structure is marked. The reason why there is no other option is that the [E] feature cannot be located on a lexical v/V head. Therefore, either ellipsis would not take place, leaving the uninterpretable quantified DP overt, or ellipsis would affect the contrastive verb too: in either case, the structure would not converge.

To sum up, Hungarian comparative subclauses that contain an overt, F-marked finite verb but no overt quantified expression differ in a predictable way from ones that prohibit the presence of a GIVEN verb. That is, the ellipsis mechanisms are essentially the same in both cases: it is invariably an [E] feature located on a functional head that causes the complement to be elided at PF. On the other hand, the derivation of ones containing a contrastive verb involves an extra movement step, which results in degraded acceptability.

6.3.4 More on cross-linguistic differences

As has been seen, Standard English and Hungarian represent two rather different patterns in terms of comparative subclause formation. Yet, as I also demonstrated, these differences can be reduced to general requirements and they do not result from construction-specific rules.

First, the reason why (Standard) English exhibits Comparative Deletion but Hungarian does not is that the Overtness Requirement requires relative operators (including comparative operators) to be phonologically visible if there is other overt material in [Spec,CP]. Since Standard English has no overt comparative operators, deletion is required; by contrast, Hungarian has only overt comparative operators and deletion does not (and cannot) take place in [Spec,CP]. In this way, the Overtness Requirement is responsible for the difference between the English example in (56a) and the Hungarian one in (56b):

(56)   a. Mary bought more cats than Peter bought.

   b. Mari több macskát vett,   mint ahány   macskát Péter
      Mary more cat.ACC bought.3SG than how.many cat.ACC Peter
      vett.
      bought.3SG
      'Mary bought more cats than Peter did.'

The difference in (56) can be detected in maximally non-elliptical clauses; however, clauses that are derived via ellipsis tend to look the same:

(57)   a. Mary bought more cats than Peter (did).

   b. Mari több macskát vett,   mint Péter.
      Mary more cat.ACC bought.3SG than Peter
      'Mary bought more cats than Peter did.'

As can be seen, the lexical verb and the quantified DP are missing in both cases. I showed in the previous sections that the deletion mechanism is essentially the same in the two languages: that is, an [E] feature is located on a functional head and the complement of that functional head is the domain of ellipsis. In English, the functional vP can be headed by the dummy auxiliary (here: *did*), which is not an option in Hungarian as Hungarian does not have such auxiliaries. Apart from that, it seems that ellipsis works in the same way in the two languages; yet, there are some questions to be clarified.

One point of difference concerns structures such as (58) below:

(58)   Mary is taller than Peter.

I argued in §6.2 that either the vP domain (as a phase) is not spelt out at PF in such constructions, or there is no underlying TP (see also Bacskai-Atkari 2014b); in either case, no ellipsis takes place here. This option was not attested for Hungarian and the reason behind this is that while in English a subject DP, as *Peter* in (58), normally moves to the specifier of the TP/IP, the head of which cannot host the [E] feature, in Hungarian a contrastive DP like *Péter* in (57b) moves to the [Spec,FP] position, the head of which is a proper functional head that can host the [E] feature. In other words, English has to resort to either the lack of spellout or to certain structural changes in order to derive at least a subset of comparative constructions. This is not the case in Hungarian due to the peculiar properties of the Hungarian clause which can generally be observed (and which are not construction-specific). If there are multiple contrastive elements, or when the verb itself is contrastive, then it is possible for a contrastive element to be a topic in Hungarian. However, topics are essentially adjoined and prosodically count as extrametrical elements; as a consequence, there must be some overt element between the VP and the topic field so that main sentential stress may be assigned. To conclude, if there is a single overt DP in the Hungarian comparative subclause, as in (57b), it is in the [Spec,FP] position, as opposed to English.

The second important difference concerns the way ellipsis seems to operate in the two languages: whereas contrastive elements in English were shown to be able to withstand linear, left to right deletion, this is not attested in Hungarian. The reason behind this is quite simple: in Hungarian, contrastive elements move to the left and are hence located above the functional head responsible for ellipsis and thus there is simply no element that could withstand ellipsis following the deletion of a string of non-contrastive elements. In English, however, contrastive elements appear clause-finally and, since ellipsis works in a left to right fashion, the only way to have both ellipsis and overt contrastive elements is precisely the one described as F-marked elements stopping the linear deletion process. Furthermore, the difference between English and Hungarian in this respect follows from the way sentential stress is assigned: in English, stress falls on the rightmost constituent in the Intonational Phrase, while in Hungarian it falls on the leftmost constituent (see Szendrői 2001). In this way, ellipsis in comparative subclauses (and in other constructions) can be directly linked to the way the syntax-prosody mapping operates in a given language. Since the detailed examination of this issue would clearly fall outside the scope of the present book, I will not venture to investigate it any further here.

Finally, let me highlight an important aspect of the analysis proposed here: this concerns the location of the [E] feature on functional heads and the directionality of ellipsis. Based on Merchant (2001), the [E] feature is located on some functional head, such as a C or a v head, and ellipsis affects the complement of that functional head, which is located to the right. As I showed, this does not exclude the possibility of contrastive elements appearing clause-finally but ellipsis still operates in a strictly left to right fashion. This predicts that ellipsis can operate in a certain domain only if the functional head precedes its complement: that is, if the projection in question (a CP or a vP) is head-initial. A head-final functional projection is not able to license ellipsis because in that case ellipsis would have to apply retrospectively.

The difference between head-initial and head-final projections is attested in German. In German, the CP is head-initial and, as also pointed out by Merchant (2004; 2013), sluicing is attested as in English: that is, carried out by an [E] feature on a C head. Compare the examples in (59) from English and German:

(59) a. Ralph saw someone, but I don't know **who** ~~he saw~~.

      b. Ralf hat jemanden gesehen, aber ich weiß nicht, **wen** ~~er~~
          Ralph has someoneACC seen   but I know.1SG not who.ACC he
          ~~gesehen hat.~~
          seen   has
          'Ralph saw someone but I don't know who.'

In both cases, there is a *wh*-pronoun located in a [Spec,CP] position and the complement of the C, equipped with an [E] feature, is elided.

However, in German, the VP and all vPs are head-final (cf. Haider 1985: 34), and VP-ellipsis is not attested in the way it is in English (see the discussion in Chapter 4 for more details). As was pointed out in Chapter 4, this is responsible for the difference in the acceptability[8] of the examples for comparatives in (60):

---

[8]See Kennedy & Merchant 2000 regarding the grammaticality of the English data. My informants have differing judgements regarding the acceptability of the gapping structure, as opposed to the pseudogapping structure: while for most of them it is grammatical, some of them find it rather marked. There seems to be even more variation in German regarding the version of (60b) where the finite verb is not elided, whereby the differences are apparently not regional. These questions cannot be discussed here in more detail, but should be clarified by experimental studies.

(60)   a.   Ralph has a bigger flat than Michael ~~has~~ a house.

       b.   *Ralf   hat eine größere Wohnung als   Michael ein Haus ~~hat~~.

           Ralph has a.F   bigger.F flat   than Michael a.F house has

           'Ralph has a bigger flat than Michael a house.'

The reason why (60a) is possible is that the [E] feature can be located on a v head in English since the complement follows that v head: hence, the lexical verb (*has*) is elided and the object DP stops deletion. However, this is not possible in German because the v head taking the VP (*ein Haus hat*) as its complement follows the VP and even if an [E] feature were located on this v, that would not (and could not) carry out ellipsis.

The advantage of this analysis is that it connects the lack of the availability of the [E] feature on a given functional head to the relative position of that head, contrary to Merchant (2013), who proposes that this is a lexical difference, in that English has both an E_S and an E_V feature, while German lacks the E_V feature and has no VP-ellipsis (but has sluicing). Though the proposal of Merchant (2013) in this respect is descriptively adequate, it fails to link this property to some other, more general property of the grammar.

I propose that the reason why a head-final functional projection cannot license ellipsis is not because of a lexical difference from head-initial projections that would ban the appearance of an [E] feature on a head-final vP: it is simply that the PF mechanism defined by the [E] feature does not (and cannot) operate backwards. This also implies that there is essentially no restriction on the appearance of the [E] feature: in principle, it can appear on the head of a head-final projection but it will have no effect on the final structure.

Again, I cannot examine these issues any further since it would necessarily involve constructions other than comparatives. What is important for us here is that ellipsis in comparative subclauses seems to operate in a principled way, in that it is carried out by similar mechanisms in various languages, irrespective of whether these languages show Comparative Deletion or not. The differences that do arise can be attributed to general requirements that follow either from the way syntax-prosody mapping works in the given language or from whether functional projections are head-initial or head-final.

7 Conclusion

The aim of this book was to provide an analysis for the syntactic structure of comparatives, with special attention paid to the derivation of the subclause. Naturally, the analysis given here is not broad enough to cover all issues connected to comparatives; still, the ones that have been dealt with are of crucial importance and the proposed account explains how the comparative subclause is connected to the matrix clause, how the subclause is formed in the syntax and what additional processes contribute to its final structure. In addition, the main interest of my research was to cast light upon these problems in cross-linguistic terms and to provide a model that allows for variation. This also enables one to give a more adequate explanation for the phenomena found in English comparatives, since the properties of English structures can then be linked to general settings of the language, and hence need no longer be considered as idiosyncratic features of the grammar of English.

In Chapter 2, I provided a unified analysis of degree expressions, with the aim of relating the structure of comparatives to that of other (the absolute and the superlative) degrees. Building on results of previous analyses such as Bresnan (1973), Izvorski (1995), Corver (1997) and Lechner (1999; 2004), I proposed a feature-based account that may explain various differences both with respect to the degree morpheme and the lexical adjective itself, either in English or cross-linguistically. It was shown that gradable adjectives are located within a degree phrase (DegP), which in turn projects a quantifier phrase (QP), and that these two functional layers are always present for gradable adjectives, irrespective of whether there is a phonologically visible element in these layers. The difference can be captured by considering (1):

(1) a. Mary is **tall**.
     b. Mary is **taller** than John.

While in (1a) only a bare adjective (*tall*) is visible, in (1b) the comparative degree morpheme (*-er*) and the comparative subclause (*than John*) are also overt. Nevertheless, building on degree semantics, I argued that the DegP and the QP are necessary also in the case of (1a) since the degree interpretation has to be present syntactically as well; in addition, modifiers also provide arguments for the existence of the QP layer. One of the strongest arguments comes from structures like (2):

(2)   Mary is **more intelligent** than John.

In this case, the degree morpheme *-er* appears as part of *more* and not as a suffix on the lexical adjective itself; as was shown, *more* is in fact a composite of the Q head *much* and the Deg head *-er*. The proposed structure is given in (3):

(3)

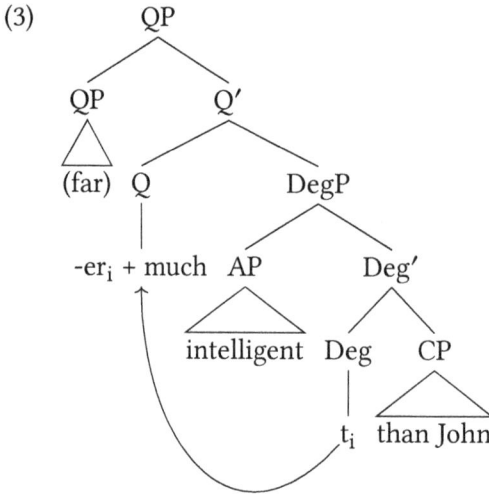

As can be seen, the lexical AP and the XP expressing the standard value (here the CP *than John*) are both arguments of the degree head, in line with Lechner (1999; 2004). In addition, there is a QP layer projected on top of the DegP, such that the Deg head moves up to the Q head; the specifier of the QP may in turn host other (QP) modifiers. The Deg head is zero in (1a) and is filled by *-er* in (1b) and in (2). The movement of the Deg head up to the Q head accounts for the formation of *more*; in all the other cases, the morpheme *-er* is attached to the lexical adjective following it at PF.

Since the comparative subclause is the complement of the degree head, the Deg head can impose selectional restrictions on it, which explains the difference between the complement of the Deg head *-er* and that of *as*. Relevant examples are given in (4):

(4)   a.   Mary is **taller** [than John].

       b.   *Mary is **taller** [as John].

       c.   *Mary is **as tall** [than John].

       d.   Mary is **as tall** [as John].

Though all of these restrictions are associated with the Deg head rather than with the adjective, I also considered cases where the adjective has arguments of its own, as in (5):

(5)   Mary is proud [of her husband].

In (5), the adjective *proud* takes the PP as its complement, and thus the PP is base-generated as the complement of the A head. Problems arise when such complements appear in comparative structures, as in (6):

(6)   Mary is prouder [of her husband] than Susan is.

Since the PP appears after the degree head, it is obvious that it undergoes extraposition of some sort. I argued that this extraposition is not syntactic in nature but follows from the fact that the PP can be spelt out on its own as a phase (just like the comparative subclause) and hence appears in the PF string later than the adjective.

The analysis can account for differences between gradable and non-gradable adjectives; in addition, it was shown that the distinction between predicative and attributive adjectives can also be captured in that predicative-only adjectives are equipped with a [−nom] feature while attributive-only adjectives are equipped with a [+nom] feature, all other adjectives allowing both options. By way of agreement with the degree head, this feature percolates up to the entire QP and defines whether it can, may or must agree with a nominal expression. On the other hand, certain Deg heads may also be inherently marked as either [+nom] or [−nom], which accounts for why superlatives are invariably attributive.

In Chapter 3, I presented a novel analysis of Comparative Deletion by reducing it to an overtness constraint holding on operators. In this way, Comparative Deletion can be reduced to morphological differences, and cross-linguistic variation is not conditioned by way of postulating an arbitrary parameter that defines whether a certain language has Comparative Deletion or not. This account is strongly feature-based in the sense that differences are ultimately dependent on whether a certain language has overt operators equipped with the relevant − [+compr] and [+rel] − features.

As was seen, the phenomenon of Comparative Deletion traditionally denotes the absence of an adjectival or nominal expression from the comparative sub-clause:

(7)   a. Ralph is more qualified than Jason is ~~x-qualified~~.
       b. Ralph has more qualifications than Jason has ~~x-many qualifications~~.
       c. Ralph has better qualifications than Jason has ~~x-good qualifications~~.

In all of the examples above in (7), x denotes a certain degree or quantity to which a certain entity is qualified, good etc. As far as Standard English is concerned, this is an operator with no phonological content. Earlier analyses of Comparative Deletion simply acknowledged that in predicative comparatives such as (7a) an adjectival expression is deleted. By contrast, in nominal comparatives such as (7b) and in attributive comparatives such as (7c) a nominal expression is deleted.

I rejected the possibility of Comparative Deletion taking place at the base-generation site and therefore the representations in (7) are only descriptively adequate. One of the greatest problems regarding the claim that Comparative Deletion takes place at the base-generation site is that it should target different constituents obligatorily, since the overt presence of the quantified expressions in (7) would lead to ungrammatical constructions. I argued that such an operation could not be conditioned and that Comparative Deletion must be the result of more general processes.

Another problem concerning Comparative Deletion and the deletion site concerns information structural properties. In subcomparative structures, an adjectival or nominal element may be left overt in the subclause; contrary to the examples in (7), these elements are not logically identical to an antecedent in the matrix clause:

(8)   a. The table is longer than the desk is **wide**.
       b. Ralph has more books than Jason has **manuscripts**.
       c. Ralph wrote a longer book than Jason did **a manuscript**.

One of the central questions often discussed in the relevant literature is whether constructions like the ones in (8) are exempt from Comparative Deletion and are hence essentially different from the ones in (7), or whether Comparative Deletion applies in both types.

I argued that Comparative Deletion takes place at the left periphery in the sub-clause in a [Spec,CP] position in all cases given in (7) and (8) due to an Overtness

Requirement that requires the presence of an overt operator if there is lexical material (an AP or an NP) located in an operator position. Since Standard English has no overt operators, the deletion of the higher copy always takes place in [Spec,CP]. As was shown, the lower copy may then be realised overtly, but this happens only if it is contrastive: this condition is satisfied in (8) but not in (7), and lower copies are therefore not pronounced in cases like (7).

Given that deletion takes place in a [Spec,CP] position if the Overtness Requirement is not satisfied, it is not surprising that a visible operator can appear in this position, which is possible for certain dialects of English that accept, for instance, *how* as a comparative operator:

(9)   % Ralph is more qualified than **how qualified** Jason is.

As I argued, structures like (9) involve operator movement in the same way the ones in (7) and (8) do; the difference is that *how* can appear overtly in the [Spec,CP] position because it does not violate the Overtness Requirement.

In addition to instances like (9), Chapter 3 also showed that there are languages and language varieties that allow the degree element to be combined with a lexical AP/NP to appear overtly in the [Spec,CP] position, as is the case in Hungarian (cf. Kenesei 1992):

(10)   a.   Mari magasabb, mint **amilyen magas** Péter.
            Mary taller   than how   tall   Peter
            'Mary is taller than Peter.'

       b.   Marinak több macskája   van, mint **ahány**   macskája
            Mary.DAT more cat.POSS.3SG is   than how.many cat.POSS.3SG
            Péternek van.
            Peter.DAT is
            'Mary has more cats than Peter has.'

       c.   Marinak   nagyobb macskája   van, mint **amilyen nagy macskája**
            Mary.DAT bigger   cat.POSS.3SG is   than how   big cat.POSS.3SG
            Péternek van.
            Peter.DAT is
            'Mary has a bigger cat than Peter has.'

As was seen, Hungarian allows the overt presence of the degree elements; again, this was shown to be so because the Overtness Requirement is satisfied in cases like (10). Since the Overtness Requirement is not specifically related to comparatives, the parametric variation attested across languages can also be linked to more general properties instead of treating Comparative Deletion as a parameter.

Strongly related to the status of operators, Chapter 3 also examined the question of how the internal structure of degree expressions plays a role in the different behaviour of individual comparative operators. In Hungarian, for instance, the operator *amilyen* 'how' may appear together with the adjective, as in (10a), though the adjective may not be stranded, as illustrated in (11):

(11)   * Mari magasabb, mint **amilyen** Péter **magas.**
        Mary taller   than how   Peter tall

       'Mary is taller than Peter.'

Chapter 3 argued that the reason behind this is that the operator *amilyen* is a Deg head and as such it cannot be extracted from the degree expression that it is the head of. Adopting the general structure for degree expressions given in Chapter 2, I made the claim that there are two possible operator positions:

(12)

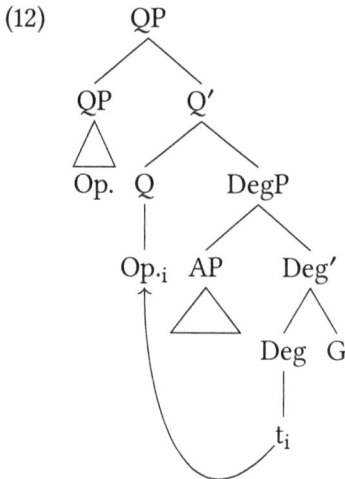

As can be seen, one operator position is the Deg head, and operators of this type ultimately undergo movement to the Q head position. These heads then cannot be extracted from within the entire QP projection, and the lexical AP (if they take any) necessarily moves together with them. Some of these operators were also shown to be able to act as proforms, hence standing for the DegP without a visible lexical AP there. On the other hand, there are operators that are QP modifiers located in the [Spec,QP] position: these cannot be proforms but since they are phrase-sized, they are able to move out on their own, at least if the entire QP functions as a predicate in the clause. This can be observed in the case of the Hungarian operator *amennyire* 'how much', illustrated in (13):

(13) a. Mari magasabb, mint **amennyire magas** Péter.
          Mary taller   than how.much tall   Peter
          'Mary is taller than Peter.'

     b. Mari magasabb, mint **amennyire** Péter **magas**.
          Mary taller   than how.much Peter tall
          'Mary is taller than Peter.'

The extractability of operators is thus responsible for whether the AP may be stranded or not; in other words, extractability is not directly linked to Comparative Deletion, which is ultimately a surface reflex of the Overtness Requirement that holds for copies in a [Spec,CP] position, but it depends on the position of the operator in the functionally extended degree expression.

As far as Hungarian is concerned, Chapter 3 also showed that if the adjective is overt, the operator has to be overt as well; this is due to the fact that Hungarian does not have zero comparative operators, as shown by (14):

(14) a. Mari magasabb, mint **(*magas)** Péter.
          Mary taller   than tall   Peter
          'Mary is taller than Peter.'

     b. Mari magasabb, mint Péter **(*magas)**.
          Mary taller   than Peter tall
          'Mary is taller than Peter.'

My analysis of Comparative Deletion takes into account that languages differ with respect to the presence/absence of the operator in a more intricate way than one that could be formulated on a +/– basis. The factors responsible for cross-linguistic variation are related to the internal structure of degree expressions, the overtness of degree operators and also to information structural properties. However, Comparative Deletion is not a direct reflex of the information structural status of lexical projections associated with the degree elements but it is a factor that plays a role as far as the realisation of lower copies in a movement chain is concerned and may also be linked to the preferred position of a lexical AP in the comparative subclause if the AP can be stranded.

Chapter 4 aimed at providing an adequate explanation for the phenomenon of Attributive Comparative Deletion, as attested in English, by way of relating it to the regular mechanisms underlying Comparative Deletion, as described in Chapter 3. I showed that Attributive Comparative Deletion can only be understood as a descriptive term referring to a phenomenon that is a result of the interaction of more general syntactic processes, since there is no reason to postulate any special mechanism underlying it in the grammar. The elimination of such a mechanism allows one to achieve a unified analysis of all types of comparatives. In addition, Chapter 4 argued that Attributive Comparative Deletion is not a universal phenomenon, and its presence in English can be conditioned by independent, more general rules, while the absence of such restrictions leads to the absence of Attributive Comparative Deletion in other languages.

Attributive Comparative Deletion is a phenomenon that involves the obligatory deletion of the quantified AP and the lexical verb from the comparative subclause, if the quantified AP functions as an attribute within a nominal expression. Consider the examples given in (15):

(15) a.   Ralph bought a bigger cat than George did ~~buy~~ a ~~big~~ cat flap.
      b.   Ralph bought a bigger cat than George ~~bought~~ a ~~big~~ cat flap.
      c. * Ralph bought a bigger cat than George bought a ~~big~~ cat flap.
      d. * Ralph bought a bigger cat than George bought a big cat flap.
      e. * Ralph bought a bigger cat than George ~~bought~~ a big cat flap.
      f. * Ralph bought a bigger cat than George did ~~buy~~ a big cat flap.

Both the adjective (*big*) and the lexical verb (*buy*) have to be eliminated from the comparative subclause; this is possible either by eliminating the tensed lexical verb, as in (15b), or by deleting the lexical verb and leaving the auxiliary *do* bearing the tense morpheme intact, as in (15a). Since the verb and the adjective both have to be deleted, the examples in (15c)–(15f) are ungrammatical.

As Chapter 4 argued, this is because the degree expression in the subclause is not licensed to appear in a particular position within the extended nominal expression. In other words, the obligatory elimination of the adjective is not due to the fact that it is GIVEN; the overt presence of the attributive adjective is ungrammatical even if it is different from its matrix clausal counterpart, as shown in (16):

(16) a. * Ralph bought a bigger cat than George ~~bought~~ a wide cat flap.
      b. * Ralph bought a bigger cat than George did ~~buy~~ a wide cat flap.

On the other hand, the deletion of the lexical verb was shown to be required only if part of the DP is overt; in case the entire DP is eliminated, the lexical verb can stay overt, as shown in (17):

(17)   Ralph bought a bigger cat than George bought ~~a big cat~~.

These phenomena raise a number of questions that were answered in Chapter 4. The major questions are why the adjective is not allowed to remain overt even if it is contrastive, why the verb is also affected and how the lexical verb and the adjective can be deleted, as they do not seem to be adjacent in (15a) and (15b). I adopted the proposal made by Kennedy & Merchant (2000) regarding the syntactic position of the quantified AP in the nominal expression in structures like (15a) and (15b). According to this, the quantified AP moves to the left edge of the extended nominal projection and is hence adjacent to the lexical verb at PF. I also made the claim that the inversion option is available because in nominal expressions such as *a cat* there is no DP layer and the quantified expression may move to [Spec,FP], while in structures containing a DP layer the DP is a boundary to such movement operations. The structure for the quantified expression in the subclause of attributive comparative constructions is as follows:

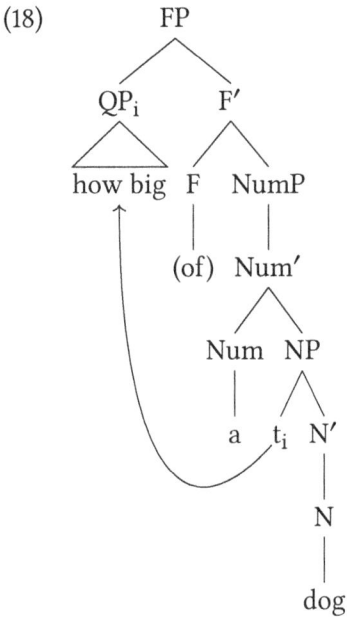

(18)

```
              FP
            /    \
         QP_i     F'
        /    \   /  \
   how big    F   NumP
              |     |
            (of)   Num'
                  /    \
                Num     NP
                 |     /  \
                 a   t_i    N'
                           |
                           N
                           |
                          dog
```

(QP_i moves to Spec,FP from the position of t_i within NP)

I argued that the quantified AP has to be eliminated because of the Overtness Requirement: the quantified AP moves to an operator position (the specifier of the FP projection) and, just as in the [Spec,CP] position, lexical material is licensed to appear here only if the operator is overt. Since this condition is not met in the case of the comparative operator in English, the AP has to be deleted. However, there is no separate mechanism that could carry it out and so a more general process has to apply, which is VP-ellipsis. Given that VP-ellipsis inevitably affects the lexical verb, it is explained why the verb has to be deleted.

In addition, Chapter 4 aimed at addressing the relation between Attributive Comparative Deletion and ordinary Comparative Deletion. I showed that the higher copy of the quantified DP is deleted in a [Spec,CP] position in attributive comparatives as well, and attributive comparatives are thus not exceptional in this respect. On the other hand, the reason for the ungrammaticality of the quantified AP in the [Spec,FP] position of the extended nominal expression is due to the same Overtness Requirement that was claimed to be responsible for the obligatory elimination of the higher copy in the [Spec,CP] position.

Furthermore, I took cross-linguistic differences into consideration, and it was shown that in Hungarian the full structure may be visible in the subclause:

(19) Rudolf   nagyobb macskát vett,   mint amilyen széles macskaajtót
      Rudolph bigger   cat.ACC bought.3SG than how   wide cat.flap.ACC
      Miklós vett.
      Mike   bought.3SG
      'Rudolph bought a bigger cat then Mike did a cat flap.'

This is so because the comparative operator is visible in Hungarian and hence the entire quantified nominal expression can be overt, as in (19).

Chapter 4 also pointed out that German does not allow Attributive Comparative Deletion either:

(20) *Ralf   hat eine   größere   Wohnung als   Michael ein   Haus.
       Ralph has a.ACC.F bigger.ACC.F flat   than Michael a.ACC.N house
      'Ralph has a bigger flat than Michael a house.'

The reason for this is that German does not have the kind of inversion that English has within the extended nominal expression, and the adjective is never located in a position that would cause ungrammaticality; in addition, it is not adjacent to the verb either. The non-adjacency of the adjective and the verb is also due to the fact that the VP is head-final in German: thus, VP-ellipsis cannot apply in the way it does in English. The analysis presented in Chapter 4 is hence able to account for cross-linguistic differences as well, since these are in fact reducible to more general properties of the respective languages.

Regarding the mechanisms underlying the phenomenon of Comparative Deletion and that of Attributive Comparative Deletion, I argued that the Overtness Requirement regulates the realisation of the higher copy, while the realisation of the lower copy is essentially tied to the lexical XP being contrastive. In Chapter 5, I examined some languages that cannot realise contrastive lower copies either.

As far as the higher copy is concerned, the Overtness Requirement on left-peripheral elements is decisive, since this states that overt lexical material is licensed in an operator position only if the operator itself is overt. I argued that there are four major logical possibilities, depending on whether the operator moves on its own, and whether the operator is overt or not. If the operator is able to strand a lexical AP or NP (or there is no lexical XP base-generated together with the operator at all), the lexical XP is spelt out in its base position, and the overtness of the operator is immaterial, as is the information structural status of the lexical XP. If an overt operator takes the lexical XP along to the [Spec,CP], the lexical XP is licensed irrespective of its information structural status. However, if a phonologically zero operator takes the lexical XP to the clausal left periphery, the entire phrase in [Spec,CP] must be deleted in order to avoid a violation of the Overtness Requirement. In this case, the lower copy of the movement chain (in the base position) is realised overtly if it is contrastive. This leads to an asymmetry between contrastive and non-contrastive XPs: if the XP is contrastive, the absence of any overt copy results in the surface phenomenon traditionally referred to as Comparative Deletion. The realisation of contrastive XPs, on the other hand, appears to be straightforward, at least in English.

Using data from Slavic, Chapter 5 demonstrated that the availability of the lower copy for overt realisation is not universal. Consider the Polish in (21):

(21) a. * Maria jest wyższa niż Karol   jest **wysoki**.
          Mary is   taller   than Charles is   tall

      'Mary is taller than Charles.'

      b. */?? Stół jest dłuższy niż   biuro jest **szerokie**.
             desk is   longer than office is   wide

      'The desk is longer than the office is wide.'

While the ungrammaticality of (21a) is expected on the basis of the English pattern, the fact that Polish apparently lacks predicative subcomparatives in the English way, that is, the ungrammaticality of (21b), is not expected. As was shown in Chapter 5, Polish is not unique in this respect: Czech shows the same distribution, too. I argued that the realisation of the lower copy is dependent on more general properties of movement chains in a certain language, which results in a difference between English and Polish/Czech. In particular, as demonstrated by Bošković (2002), *wh*-elements have to undergo fronting in multiple *wh*-fronting languages such as Polish independently of an active [wh] feature on C: that is, while the first moved *wh*-constituent checks off the [wh] feature on C and thus it undergoes ordinary *wh*-movement, the further *wh*-elements merely undergo obligatory fronting. This is presumably because these elements are equipped with an EDGE feature. Bošković (2002) shows that apparent exceptions to the fronting requirement are relatively rare and they are subject to certain conditions; further, these instances do not involve the lack of fronting but rather the realisation of a lower copy of a movement chain. I argued that since these requirements are absent from comparative constructions, the realisation of a contrastive lower copy is not possible in these languages.

I argued that there are thus three major factors determining the overt realisation of the quantified expression: whether the operator is overt, whether it is extractable, and whether lower copies of a movement chain can be realised if the pronunciation of the higher copy would cause the derivation to crash at PF. The possibilities are summarised in the representation given in (22):

(22)

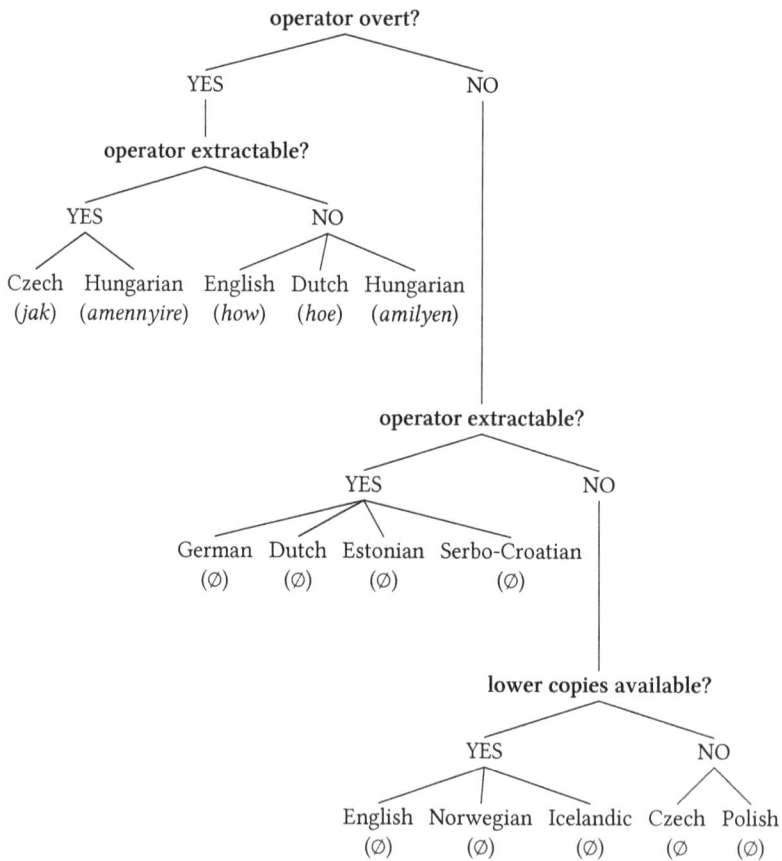

The most important finding in this respect is that the English pattern, where Comparative Deletion refers to the obligatory elimination of a non-contrastive AP from the comparative subclause, is not universal at all: in fact, it is highly language-specific, and it can only be regarded as a result of several factors. Thus, Comparative Deletion cannot be regarded as a universal phenomenon or a parameter either, and the analysis of the particular English pattern cannot be solely based on Standard English data but must take other languages and non-standard varieties into consideration.

Finally, Chapter 6 aimed at accounting for optional ellipsis processes that play a crucial role in the derivation of typical comparative subclauses. These processes are not directly related to the structure of degree expressions and the elimination of the quantified expression from the subclause; nevertheless, they were shown to interact with the mechanisms underlying Comparative Deletion or the absence thereof.

In English predicative structures, shown in (23), this involves the elimination of the copula from subclauses such as the one given in (23b), as opposed to the one given in (23a):

(23)   a. Ralph is more enthusiastic than Jason is.
       b. Ralph is more enthusiastic than Jason.

In nominal comparatives, as shown in (24), the lexical verb may be deleted:

(24)   a. Ralph bought more houses than Michael bought flats.
       b. Ralph bought more houses than Michael did flats.
       c. Ralph bought more houses than Michael did.
       d. Ralph bought more houses than Michael.

Verb deletion may result either in a subclause without any verbal element, as in (24d), or the tense morpheme may be carried by the dummy auxiliary, as in (24b) and (24c). In addition, depending on whether the object contains a contrastive noun or not, the object nominal expression remains overt, as in (24a) and (24b), or does not appear overtly, as in (24c) and (24d). A very similar pattern arises in attributive comparatives, as shown in (25):

(25)   a. Ralph bought a bigger house than Michael did a flat.
       b. Ralph bought a bigger house than Michael did.
       c. Ralph bought a bigger house than Michael.

The main question was whether the deletion of the lexical verb is merely the deletion of the verbal head or whether there is VP-ellipsis at hand; in the latter case, the possibility of having overt objects (or parts of objects) must be accounted for. Using the analysis given in Chapter 4, Chapter 6 argued that gapping is an instance of VP-ellipsis, which proceeds from a left-to-right fashion at PF, and the starting point of it is an [E] feature on a functional v head, in line with Merchant (2001). The endpoint of ellipsis is a contrastive phrase, if there is any. I also showed that since the [E] feature can be present on a C head as well, the derivation of comparative subclauses at PF may involve ellipsis starting from an [E] feature either on a C or a v head. Since the final string may be ambiguous, one of the central questions is whether a uniform kind of ellipsis mechanism may account for these ambiguities; this was indeed shown to be possible.

On the other hand, the fact that reduced comparative subclauses also exist in Hungarian raises the question of how languages that have overt comparative operators exclusively may show the elimination of the entire degree expression, given that there is no Comparative Deletion in these languages. For instance, predicative comparatives in Hungarian show the variation given in (26):

(26) a. Mari magasabb volt, mint **amilyen magas** Péter **volt**.
          Mary taller   was.3SG than how   tall   Peter was.3SG
          'Mary was taller than Peter.'

      b. Mari magasabb volt,   mint Péter.
          Mary taller   was.3SG than Peter
          'Mary was taller than Peter.'

In (26a) the subclause contains all the elements overtly, while the degree expression and the verb are absent from (26b). The same can be observed in nominal comparatives, as illustrated in (27):

(27) a. Mari több macskát vett,   mint **ahány**   **macskát** Péter
          Mary more cat.ACC bought.3SG than how.many cat.ACC   Peter
          vett.
          bought.3SG
          'Mary bought more cats than Peter did.'

      b. Mari több macskát vett,   mint Péter.
          Mary more cat.ACC bought.3SG than Peter
          'Mary bought more cats than Peter did.'

Finally, attributive comparatives also show this pattern, as illustrated in (28):

(28) a. Mari nagyobb macskát vett,   mint **amilyen nagy macskát**
        Mary bigger   cat.ACC bought.3SG than how   big   cat.ACC
        Péter **vett**.
        Peter bought.3SG

        'Mary bought a bigger cat than Peter did.'

    b. Mari nagyobb macskát vett,   mint Péter.
        Mary bigger   cat.ACC bought.3SG than Peter

        'Mary bought a bigger cat than Peter did.'

In all of these cases the sentences of a given pair have the same meaning. The main research question was whether the deletion of the degree expression is independent from that of the verb or not. As Chapter 6 showed, these are not two independent processes, since the verb cannot be overt in the absence of an overt degree expression. I argued that this is so because it is ungrammatical to have an operator in its base position in Hungarian, but since there is no separate mechanism that would eliminate the degree expression, a more general ellipsis process has to apply, which is essentially VP-ellipsis. The ellipsis mechanism is fairly similar to the one attested in English and the differences were linked to the slightly different internal structure of the functional layers in the two languages. Otherwise ellipsis is carried out by an [E] feature on the highest possible functional head in Hungarian too; the ellipsis domain for the subclauses in (26b), (27b) and (28b) is given in (29):

(29)

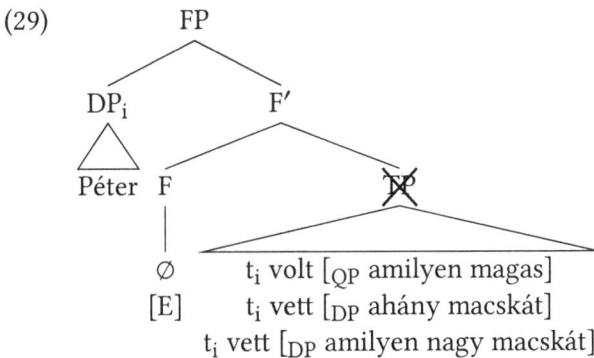

```
                    FP
              _____|_____
             /             \
           DPᵢ              F′
          / \          _____|_____
         /   \        /           \
      Péter  F                     X̸P̸
             |           _____|_____
             |          /                     \
             Ø        tᵢ volt [QP amilyen magas]
            [E]       tᵢ vett [DP ahány macskát]
                      tᵢ vett [DP amilyen nagy macskát]
```

As can be seen, both the verb (the copula or a lexical verb) and the quantified expression (either a QP or a DP containing a QP) are located in the ellipsis domain, which is the complement of the F head: the FP itself is the leftmost projection that can host the [E] feature.

I argued that in case the verb is contrastive, ellipsis is slightly different. If the contrastive verb is a copula, then the [E] feature can be located on a lower functional head (the head of the PredP, predicative phrase) and hence the ellipsis site is located lower. The copula itself is base-generated in Pred but moves regularly further up to T and to the F head. However, if the contrastive verb is a lexical verb, this is not base-generated in Pred but moves there only from a lower (V) head: this involves a movement step that normally does not take place, since the movement of the verb is not triggered to a functional head containing [E]. The resulting configurations are thus marked, even though they are not ungrammatical.

I showed that the difference between English and Hungarian in terms of gapping effects is chiefly a result of the different prosody in the two languages: while the Intonational Phrase is right-headed in English, it is left-headed in Hungarian. Therefore, while contrastive elements are located at the right edge of the ellipsis domain in English, in Hungarian they are to the left of the functional head hosting the [E] feature and consequently not part of the ellipsis domain. Chapter 6 also showed that since there is strong directionality in terms of ellipsis, in that it proceeds in a strict left-to-right fashion, this kind of ellipsis works only in head-initial phrases since the ellipsis domain (the complement) has to follow the head hosting the [E] feature. This accounts for why German does not have VP-ellipsis in the way English does: the German VP and all vP layers are head-final while in English all VP projections are head-initial. Cross-linguistic differences concerning optional ellipsis processes can thus be reduced to more general properties that hold in individual languages, and hence ellipsis processes are not construction-specific.

References

Abney, Steven Paul. 1987. *The English Noun Phrase and its sentential aspect*. Cambridge, MA: Massachusetts Institute of Technology dissertation.

Austin, John Langshow. 1962. *How to do things with words*. Oxford: Oxford University Press.

Bacskai-Atkari, Julia. 2010a. On the nature of comparative subclauses: A crosslinguistic approach. *The Odd Yearbook* 8. 1–37.

Bacskai-Atkari, Julia. 2010b. Parametric variation and Comparative Deletion. *The Even Yearbook* 9. 1–21.

Bacskai-Atkari, Julia. 2012a. English comparatives and parameters. In Mária Gósy & Attila Péteri (eds.), *Tanulmányok: Nyelvtudományi Doktori Iskola*, 23–37. Budapest: Eötvös Loránd University.

Bacskai-Atkari, Julia. 2012b. Reducing Attributive Comparative Deletion. *The Even Yearbook* 10. 1–25.

Bacskai-Atkari, Julia. 2013a. On the syntax-prosody mapping in Hungarian comparatives. In Péter Szigetvári (ed.), *VLlxx: Papers in linguistics presented to László Varga on his 70th birthday*, 257–277. Budapest: Tinta Könyvkiadó.

Bacskai-Atkari, Julia. 2013b. Reanalysis in Hungarian comparative subclauses. In Christer Platzack & Valéria Molnár (eds.), *Approaches to Hungarian 13: Papers from the 2011 Lund conference*, 5–32. Amsterdam: John Benjamins.

Bacskai-Atkari, Julia. 2014a. Cyclical change in Hungarian comparatives. *Diachronica* 31(4). 465–505.

Bacskai-Atkari, Julia. 2014b. Structural case and ambiguity in reduced comparative subclauses in English and German. *Acta Linguistica Hungarica* 61(4). 363–378.

Bacskai-Atkari, Julia. 2014c. *The syntax of comparative constructions: Operators, ellipsis phenomena and functional left peripheries*. Potsdam: Universitätsverlag Potsdam.

Bacskai-Atkari, Julia. 2015. Information structure and clausal comparatives in Czech and Polish. In Gerhild Zybatov, Petr Biskup, Marcel Guhl, Claudia Hurtig, Olav Mueller-Reichau & Maria Yastrebova (eds.), *Slavic grammar from a formal perspective: The 10th anniversary FDSL [Formal Description of Slavic Languages] conference, Leipzig 2013*, 27–42. Frankfurt am Main: Peter Lang.

Bacskai-Atkari, Julia. 2016. Towards a cross-linguistic typology of marking polarity in embedded degree clauses. *Acta Linguistica Hungarica* 63(4). 389–409.

Bacskai-Atkari, Julia. 2017. Ambiguity and the internal structure of comparative complements in Greek. In Thanasis Georgakopoulos, Theodossia-Soula Pavlidou, Miltos Pechlivanos, Artemis Alexiadou, Jannis Androutsopoulos, Alexis Kalokairinos, Stavros Skopeteas & Katerina Stathi (eds.), *Proceedings of the ICGL12 [12th International Conference on Greek Linguistics], Vol. 1*, 231–242. Berlin: Edition Romiosini/CeMoG.

Bacskai-Atkari, Julia & Gergely Kántor. 2011. Elliptical comparatives revisited. In Vadim Kimmelman, Natalia Korotkova & Igor Yanovich (eds.), *Proceedings of MOSS 2: Moscow Syntax and Semantics*, 19–34. Cambridge, MA: MIT Working Papers in Linguistics.

Bacskai-Atkari, Julia & Gergely Kántor. 2012. Deletion in Hungarian, Finnish and Estonian comparatives. *Finno-Ugric Languages and Linguistics* 1(1–2). 44–66.

Baker, Mark. 1985. Mirror theory and morphosyntactic explanation. *Linguistic Inquiry* 16(3). 373–415.

Baker, Mark. 1988. *Incorporation: A theory of grammatical function changing*. Chicago, IL: University of Chicago Press.

Bally, Charles. 1944. *Linguistique générale et linguistique française*. Berne: A. Francke.

Beard, Robert. 1991. Decompositional composition: The semantics of scope ambiguities and 'bracketing paradoxes'. *Natural Language & Linguistic Theory* 9(2). 195–229.

Beck, Sigrid. 2011. Comparison constructions. In Klaus von Heusinger, Claudia Maienborn & Paul Portner (eds.), *Semantics: An international handbook of natural language meaning 2*, 1341–1389. Berlin: Mouton de Gruyter.

Bhatt, Rajesh & Shoichi Takahashi. 2011. Reduced and unreduced phrasal comparatives. *Natural Language & Linguistic Theory* 29(3). 581–620.

Billings, Loren & Catherine Rudin. 1996. Optimality and superiority: A new approach to overt multiple *wh*-ordering. In Jindřich Toman (ed.), *Formal approaches to Slavic linguistics: The College Park Meeting*, 35–60. Ann Arbor, MI: Michigan Slavic Publications.

Bobaljik, Jonathan David. 1995. *Morphosyntax: The syntax of verbal inflection*. Cambridge, MA: Massachusetts Institute of Technology dissertation.

Bobaljik, Jonathan David. 2002. A-chains at the PF-interface: Copies and 'covert' movement. *Natural Language & and Linguistic Theory* 20(2). 197–267.

Bobaljik, Jonathan David & Susi Wurmbrand. 2005. The domain of agreement. *Natural Language & Linguistic Theory* 23(4). 809–865.

Bolinger, Dwight. 1972. *Degree words*. The Hague: Mouton.

Borsley, Robert D. & Ewa Jaworska. 1981. Some remarks on equatives and related phenomena. *Studia Anglica Posnaniensia* 13. 79–108.

Bošković, Željko. 2002. On multiple *wh*-fronting. *Linguistic Inquiry* 33(3). 351–383.

Bošković, Željko. 2005. On the locality of Left Branch Extraction and the structure of NP. *Studia Linguistica* 59(1). 1–45.

Bošković, Željko. 2012. On NPs and clauses. In Günther Grewendorf & Thomas Ede Zimmermann (eds.), *Discourse and grammar: From sentence types to lexical categories*, 179–242. Berlin: Walter de Gruyter.

Bošković, Željko & Jairo Nunes. 2007. The copy theory of movement: A view from PF. In Norbert Corver & Jairo Nunes (eds.), *The copy theory of movement*, 13–74. Amsterdam: John Benjamins.

Bowers, John. 1987. Extended X-bar theory, the ECP and the Left Branch Condition. In Megan Crowhurst (ed.), *Proceedings of the 6th West Coast Conference on Formal Linguistics*, 47–62. Stanford, CA: Stanford Linguistics Association.

Brame, Michael. 1986. Ungrammatical notes 11: Much ado about *much*. *Linguistic Analysis* 16. 3–24.

Bresnan, Joan. 1972. *Theory of complementation in English syntax*. Cambridge, MA: Massachusetts Institute of Technology dissertation.

Bresnan, Joan. 1973. The syntax of the comparative clause construction in English. *Linguistic Inquiry* 4(3). 275–343.

Bresnan, Joan. 1975. Comparative Deletion and constraints on transformations. *Linguistic Analysis* 1(1). 25–74.

Bresnan, Joan. 1977. Transformations and categories in syntax. In Robert E. Butts & Jaako Hintikka (eds.), *Basic problems in methodology and linguistics*, 261–282. Dordrecht: Reidel.

Brody, Michael. 1990. Some remarks on the focus field in Hungarian. *UCL Working Papers in Linguistics* 2. 201–225.

Brody, Michael. 1995. Focus and checking theory. In István Kenesei (ed.), *Approaches to Hungarian 5*, 29–44. Szeged: JATE.

Büring, Daniel. 2006. Focus projection and default prominence. In Valéria Molnár & Susanne Winkler (eds.), *The architecture of focus*, 321–346. Berlin: Mouton de Gruyter.

Chen, Matthew Y. 1987. The syntax of Xiamen tone sandhi. *Phonology Yearbook* 4. 109–150.

Chomsky, Noam. 1977. On *wh*-movement. In Peter W. Culicover, Thomas Wasow & Adrian Akmajian (eds.), *Formal syntax*, 71–132. New York, NY: Academic Press.

Chomsky, Noam. 1991. Some notes on economy of derivation and representation. In Robert Freidin (ed.), *Principles and parameters in comparative grammar*, 417–454. Cambridge, MA: MIT Press.

Chomsky, Noam. 1995. *The Minimalist Program*. Cambridge, MA: MIT Press.

Chomsky, Noam. 2001. Derivation by phase. In Michael Kenstowicz (ed.), *Ken Hale: A life in language*, 1–52. Cambridge, MA: MIT Press.

Chomsky, Noam. 2004. Beyond explanatory adequacy. In Adriana Belletti (ed.), *The cartography of syntactic structures 3: Structures and beyond*, 104–131. Oxford: Oxford University Press.

Chomsky, Noam. 2008. On phases. In Robert Freidin et al. (eds.), *Foundational issues in linguistic theory: Essays in honor of Jean-Roger Vergnaud*, 133–166. Cambridge, MA: MIT Press.

Comorovski, Ileana. 1996. *Interrogative phrases and the syntax-semantics interface*. Dordrecht: Kluwer.

Coppock, Elizabeth. 2001. Gapping: In defense of deletion. In Mary Andronis, Christopher Ball, Heidi Elston & Sylvain Neuvel (eds.), *Proceedings of the Chicago Linguistics Society [CLS] 37 Vol. 1: The Main Session*, 133–148. Chicago, IL: University of Chicago.

Corver, Norbert. 1990. *The syntax of Left Branch Extractions*. Tilburg: Tilburg University dissertation.

Corver, Norbert. 1992. Left Branch Extraction. In Kimberly Broderick (ed.), *Proceedings of NELS [North East Linguistic Society] 22*, 67–84. Amherst, MA: Graduate Linguistic Student Association of the University of Massachusetts.

Corver, Norbert. 1993. A note on subcomparatives. *Linguistic Inquiry* 24(4). 773–781.

Corver, Norbert. 1997. *Much*-support as a last resort. *Linguistic Inquiry* 28(1). 119–164.

Cresswell, Max J. 1976. The semantics of degree. In Barbara Partee (ed.), *Montague grammar*, 261–292. New York, NY: Academic Press.

Croitor, Blanca & Ion Giurgea. 2016. Relative superlatives and Deg-raising. *Acta Linguistica Hungarica* 63(4). 411–442.

den Besten, Hans. 1989. *Studies in West Germanic syntax*. Amsterdam: Rodopi.

den Dikken, Marcel. 2006. *Relators and linkers: The syntax of predication, predicative inversion, and copulas*. Cambridge, MA: MIT Press.

Doetjes, Jenny. 2008. Adjectives and degree modification. In Louise McNally & Christopher Kennedy (eds.), *Adjectives and adverbs: Syntax, semantics, and discourse*, 123–155. Oxford: Oxford University Press.

Drummond, Alex, Norbert Hornstein & Howard Lasnik. 2010. A puzzle about P-stranding and a possible solution. *Linguistic Inquiry* 41(4). 689–692.

É. Kiss, Katalin. 1987. *Configurationality in Hungarian*. Dordrecht: Reidel.

É. Kiss, Katalin. 2002. *The syntax of Hungarian*. Cambridge: Cambridge University Press.

É. Kiss, Katalin. 2007. Topic and Focus: Two structural positions associated with logical functions in the left periphery of the Hungarian sentence. In Caroline Féry, Gisbert Fanselow & Manfred Krifka (eds.), *Interdisciplinary Studies on Information Structure (ISIS) 6: The notions of information structure*, 69–82. Potsdam: Universitätsverlag Potsdam.

É. Kiss, Katalin. 2008a. Free word order, (non-)configurationality and phases. *Linguistic Inquiry* 39(3). 441–474.

É. Kiss, Katalin. 2008b. The structure of the Hungarian VP revisited. In Christopher Piñón & Szilárd Szentgyörgyi (eds.), *Approaches to Hungarian 10*, 31–58. Budapest: Akadémiai Kiadó.

É. Kiss, Katalin. 2009. Is free postverbal order in Hungarian a syntactic or a PF phenomenon? In Nomi Erteschik-Shir & Lisa Rochman (eds.), *The sound patterns of syntax*, 53–71. Oxford: Oxford University Press.

Fanselow, Gisbert. 2004. Münchhausen-style head movement and the analysis of verb second. In Ralf Vogel (ed.), *Three papers on German verb movement*, 9–49. Potsdam: Universitätsverlag Potsdam.

Felser, Claudia. 2004. Wh-copying, phases, and successive cyclicity. *Lingua* 114. 543–574.

Fiengo, Robert & Robert May. 1994. *Indices and identity*. Cambridge, MA: MIT Press.

Fowlie, Meaghan. 2010. More multiple multiple spellout. Manuscript. UCLA. Available at http://mfowlie.bol.ucla.edu/documents/fowlie_moremms.pdf (last accessed: 20 December 2016).

Fradin, Bernard. 2007. On the semantics of denominal adjectives. In Angela Ralli, Geert Booij, Sergio Scalise & Athanasios Karasimos (eds.), *Morphology and dialectology: On-line proceedings of the Sixth Mediterranean Morphology Meeting (MMM6). Ithaca, 27–30 September 2007*, 84–98. Ithaca: University of Patras.

G. Varga, Györgyi. 1992. A névmások. In Loránd Benkő (ed.), *A magyar nyelv történeti nyelvtana II/1.: A kései ómagyar kor: Morfematika*, 455–569. Budapest: Akadémiai Kiadó.

Gallego, Ángel J. 2010. *Phase theory*. Amsterdam: John Benjamins.

Grebenyova, Lydia. 2004. Sluicing and Left-Branch Extraction out of islands. In Vineeta Chand (ed.), *WCCFL 23: The proceedings of the 23rd West Coast Conference on Formal Linguistics*, 164–172. Somerville, MA: Cascadilla Press.

Haider, Hubert. 1985. Chance and necessity in diachronic syntax: Word order typologies and the position of Modern Persian relative clauses. In Jacek Fisiak (ed.), *Papers from the VIth International Conference on Historical Linguistics, Poznań, 22–26 August 1983*, 199–216. Amsterdam: John Benjamins.

Haider, Hubert & Inger Rosengren. 1998. Scrambling. *Sprache und Pragmatik* 49. 1–104.

Hankamer, Jorge. 1973. Why there are two *than*'s in English. In Claudia Corum, Thomas Cedric Smith-Stark & Ann Weiser (eds.), *Papers from the 9th Regional Meeting of the Chicago Linguistic Society [CLS]*, 179–191. Chicago, IL: Chicago Linguistic Society.

Heim, Irene. 1985. Notes on comparatives and related matters. Austin, TX. Manuscript. University of Texas, Austin. http://semanticsarchive.net/Archive/zc0ZjY0M/Comparatives%2085.pdf. Accessed: 30.03.2017).

Heim, Irene. 1999. Notes on superlatives. Cambridge, MA. Manuscript. Massachusetts Institute of Technology.

Heim, Irene. 2000. Degree operators and scope. In Brendan Jackson & Tanya Matthews (eds.), *SALT [Semantics and Linguistic Theory] X*, 214–239. Ithaca, NY: Cornell University.

Horrocks, Geoffrey & Melita Stavrou. 1987. Bounding theory and Greek syntax: Evidence for *wh*-movement in NP. *Journal of Linguistics* 23. 79–108.

Horvath, Julia. 1986. *FOCUS in the theory of grammar and the syntax of Hungarian*. Dordrecht: Foris.

Horvath, Julia. 1997. The status of Wh-expletives and the partial Wh-movement construction of Hungarian. *Natural Language & Linguistic Theory* 15(3). 509–572.

Huddleston, Rodney. 1967. More on the English comparative. *Journal of Linguistics* 3. 91–102.

Inkelas, Sharon. 1989. *Prosodic constituency in the lexicon*. Stanford, CA: Stanford University dissertation.

Izvorski, Roumyana. 1995. A DP-shell for comparatives. In Antonietta Bisetti, Laura Brugè, João Costa, Rob Goedemans, Nicola Munaro & Ruben van der Vijver (eds.), *Console III proceedings*, 99–121. The Hague: Holland Academic Graphics.

Jackendoff, Ray. 1977. *X' syntax: A study in phrase structure*. Cambridge, MA: MIT Press.

Jäger, Agnes. 2010. Der Komparativzyklus und die Position der Vergleichspartikeln. *Linguistische Berichte* 224. 467–493.

Jayaseelan, Karattuparambil A. 1990. Incomplete VP deletion and gapping. *Linguistic Analysis* 20. 64–81.

Johnson, Kyle. 1997. When verb phrases go missing. *GLOT* 2(5). 3–9.

Johnson, Kyle. 2004. In search of the English middle field. Cambridge, MA. Manuscript. Massachusetts Institute of Technology.

Kántor, Gergely. 2008a. A phase-based approach to rightward movement in comparatives. *Newcastle Working Papers in Linguistics* 14. 81–99.

Kántor, Gergely. 2008b. On Hungarian relative operators. *The Even Yearbook* 8. 1–12.

Kántor, Gergely. 2010. *Syntactic processes and interface phenomena in comparatives*. Budapest: Eötvös Loránd University dissertation.

Kayne, Richard. 1983. Connectedness. *Linguistic Inquiry* 14(2). 223–250.

Kayne, Richard. 1994. *The antisymmetry of syntax*. Cambridge, MA: Massachusetts Institute of Technology.

Kenesei, István. 1992. On Hungarian complementisers. In István Kenesei & Csaba Pléh (eds.), *Approaches to Hungarian 4*, 37–50. Szeged: JATE.

Kenesei, István. 1995. On bracketing paradoxes in Hungarian. *Acta Linguistica Hungarica* 43(1–2). 153–173.

Kenesei, István. 2006. Focus as identification. In Valéria Molnár & Susanne Winkler (eds.), *The architecture of focus*, 137–168. Berlin: Mouton de Gruyter.

Kenesei, István. 2014. On a multifunctional derivational affix: Its use in relational adjectives or nominal modification, and phrasal affixation in Hungarian. *Word Structure* 7(2). 214–239.

Kenesei, István & Irene Vogel. 1989. Prosodic phonology in Hungarian. *Acta Linguistica Hungarica* 39(1–2). 149–193.

Kenesei, István & Irene Vogel. 1995. Focus and phonological structure. Newark, NJ. Manuscript. University of Delaware. http://www.nytud.hu/kenesei/publ/kenesei_vogel_1995.pdf. Accessed 24.01.2017).

Kennedy, Christopher. 1997. *Projecting the adjective: The syntax and semantics of gradability and comparison*. Santa Cruz, CA: University of California dissertation.

Kennedy, Christopher. 1999. *Projecting the adjective: The syntax and semantics of gradability and comparison*. New York, NY: Garland.

Kennedy, Christopher. 2002. Comparative Deletion and optimality in syntax. *Natural Language & Linguistic Theory* 20(3). 553–621.

Kennedy, Christopher & Louise McNally. 2005. Scale structure, degree modification, and the semantics of gradable predicates. *Language* 81(2). 345–381.

Kennedy, Christopher & Jason Merchant. 1997. Attributive comparatives and bound ellipsis. Santa Cruz, CA. Linguistics Research Center Report LRC-97-03, University of California. http://semantics.uchicago.edu/kennedy/docs/km-lcr.pdf. Accessed 26.03.2018.

Kennedy, Christopher & Jason Merchant. 2000. Attributive Comparative Deletion. *Natural Language & Linguistic Theory* 18(1). 89–146.

Kuno, Susumu. 1981. The syntax of comparative clauses. In Roberta Hendrick, Carrie S. Masek & Mary Frances Miller (eds.), *Papers from the 17th Regional Meeting of the Chicago Linguistics Society [CLS]*, 136–155. Chicago, IL: Chicago Linguistics Society.

Larson, Richard Kurth. 1987. "Missing prepositions" and the analysis of English free relative clauses. *Linguistic Inquiry* 18(2). 239–266.

Larson, Richard Kurth. 1988. On the double object construction. *Linguistic Inquiry* 19(3). 335–391.

Larson, Richard Kurth & Naoko Takahashi. 2007. Order and interpretation in prenominal relative clauses. In Meltem Kelepir & Balkız Öztürk (eds.), *Proceedings of the Workshop on Altaic Formal Linguistics [wals] II*, 101–120. Cambridge, MA: MITWPL.

Lasnik, Howard. 1995. A note on pseudogapping. *MIT Working Papers in Linguistics* 27. 143–163.

Lechner, Winfried. 1999. *Comparatives and DP-structures*. Cambridge, MA: University of Massachusetts Amherst dissertation.

Lechner, Winfried. 2001. Reduced and phrasal comparatives. *Natural Language & Linguistic Theory* 19(4). 683–735.

Lechner, Winfried. 2004. *Ellipsis in comparatives*. Berlin: Mouton de Gruyter.

Lees, Robert B. 1961. Grammatical analysis of the English comparative construction. *Word* 17. 171–185.

Lee-Schoenfeld, Vera. 2007. *Beyond coherence: The syntax of opacity in German*. Amsterdam: John Benjamins.

Lerner, Jan & Manfred Pinkal. 1992. Comparatives and nested quantification. In Martin Stokhof & Paul Dekker (eds.), *Proceedings of the Eighth Amsterdam Colloquium on Logic, Language and Information*, 329–347. Amsterdam: University of Amsterdam, Institute for Logic, Language & Computation.

Lerner, Jan & Manfred Pinkal. 1995. Comparative Ellipsis and variable binding. In Mandy Simons & Teresa Galloway (eds.), *Proceedings from the Conference on Semantics and Linguistic Theory (SALT), University of Texas, Austin*, 222–236. Ithaca: Cornell University, Department of Linguistics.

Levin, Nancy. 1986. *Main-verb ellipsis in spoken English*. New York, NY: Garland.

Marušič, Franc. 2005. What happens when phases get individualistic: On LF-only & PF-only phases. *Anuario del Seminario de Filología Vasca "Julio de Urquijo"* 39(2). 121–140.

Marušič, Franc & Rok Žaucer. 2006. On the intensional *feel-like* construction in Slovenian: A case of a phonologically null verb. *Natural Language & Linguistic Theory* 24(4). 1093–1159.

Matushansky, Ora. 2008. On the attributive nature of superlatives. *Syntax* 11(1). 26–90.

McCarthy, John & Alan Prince. 1993. Generalised alignment. In Geert Booij & Jaap van Marle (eds.), *Yearbook of morphology*, 79–154. Dordrecht: Kluwer.

McCawley, James D. 1988. *The syntactic phenomena of English*. Chicago, IL: University of Chicago Press.

McNally, Louise & Gemma Boleda. 2004. Relational adjectives as properties of kinds. In Olivier Bonami & Patricia Cabredo Hofherr (eds.), *Empirical issues in formal syntax and semantics 5*, 179–196. Berlin: Lang.

Merchant, Jason. 2001. *The syntax of silence: Sluicing, islands, and the theory of ellipsis*. Oxford: Oxford University Press.

Merchant, Jason. 2004. Fragments and ellipsis. *Linguistics and Philosophy* 27. 661–738.

Merchant, Jason. 2008. Variable island repair under ellipsis. In Kyle Johnson (ed.), *Topics in ellipsis*, 132–153. Cambridge: Cambridge University Press.

Merchant, Jason. 2009. Phrasal and clausal comparatives in Greek and the abstractness of syntax. *Journal of Greek Linguistics* 9. 134–164.

Merchant, Jason. 2013. Voice and ellipsis. *Linguistic Inquiry* 44(1). 77–108.

Miller, Philip. 1992. *Clitics and constituents in Phrase Structure Grammar*. New York, NY: Garland.

Moltmann, Friederike. 1992. *Coordination and comparatives*. Cambridge, MA: Massachusetts Institute of Technology dissertation.

Müller, Gereon. 2003. Phrase Impenetrability and *wh*-intervention. Leipzig. Manuscript. University of Leipzig.

Napoli, Donna Jo. 1983. Comparative Ellipsis: A phrase structure account. *Linguistic Inquiry* 14(4). 675–694.

Neeleman, Ad & Fred Weerman. 1999. *Flexible syntax: A theory of Case and arguments.* Dordrecht: Kluwer.

Nespor, Marina & Irene Vogel. 1986. *Prosodic phonology.* Dordrecht: Foris.

Nissenbaum, Jonathan W. 2000. *Investigations of covert phrase movement.* Cambridge, MA: Massachusetts Institute of Technology dissertation.

Nunes, Jairo. 1999. Linearization of chains and phonetic realization of chain links. In Samuel David Epstein & Norbert Hornstein (eds.), *Working minimalism*, 217–249. Cambridge, MA: MIT Press.

Ortiz de Urbina, Jon. 1993. Feature percolation and clausal pied-piping. In José Ignacio Hualde & Jon Ortiz de Urbina (eds.), *Generative studies in Basque linguistics*, 189–220. Amsterdam: John Benjamins.

Pesetsky, David. 1985. Morphology and Logical Form. *Linguistic Inquiry* 16(2). 193–248.

Pesetsky, David. 1987. Wh-in situ: Movement and unselective binding. In Eric Reuland & Alice ter Meulen (eds.), *The representation of (in)definiteness*, 98–129. Cambridge, MA: MIT Press.

Pesetsky, David. 1989. The Earliness Principle. Cambridge, MA. Manuscript. Massachusetts Institute of Technology.

Pesetsky, David. 1997. Optimality theory and syntax: Movement and pronunciation. In Diana Archangeli & D. Terence Langendoen (eds.), *Optimality Theory: An overview*, 134–170. Oxford: Blackwell.

Pesetsky, David. 1998. Some optimality principles of sentence pronunciation. In Pilar Barbosa, Daniel Fox, Paul Hagstrom, Martha McGinnis & David Pesetsky (eds.), *Is the best good enough?*, 337–383. Cambridge, MA: MIT Press & MITWPL.

Pinkham, Jessie. 1982. *The formation of comparative clauses in French and English.* Bloomington, IN: Indiana University Bloomington dissertation.

Pinkham, Jessie. 1985. *The formation of comparative clauses in French and English.* New York, NY: Garland.

Poletto, Cecilia. 1995. Complementizer deletion and verb movement in Italian. *University of Venice Working Papers in Linguistics* 5(2). 49–79.

Postal, Paul. 1998. *Three investigations of extraction.* Cambridge, MA: MIT Press.

Price, Susan. 1990. *Comparative constructions in Spanish and French syntax.* London: Routledge.

Reglero, Lara. 2006. Spanish subcomparatives: The "obligatory gapping" strategy. In Nuria Sagarra & Almeida Jacqueline Toribio (eds.), *Selected proceedings of the 9th Hispanic Linguistics Symposium [hls]*, 67–78. Somerville, MA: Cascadilla Proceedings.

Reich, Ingo. 2007. Toward a uniform analysis of short answers and gapping. In Kerstin Schwabe & Susanne Winkler (eds.), *On information structure: Meaning and form*, 467–484. Amsterdam: John Benjamins.

Richards, Norvin. 1997. *What moves where when in which language?* Cambridge, MA: Massachusetts Institute of Technology dissertation.

Richter, Franz & Manfred Sailer. 1998. Complementizers and finite verbs in German sentence structure. In Tibor Kiss & Detmar Meurers (eds.), *Proceedings of the ESSLLI-98 [European Summer School in Logic, Language and Information 1998] Workshop on Current Topics in Constraint-based Theories of Germanic Syntax*, 133–148. Saarbrücken: University of Saarbrücken.

Rizzi, Luigi. 1997. The fine structure of the left periphery. In Liliane Haegeman (ed.), *Elements of grammar*, 281–337. Dordrecht: Kluwer.

Rizzi, Luigi. 1999. On the position "Int(errogative)" in the left periphery of the clause. Siena. Manuscript. University of Siena. www.ciscl.unisi.it/doc/doc_-pub/int.doc. Accessed 02.01.2017).

Rizzi, Luigi. 2004. Locality and left periphery. In Adriana Belletti (ed.), *Structures and beyond: The cartography of syntactic structures, Volume 3*, 223–251. Oxford: Oxford University Press.

Roberts, Ian. 1997. Restructuring, head movement, and locality. *Linguistic Inquiry* 28(3). 423–460.

Ross, John Robert. 1967. *Constraints on variables in syntax*. Cambridge, MA: Massachusetts Institute of Technology dissertation.

Ross, John Robert. 1986. *Infinite syntax*. Norwood, MA: Ablex Publishing.

Rudin, Catherine. 1988. On multiple questions and multiple WH fronting. *Natural Language & Linguistic Theory* 6(4). 445–501.

Runner, Jeffrey. 1998. *Noun phrase licensing and interpretation*. New York, NY: Garland.

Sag, Ivan. 1976. *Deletion and Logical Form*. Cambridge, MA: Massachusetts Institute of Technology dissertation.

Sato, Yosuke & Yoshihito Dobashi. 2012. Functional categories and prosodic phrasing in English: Evidence from that-trace effects and pronominal object shift. Manuscript. http://ling.auf.net/lingbuzz/001499. Accessed 24.01.2017).

Schütze, Carson T. 2001. On the nature of default case. *Syntax* 4(3). 205–238.

Schwarzschild, Roger. 1999. Givenness, AvoidF and other constraints on the placement of accent. *Natural Language Semantics* 7. 141–177.

Searle, John Rogers. 1969. *Speech acts*. Cambridge: Cambridge University Press.

Selkirk, Elisabeth O. 1984. *Phonology and syntax: The relation between sound and structure*. Cambridge, MA: MIT Press.

Selkirk, Elisabeth O. 1986. On derived domains in sentence phonology. *Phonology Yearbook* 3. 371–405.

Selkirk, Elisabeth O. 1996. Sentence prosody: Intonation, stress and phrasing. In John A. Goldsmith (ed.), *The handbook of phonological theory*, 550–569. London: Blackwell.

Selkirk, Elisabeth O. 2005. Comments on intonational phrasing in English. In Sonia Frota, Marina Vigario & Maria Joao Freitas (eds.), *Prosodies*, 11–58. Berlin: Mouton de Gruyter.

Šimík, Radek & Marta Wierzba. 2012. Givenness and scrambling in Czech: Experimental evidence for a stress-based approach. Potsdam. Manuscript. University of Potsdam / SFB-632.

Sproat, Richard. 1992. *Unhappier* is not a "Bracketing Paradox". *Linguistic Inquiry* 23(2). 347–352.

Stepanov, Arthur. 1998. On wh-fronting in Russian. In Pius N. Tamanji & Kiyomi Kusumoto (eds.), *NELS [North East Linguistic Society] 28*, 453–467. Amherst: University of Massachusetts, GLSA.

Stjepanović, Sandra. 1999. *What do second position cliticization, scrambling, and multiple wh-fronting have in common?* University of Connecticut dissertation.

Svenonius, Peter. 2004. On the edge. In David Adger, Cécile de Cat & George Tsoulas (eds.), *Peripheries: Syntactic edges and their effects*, 259–287. Dordrecht: Kluwer.

Szendrői, Kriszta. 2001. *Focus and the phonology–syntax interface*. London: University College London dissertation.

Truckenbrodt, Hubert. 1999. On the relation between syntactic phrases and phonological phrases. *Linguistic Inquiry* 30(2). 219–255.

Tsimpli, Ianthi Maria & Maria Dimitrakopoulou. 2007. The Interpretability Hypothesis: Evidence from wh-interrogatives in second language acquisition. *Second Language Research* 23(2). 215–242.

Uriagereka, Juan. 2006. Complete and partial Infl. In Cedric Boeckx (ed.), *Agreement systems*, 267–298. Amsterdam: John Benjamins.

van Craenenbroeck, Jeroen & Anikó Lipták. 2006. The crosslinguistic syntax of sluicing: Evidence from Hungarian relatives. *Syntax* 9(3). 248–274.

Vicente, Luis. 2010. On the syntax of adversative coordination. *Natural Language & Linguistic Theory* 28(2). 381–415.

Wachowicz, Krystyna A. 1974. Against the universality of a single Wh-question movement. *Foundations of Language* 11. 155–166.

Webelhuth, Gert. 1992. *Principles and parameters of syntactic saturation*. Oxford: Oxford University Press.

Winkler, Susanne. 2005. *Ellipsis and focus in generative grammar*. Berlin: Mouton de Gruyter.

Wunderlich, Dieter. 2001. Two comparatives. In István Kenesei & Robert M. Harnish (eds.), *Perspectives on semantics, pragmatics, and discourse: A festschrift for Ferenc Kiefer*, 75–89. Amsterdam: John Benjamins.

Yoon, Jeong-Me. 2001. Feature percolation, movement and cross-linguistic variation in pied-piping. In Benjamin Ka-Yin T'sou, Olivia O.Y. Kwong & Tom B.Y. Lai (eds.), *Language, information and computation: Proceedings of the 15th Pacific Asia Conference*, 283–292. Hong Kong: City University of Hong Kong.

Zamparelli, Roberto. 2008. Bare predicate nominals in Romance languages. In Henrik Høeg Müller & Alex Klinge (eds.), *Essays on nominal determination: From morphology to discourse management*, 101–130. Amsterdam: John Benjamins.

Name index

Language index

Subject index

www.ingramcontent.com/pod-product-compliance
Lightning Source LLC
Chambersburg PA
CBHW082147150426
42812CB00076B/2283